TAKING A LIT
SAILING SHIP

TAKING A LITTLE SAILING SHIP

A VIEW OF THE WORLD FROM
A THIRTY-FOOT SCHOONER

KLAUS GEHRIG

NIMBUS
PUBLISHING LTD

Nimbus Publishing Limited
P.O. Box 9301, Station A
Halifax, N.S.
B3K 5N5

Cover design: Steven Slipp, GDA, Halifax
Cover photograph: Klaus Gehrig

Canadian Cataloguing in Publication Data

Gehrig, Klaus, 1946-

Taking a Little Sailing Ship

ISBN 0-921054-63-7

1. Voyages around the world—1981—I. Title.
G440.G43G43 1991 910.4'1 C90-097711-6

Contents

A Book

*T*here was a time when I thought that I would never write a book. I even told myself that I could never do it—for in a book, I thought, one should include every thing, every emotion, every impression ... It would take a lifetime, and nobody has a lifetime to write a book—first one has to live. I have mellowed—I'm writing a book.

A Boat

We say we are intelligent beings living on the Planet Earth, but we are simply entities that exist for a brief time and then turn to dust on the crust of a particle in a vast space that we call the Universe.

Before man acknowledged that the Earth is a sphere, most people didn't care whether it was or not, but concerned themselves with shelter and food, and maybe pleasures and riches. It occurred to only a few to find out.

Today it is about the same. To find one's place in society, to pull off a convincing love affair or to plan ahead, leaves little time to experience the world around us. True, we can see a majestic mountain on a screen, but it is not the same as being on the mountain, feeling it pulsate. A photograph does not inspire a sense of loftiness and grandeur in the same way.

Knowing that the Earth is round is not the same as drifting, struggling and sailing around its girth.

This book is about that experience.

A few days before we set out on our five-year voyage an article appeared in the *Squamish Times* with the heading, "Sailing around the world is this pair's dream."

Now at least I know the difference between a dream and the reality of coping with hardship, or in fact, distinguishing between real and apparent hardship, and of experiencing extraordinary events without being stupefied by them.

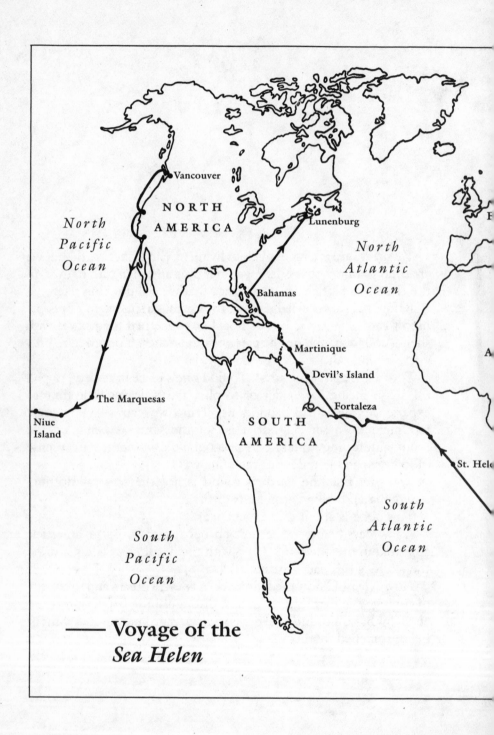

Niue
Island

The Marquesas

Vancouver

**NORTH
AMERICA**

Lunenburg

*North
Pacific
Ocean*

Bahamas

*North
Atlantic
Ocean*

Martinique

Devil's Island

Fortaleza

**SOUTH
AMERICA**

St. Hele

*South
Pacific
Ocean*

*South
Atlantic
Ocean*

Voyage of the
Sea Helen

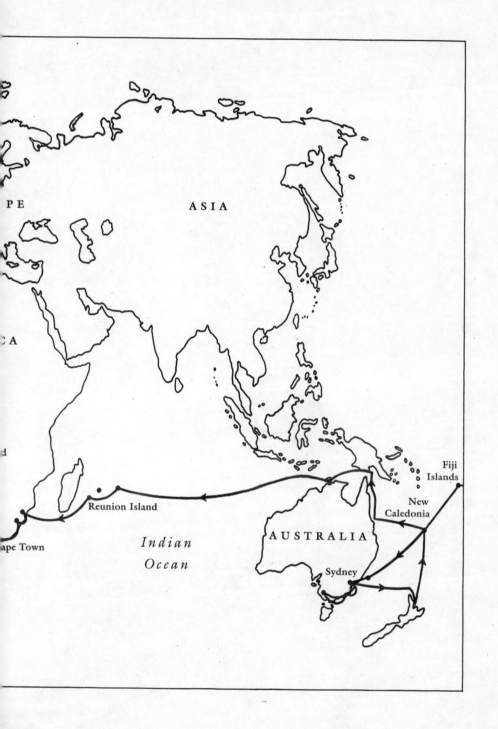

CHAPTER ONE

Beyond Building a Boat

Without ever knowing the mechanics of them, I was always fascinated with sailing ships, because they ventured to faraway and exotic places.

As a young lad, I was torn between making a break to sea or following the advice of my mother and my vocation counsellor. I was even willing to be a sailor on a modern commercial freighter, but finally I showed my conservative side by taking up an apprenticeship in the local automobile factory. Besides, there wasn't a seaport in the heart of Bavaria, where I lived.

I never regretted the apprenticeship for those were happy days, and the age of computer technology and space exploration was upon us. But I never stopped longing for exotic places and the ships that go there.

After my apprenticeship, however, I forgot about boats and went to Canada where, for the next five years, I lived, worked and thought. Suddenly at the age of twenty-three, still never having sailed, I made up my mind to build a sailing ship of my own.

By coincidence, I was introduced to two people who were into boating—boat building, to be more precise. They spent a great deal of time talking about boats, using names and terms so strange and mysterious that they appeared to belong to an initiated élite. They were each building a boat, in wood and in fiberglass. One of them, Brian, had actually been a crew member on a sailing ship and, with just a bit of coaxing, recounted tales of the sea with a practiced tongue.

I had heard enough and one day blurted out that I would build a sailing ship myself, but it would be in steel, the material I know best. After a few moments of shocked silence, Hugh, the other boat builder, and an engineer by profession, reached into a shelf behind his chair and pulled out a study plan for a thirty-foot schooner!

"Here is a little steel boat," he said, passing me the sheet with the air of someone with things at his fingertips.

What a wonderful little ship she looked on the drawing, with two masts instead of just one.

"That's the one I'll build!" I said instantly.

The design I was holding in my hand was the "Little Maid of Kent" by John Atkin, an auxiliary schooner in steel, thirty feet on deck, twenty-four on the waterline, ten-and-a-half feet across the beam, and four-and-a-half feet from the waterline to the deepest part of her keel. It was a ship small enough for me to tackle both physically and financially.

At this time I already knew a beautiful young waitress, who despite a meagre wage and even smaller tips, appeared happy. Of all the people in this inexpensive café her favourite customer was me, or so I assumed.

Over a period of seven years, with the idea of cruising to faraway places, my favourite waitress, Marie-José, and I built our thirty-foot schooner in Squamish, British Columbia, forty miles north of Vancouver.

We worked after or before regular working hours on a paying job and then only if the weather permitted. There were frustrations, setbacks and outright problems; but we finally experienced the tremendous feeling of anticipation that accompanies a brilliant sunrise at the beginning of a new day. We were about to begin our voyage.

* * *

Around the boat, it is still. We are in very protected waters tied to a dock. Marie-José produces a few clicks and clangs on the stove as she lights it up to prepare breakfast. The burners hiss and send faintly scented warm air through the cabin, soon accompanied by the aroma of coffee. It is not yet 0400 hours. All we have to do before 0400 hours is warm up the engine about ten minutes, light up the kerosene lanterns and undo the mooring lines.

We sit on the bunks, with the cabin table between us. I have the feeling that I might have slept in had Marie-José not woken me. We look at each other over the tops of the cups clutched in our hands. We have seemingly thought about everything we need to sail our boat to a faraway place, and even about the many items that we could

2

have, but don't. What we have is what we really need; what we don't
have we don't really need.

We have thought about ourselves to the degree that we can fathom
our feelings, which is perhaps not very far. It is not the time now to
talk it all over, we have had years to do that. Still, there was never a
moment quite like this one. We each experience it in our own way.

There are footsteps on the wharf, a faint calling of our names. A
faint call is all that is required in the stillness. It is Leo, his wife and
the two young boys who have come to say good-bye. Leo hands me
a bottle of rum. It is a special moment for him; he has been building
his own boat for years—his wife once confided that he is part gypsy—
he wants to be free, free from many things.

The noisy patter of the one-cylinder diesel has shattered the quiet
for more than ten minutes. Leo and his boys untie our lines and
throw them to us. I endeavour not to bump or scratch any of the
other boats as we back out. Now that we are well clear my attention
is focused on the small group of people who rush to the far end of the
wharf; we wave.

*   *   *

The feeling is different now that the sky is blue and high and we are
almost out of How Sound and entering Georgia Strait. Once before
we crossed this body of water, made into an inland sea by the long
land mass labelled Vancouver Island, but this time we will keep going
around the south end of the island, through the narrow Juan de Fuca
Strait and into the open Pacific.

Only moments ago, there was a grey smudge far down the Juan de
Fuca Strait; it is now a very large freighter heading dead towards us,
most certainly travelling within the established shipping lanes. My
knees feel weak. I tug on the stiff Dacron of the foresail some more,
but I cannot hope to complete the reef before the ship is upon us. I
might never complete it—I'm not even doing it right! And am I not
supposed to give instructions to the helmsman! It would be tremendous if I could stand erect and bellow above the wind, "Two points
to starboard!" or, "Fall off twenty degrees to port!" and then give a
smart salute as we watch the ship go by.

The big grey hull bears off to starboard, passing close to our port
side. The faces that look down at us are grinning. They probably
think that we are doing this for fun! I look back at Marie-José to see

3

if she feels, as I do, that the situation was resolved in a seamanlike manner—motor vessel gives way to sailing vessel—and make a further effort to reef the foresail. I prefer to lie on the cabin top to tie the reef points; I hate the spray flying over me; I think it's my stomach. I think it's unfair, or at least unfortunate, to have to beat against wind and swell with a stomach that feels ... It's not only the stomach, it's everything.

* * *

I examine my conflicting thoughts, realizing that my will to be anywhere but in my bunk is ebbing. Clinging to the last shreds of my self-image as a great seafarer, I pull down the sails, stow them on their booms, and toss the canvas funnel (sea anchor) into the sea. Promising myself the reward of a rest in my bunk, I undertake the enormous task of lighting the kerosene lanterns for the night. I explain to Marie-José, "We just look out now and then—if we drift too close to shore we start the engine. In the morning we try to sail again ... meanwhile we hang to the sea anchor and get some rest ..." I'm glad she sees it my way. Sea anchor! It was to be used for the worst—this is not the worst! I wish the dizziness would leave me; I hate those bitter stomach juices travelling up my throat.

* * *

It is a regular sort of a day with the winds moderate, although still blowing the wrong way for us. I know what I'll do: hoist the sails (what else) and take in the sea anchor. If we can just make it to Neah Bay, the open-Pacific end of Juan de Fuca Strait, we can wait there until the weather is just right to sail into the open sea where the proper breezes blow.

We enter Neah Bay late in the afternoon with a noticeable absence of cheerfulness on board. We made it, this cannot be denied, but it took so long to come such a short distance!

Supper on the stove on a level boat transforms the world back to approximately what it had been.

* * *

We have been in Neah Bay for three days. I feel a mixture of hesitation, expectation and anticipation. If we don't go now, on a day as fine as this, when will we go? Suddenly I know that the voyage will not have begun until we are in the open sea.

The bell buoy to the entrance of Neah Bay, chained to the ocean floor, rekindles my wish to be free. It is a very fair day—the open Pacific lies before us.

With sounds of "whoosh" and "phooo," fat bodies arch alongside us—dolphins! Or are these killer whales? I can see their faces now. These animals have a strange metallic appearance. Yes, definitely! The keel of our boat is in the open sea. The water is a different colour.

"Look, Marie-José, those are our sails against the sky!" She is still slightly hesitant, uncertain, as I am. As the land recedes, the boat closes around us and we are even aware of the grains of the materials of which it is made.

"If you make it past Cape Flattery, you are on your way!" Brian had said to us. Cape Flattery is a good distance astern and it is not yet time to light the lanterns.

* * *

The breeze is a lot stronger, "stiff" is the word, this morning. "It takes about two weeks to get sorted out 'out there,'" Art had predicted, speaking from experience. Art knows something. It's our second day out here and we are not sorted out. Breakfast doesn't taste like breakfast and my head is fuzzy. No one's complaining, it's just that one should be able to think while at sea, otherwise what's the use. Perhaps that's what Art meant when he said it takes two weeks to get sorted out: it takes two weeks before one can think comfortably and coherently on a boat that is in constant motion, without being limited to, "I feel dizzy, my stomach.... I hope the wind is not getting worse ..." Perhaps after two weeks the veil will lift and there will be some clarity to my thoughts.

* * *

It is like commanding a half-asleep man to do a dozen push-ups. Finally giving up the notion that the weather will turn fine, I toss the sea anchor over the stern. On the point of total exhaustion, I lower the main and foresail and reef the jib to its smallest size.

I am disillusioned because I'm sick. I knew the sea would be "like that," but I didn't think that I would be like that. Marie-José, I'm glad, does not feel seasick. Still, it's an amazing comfort to know that the boat is travelling in the right direction. What a surprisingly impersonal experience it is to be the master of this sailing ship! I give Marie-José a little smile—she glances at me, twice. The smile is too feeble, too influenced by my physical state, to be convincing. "If I lie

5

down once in a while I'm okay," I tell her, suggesting that there is not much to do, now that the sea anchor is down and there is no land near.

"Klaus, wake up, we must light the lanterns." I'm not asleep; I just thought that the moment could be held off a bit. I wish I had refilled the lanterns in the morning when it was still calm. They have to be lit inside the cabin with the hatch closed so that there is no draft.

The doors to the companionway have made a jarringly loud noise....

"Your safety harness!"

"Ya-agh!"

"Klaus!"

"I'm okay now, it was the smell of the kerosene." I have soot on my floater coat; but no vomit. No vomit, I'm glad!

* * *

I have an idea this morning: a song! It's a wondrous world—we should be cheerful, we should sing, we should feel that it is special out here. After only a few words, which I intended to be melodious, Marie-José cracks a smile, a compassionate one. I had no idea that a voice trained for years to render the world's great folk songs wouldn't work in places as special as the ridges and valleys of the ocean.

Marie-José is fed-up with looking at waves, and at my seasick green face. "The foremast is shaking like a leaf." I acknowledge her complaint. "The waves must be about forty feet high!" She shuts the hatch quickly. The waves threaten to climb right into the cabin, the way they are rolling after us; but they never do, the boat always lifts in time. I don't think they are forty feet high—but they are big.

It is five days since Neah Bay. The last two have been the worst. I won't write anything in the logbook today. Why should I? It's so much effort for nothing. But I must look out once in a while, maybe even step into the cockpit—Marie-José likes to see me do that, it helps her imagine that I'm in control. I should really take that jib down, we should run under bare poles; it wouldn't take long. I'll just go forward, slacken the halyard, pull down on the Dacron and lash it all down. But it will require that I go out on the bowsprit.

"No!" Marie-José is adamant. I can't really go against Marie-José's wishes, unless there is no other way. I can leave the jib up. I want to leave it up. If I lay down quickly, maybe I won't have to throw up.

Things are better when we lie together in one bunk. It is comforting to comfort her, to wipe away the tears. "Why don't we try some rum, then?" Marie-José suggests. I'm slightly taken aback, but it's an idea. "... I think it's helping!" I couldn't eat, even if Marie-José cooked; the galley is a mess.

"Look! there is water coming from under the floorboards!" The disgust in her voice overshadows the meaning of the words. It is true, there is water up to the floorboards. I built the boat...! The water, the sea, is coming in via the rudder stuffing box. My mind is already made up. I will pump the bilges whenever required, rather then crawl into the aft compartment; my stomach couldn't bear it.

We are everything we never intended to be: sad, cynical and beaten. We are drawing close to the latitude of San Francisco, a port we intended never to call at. There is a trace of wonder in knowing approximately where we are, in spite of it all. The simple knowledge of how to get a position from the sun by observing it through the sextant at noon, and the incredible coincidence that the sun was actually visible during this critical time on several days is comforting. Things are not all black if one has learned a little and has a little strength.

*   *   *

We are grateful, we are laughing, we open a bottle of wine and drink it. Let there be fog, so long as the sea is calm! It is surely a coincidence, it is weird, that the big swells should have carried us as far as San Francisco and then dissolved into a flat sea, melding with a sea of fog.

The plastic glasses make a muffled sound as we bring them together, but I forgive them, for inside me they ring sweet and clear. And Marie-José will cook a meal if I wish....

It would be an adventure to have fried eggs. It's been ten days, I think. What date is it?

*   *   *

It is true, dolphins feel like friends. They seem so tuned to the environment, so unencumbered, it is as if they are showing you the way. It is our third day in the fog.

Marie-José sees it first. It's a black buoy; no, a sailboat; no, it is a

7

black buoy—it's coming closer.

"Ahoy! You are being filmed."

"Ahoy! What?"

"We are making a movie!"

"Black Wind" reads the huge letters on the side of a black hull. What a bunch of letters to come out of the fog. It is just an ordinary sailing yacht, but if they are making a movie, they probably know where they are. I hate to do it, but I must.

"Can you give us the course to the Golden Gate?"

"It's ninety degrees. You are twenty miles from the bridge—must go now."

They have already gone.

*　*　*

I had imagined our boat gliding under the Golden Gate Bridge into San Francisco Bay, under full sail in brilliant sunshine. It is 2230 hours and we are wallowing slowly towards the arch of the bridge with the noisy patter of the engine. The bridge is visible—some lights shine from its steelwork—the fog has thinned considerably. I know that the bridge is high enough for the largest square-rig to pass underneath, yet I look up to see how our masts will fare. The foghorns blasting from the bridge are so overpowering that even though I can see the pillars, I cannot help thinking that we might strike them.

One mile inside the bay the horns are subdued—the bridge has disappeared. The anchorage is not ideal, but the anchor takes hold and the boat swings obediently—an anchor light weakly twinkles in the rigging. The aroma of coffee and herbs and spices still the mind. Restful thoughts enjoin the quiet night.

San Francisco, I'm thinking about San Francisco! I'm so agitated that I don't see it the way I might have; my mind is heavy with the realization that I'm not who I thought I was, not exactly.

The buildings on the hills, some in the shadow, some in the sun … the cable cars, conceived and built long ago and still here … fishing boats and pleasure boats in rows—they do not go far …

There are ships tied to a wharf—one must pay to view their insides—they are old—they travelled the seas—they did not come to grief—they came to rest.

What do the jugglers and the buskers in the streets mean to one

8

who is not able to sail his ship on the seas? How inspiring she looks, the girl bouncing across the street and entering a narrow door; she is probably an artist—and I'm not who I thought I was.

Would somebody buy our little ship? How much would we ask for it? I suppose the import duty would have to be paid by the buyer, not by us ... Why am I preoccupied with this? If a journey in a little sailing ship meant so much to me, but we cannot do it, why try to salvage the material things? How do I salvage the pieces of my mind? Perhaps I'm all right. I see there are physical limitations that stop us from doing what we aspire to. That always will be; and I'm still me, but things are not what I imagined.

With complete indecisiveness, we remain in the relatively sheltered waters of San Francisco Bay. We have taken a wait-and-see attitude, suppressing visions of clearing our personal belongings out of the boat as a new owner takes possession of it.

* * *

The Napa river, which branches off where the waters of San Francisco Bay penetrate inland, is sluggish and tranquil. Where the river narrows to the point that shipping is not feasible is the town of Napa. We nose into a berth in a small marina near the town.

"Have you visited some of the wineries?" The young lady with a trace of baby fat is looking at us with eyes wide. She has big eyes.

I realize that she is surprised I don't know what she means.

"The Napa wine, that's why people come to Napa."

It is such a hot day—the river makes it cool; the sound of the word "wine" makes it cool, too.

"They make wine here?"

"Yeah!"

All at once I feel that we have come to the right place. Besides, I like California girls; maybe it's the sun that makes them look sunny.

And there are Allen and Margie, who are building a boat by the river bank; and John and Helen, they have a schooner tied to a little pier in front of their house and keep inviting us to their home; Everett, a retired airline pilot, wants to know if we are interested in visiting some of the wineries. We are, especially with someone so keen.

No, we did not come to Napa Valley because of the wine. We didn't know. We came just to come, maybe to do a little painting on

,the *Sea Helen*. But now that we are here, we don't feel the way we did when we first arrived in San Francisco. The voyage down the coast wasn't really "like that." Our fears, our tears, what were they based on?

I'm thinking about how our schooner would look in a gentle breeze, with bottles of Napa wine in her belly, gliding under the Golden Gate Bridge into the open sea again, down the coast of California and ... and then we would be carrying on with our voyage....

* * *

There is indeed Napa wine in *Sea Helen*'s belly, the sun is pouring down and we are momentarily in the shadow as we gently roll beneath the arch of the Golden Gate Bridge.

The shoreline changes but the sea is locked into a gentle rhythm. Sea lions bark at us from the breakwater of Monterey Harbour and we laugh back at them.

* * *

The wind is gusting suspiciously—we are only a few hours out from Monterey.

It is not that I don't believe it, it is just that I have a hard time accepting that it is definitely blowing. What happened to our hopes for continued fine weather? I find the motion of throwing over the sea anchor (now only a motor car tire as the canvas funnel disappeared in the big swells on our way to San Francisco) all too familiar.

Marie-José, swift as the wind, suggests a sip of rum. I acknowledge it as a great idea and I'm grateful to have a mate that can function under the meanest conditions. But I cannot decide whether to have my sip now or wait until I throw up and have it on an empty stomach.

I'm miserably aware that the rum is burning its way down my throat to mingle with the bitter stomach juices. To navigate, to predict the weather (not my strong point), to cook, worse, to eat ... the images of ourselves on a sailing ship are increasingly overshadowed by images of ourselves snugly on land, in a pub, in a living room, at work, yes, even at work, where at four or five o'clock it's all over and we can go home. Here on the boat it's never over.

"The sun rises even if the sky is grey." That's a dumb philosophy, but on second thought, it is a fact. Besides, the wind does seem to have gone down a little.

*   *   *

If there was fog over the sea obliterating the land and I was told to sail in it with only my eyes and ears and a compass to guide me, I would say "No!" But when one has just weathered a gale and the fog has moved in, even before the sea has had a chance to flatten, one can only accept the circumstances. One then concentrates on the compass and tunes one's ears to pick up the sounds of the foghorns placed along the coast.

A strategically placed foghorn and a chart to show where its location is not much to go by, but somehow it is not too little if that's all there is.

With a patch of clear sky allowing for a sun shot, I find relief from the uncertainty over our position. I'm surprised that after three days we are much further down the coast than I thought we were. No, I'm not surprised, I'm disappointed that I'm so far out in my dead reckoning.

*   *   *

It seems that the best a sailor can do is to leave on a clear day and take it from there. To have sailed in the fog before is no comfort when the mist rolls in again. To wake up one brilliant sunlit morning to find that the port entered at night is backdropped by majestic mountain, is both bemusing and pleasant.

As we are in Los Angeles, where the skies are clear, we only vaguely remember the coast we sailed along. It seems only a short distance now to San Diego, to where we will really begin our voyage, where we will leave the land behind ...

We Must Get into the Spirit

*T*his is now our third day out from San Diego and for two-and-a-half days there hasn't been enough wind to stop the sails from flapping. Taking them down in the big swell would have been unbearable for us.

The sky was clear and the wind fresh enough to satisfy any sailor when, in the forenoon of November 6, we set our course for the Marquesas, the nearest South Pacific islands. The many small boats busily tacking back and forth and nodding their masts seemed to bid a gay farewell. But the wind only lasted till evening and died by the time the last day-sailors returned to port.

But us! We are not day-sailors, we are here to sail across an ocean and must get into the spirit of it.

After two-and-a-half days with not a breath of that basic necessity for a voyage under sail—wind—our spirits are not at all high, in fact, they seem dulled by the swells that give the boat such an uncomfortable motion. The islands of Los Coronado, marking the U.S./Mexican border, are visible as before—they are still bearing twenty degrees.

I never thought of tying down the wheel, as I assumed that the water would dampen the movement of the rudder enough to avoid any damage ... but now, with the rolling and heaving of the vessel, the rudder has swung so violently that it broke the steering cable. Considering that the wind may suddenly return, I set to work, feverishly.

Pulling in a new cable is a fairly simple matter in still waters; out here, I must crawl into a confined space with a stomach that doesn't feel the same as on land. The cables are in. I'm exhausted, and I'm amazed that I did it without having to do what I do now, cling to the rails and hand over my partially digested lunch to the sea. Gently, Marie-José suggests that we could turn back and maybe try again some other time. My protests are weak, for I, too, am discouraged. I feel the weight of responsibility rather than the thrill of voyaging. I know an unbearable depression will envelop me if we turn back with a boat fitted out and provisioned for a voyage across the Earth's largest ocean.

"But if we turn back, I won't go out again," I declare, as if striking a bargain with my alter ego.

We experience our dilemma again: there is safety and comfort ashore and yet we, or at least I, insist on being tossed and driven by the sea for the sake of carrying out a fancy idea.

The tremor in my voice sounds over-amplified: "I'll find someone to take the boat back for us if we can't sell it." For the second time I doubt if we will ever make it to any South Sea island. God! How do other people do it—I've heard of people that have done it before us.

"I'll tell you what," I say to Marie-José—she regards me with compassion and would be willing to make a life with me anywhere, on a farm, or in a city, or on the sea—"if there's no wind tomorrow, then we'll turn back—let's wait till tomorrow!"

We agree to give the wind an ultimatum.

* * *

To be fair I was willing to wait the better part of the day for the wind to appear, but this morning there is something different about the sea—the wind is gathering!

With wind in the sails, the controlled motion of the little ship has balanced our emotions. The land is growing small ... we stop looking back now that it has dipped below the horizon altogether; we gaze ahead as if we might be seeing new land at any time—knowing that there will be none for many days.

Now there is no return. We are going into the unknown; but we know for sure now that we are going.

CHAPTER THREE

The Marquesas,
A Faraway Place Indeed

*I*t is five days later and we are running before a strong breeze with a reefed jib and foresail. The weather is still far from ideal, but we are making fair progress along our course, and it means that we should soon reach the trade wind belt—"trade wind," such a magic word for sailors. We dare to hoist all three sails and, in spite of the ever-present squeamish feeling, pride stirs in us for our little ship, steering herself among the majestic swells.

Frequently, seemingly following a pattern, the wind dies, only to return unsteadily a few hours later.

The morning is windless. We stretch out on the foredeck, the way people sunbathe on yachts, and gaze into the mysterious deep ocean. Only one word presents itself: B*lue*—the ocean is a magical translucent blue. Now some very colourful creatures have appeared. They must have been nearby all along, but they are now around the bow, barely below the surface of the translucent blue.

"These must be dolphin fish," I venture to say. We have heard of such visitors. How alien they seem suspended in this element, with their many colours and peculiar shape. It occurs to us that it is more their environment than ours: if a storm comes up, if the ocean darkens and the swells grow steep, they simply sink below the waves and find shelter—they are at home. The way they stay with us makes their visit so personal. We throw a bait herring to them which they snap up in an instant. They cruise up slowly to a piece of cake, only to hurry away as if spooked, and take no notice of it again.

Fishing is out of the question, it would be a battle with our conscience for which we are not ready—so sensitive are we to our new environment. If I was to put a hook over, one of these creatures would probably swim up to it and snap it up; it would tug frantically

14

to free itself. I've been told that they change their colours several times as they die.

*   *   *

We are away from established shipping lanes and with the schooner usually steering herself, we fall into a habit of both of us staying awake during the day and sleeping at night. This has the familiarity of apartment dwelling: we turn out the light at night and go to sleep.

This morning, a casual glance at the compass becomes a long study—performed with open mouth. Our little apartment is heading east, instead of south-west. The wind has simply changed direction. Slightly embarrassed, I make the ship point south-west again, explaining meekly that we wouldn't have gone very far off course because the wind was light throughout the night. A slight drizzle begins and now we are becalmed once more. What seems to be the same school of fish shows up again. I still have no stomach for catching and gutting one of them; instead, I agree to try a little wine for lunch.

*   *   *

We have made very little progress in the past two days, but by now the shifting wind is calming my seasickness: the trade winds in the northern hemisphere are said to blow from the north-east and this new wind is blowing from that direction. What a disappointment, it is building up to gale force!

I'm trying to debate with myself what is harder: to smile and joke in order to put Marie-José at ease, or to take the necessary sun sights and work them out. To pull my face into a convincing smile when actually it wants to reflect the sorrowful state of my stomach, is truly a difficult task; by the time a single sun sight is worked out I feel dizzy; sweat is pouring off me.

The trade-wind gale has ended and large animals—whales—have arrived, keeping a fair distance off. Flying fish are landing on our decks frequently; a squall line on the horizon comes to our attention as we lie becalmed.

Thunder and lightning, rain and sunshine, squeeze into a time span of twenty minutes, and I believe that we are truly in the "doldrums"—an area dreaded by sailors because of the unbearable, endless, windless weeks one may be forced to spend in them.

Whenever a squall passes I'm anxious to hoist the full sails again, even to the fickle wind it leaves behind. No sooner have I sneaked into my bunk, than I'm called back on deck to reef down in a storm that has developed on the spot. The decks are already so steeply tilted that I am up to my calves in sea water when I stand to uncleat the main halyard. It is an unusual sensation to have cold rain gushing over me from above and warm sea water washing over me from below. I have already learned not to leave my clothes on, only to take them off wet afterwards; the rule now is to do this sort of job naked, except for a safety harness. Marie-José thinks I look like a Greek god, all wet and glistening. I'm ready to do it again, if that's the case.

Breezeless hours arouse speculative thoughts about our fate in this dreaded area, and as these thoughts weigh more heavily on us, we start the noisy little engine to forge ahead.

* * *

"Ah! here are these fish again, Marie-José." I was looking over the side. "Oh, no, they are mermaids!"

One of them did not hesitate to come on board. I was slightly confused—she was an older mermaid.

We both knew where we would sit. There was only one place: on the cabin top slightly ahead of midship with our lower extremities dangling onto the side deck. There, in relative seclusion, we faced out to sea.

We sat close to each other, so that when I looked into her face and saw all the wrinkles, I felt sad.

How she has aged, I thought.

Still, I felt wonderful in her presence. She was an old friend and she had not missed the opportunity to visit me as I was passing through. And she has aged well—actually hardly at all, she has delicate little wrinkles in a few places on her face.

I did not want to spoil the moments we shared, yet I could not let this opportunity go by: "Do you know if we are in the equatorial counter current?" I asked in a subdued voice, sure that she would know.

Her voice was soft and gentle: "I don't know. If you have a depth sounder you can find out."

A depth sounder? That wouldn't help here where the water is so deep, I thought! "But the weather has treated us so badly," I complained.

16

"Oh the weather," she said, again in a soft voice, "you've got all that behind you. From now on you'll have clear sailing."

Marie-José listens with interest to what I have to say. When I repeat the exact words: "Oh the weather, you have all that behind you...." she smiles and leers at the sky. Her voice is slightly higher than the mermaid's: "I guess dreams are what they are, just dreams."

I look at the sky, too. I look at the spot where we sat, on the cabin top just ahead of midship.

* * *

It took an extra day and a night. As this new day breaks, a fine wind—a smart wind blows from the south-east. We are a bit slow in accepting the fact that we are getting the first of the south-east trades.

A white bird often circles over us now. Flying fish are common. The clouds in the sky tell us that this is it—trade winds, and nothing else!

This morning is special: I deduce that sometime during the night we have crossed the equator. "Twenty miles south of the equator!" I announce with great confidence. How extraordinary it is to be able to measure the angle of the sun with a simple instrument, translate it into a few figures out of a book and say, "This is where we are!"

I experience another new sensation when I write in the log, "Only about 150 miles from the Marquesas—all hands are looking forward to our landfall." The next day the entry is even more exciting: "Should be seeing land tomorrow." At the same time I add, "Dying for some cold drinks, like a beer." Dying!—how thoughtless of me to use that word just now.

Marie-José sights land, the island of Ua Huka, on our fortieth day at sea. We are on its north-eastern side, instead of its north-western. Nuka Hiva should have been where Ua Huka is! We have read something about these islands not being charted properly. A noon sight places us to the north of the island on our French chart, and on the south side on our American chart.

It is thirty miles to Nuka Hiva, where we must make our formal entry before docking anywhere else. Our disappointment over not being able to make a snug anchorage today is replaced by contentment as we drift in the lee of Ua Huka at sunset.

"So here we are! The Marquesas, a faraway place indeed." I scrutinize everything within sight: the peculiar colours of the land-

17

scape—the shape of the islands—the sky—even the sea that we have been on all this time … to see if it's different here. A bee has appeared, if that's what it is. It is very large, and scraggy as a wild dog. We keep very still, as we do with bees at home, so it won't feel threatened and sting us.

I'm sure it's not my imagination, that smell; the islands are giving off a peculiar scent. "That's the South Sea scent!" I conclude. If it isn't another world altogether, it is at least a different world from the one we know.

We consider it a blissful night, sailing at a snail's pace toward Nuka Hiva. At sunrise it is already our second day among South Sea islands. We enter the bay that is named Taiohae.

Again scanning everything for possible dangers, and first impressions, we see about eight or ten yachts anchored at the head of the bay. I realize we are not far from others who have ventured across the ocean in a small boat to this remote spot. I see now that one I thought odd looking is actually a ketch with a broken main mast. Their experience has been different from ours.

The sun brightens the heavens and our spirits are high. I watch several snow-white birds flutter up and down the cliffs and find the word "snow" ironic when soon we will be seeking shelter from the intense tropical sun.

Ashore we are met by the local gendarme. He seems happy to see us and shows great interest in our voyage. First offering us a cigarette, he begins to fill in the necessary papers.

With the formalities behind us, we sit happily, cross-legged in the grass with a bottle of beer each and a stick of oven-fresh French bread.

CHAPTER FOUR

A Touch of Paradise

*T*he cold beer and the French bread were as unexpected as the presence of so many other yachts; we must adapt quickly and let a touch of paradise include a touch of Western civilization.

Acquiring our first bananas brings a wave of joy as does each new tropical fruit we discover. Pamplemousses are not unlike grapefruit, but they are so large, so sweet, so juicy and so flavourful. I stagger, happily, under a sack full of them, deeply breathing in the scented air. Wavelets of joy keep lapping over us—meeting local inhabitants, hearing melodious Polynesian songs, being part of this island way of life.

It would be sheer madness to wish for a "white Christmas" while listening to the people sing, and watching them sparkle. I feel I am on a slightly higher plain, regarding palm fronds and hibiscus flowers as perfect Christmas decorations.

*   *   *

"Tahitians, especially, work their derrière well," the wife of the gendarme, who is a Tahitian, tells us. She urges her daughters—she commands her daughters—to work them more. The two little girls, with just a tiny bit of self-consciousness—their skinny bums in motion—try yet a little harder and look again to their mother for approval.

"They must be more expressive with their derrières," she says. We think all the Marquesan ladies work their bums commendably, but then I suppose we don't really know how good it can get. We never thought of these movements as being practised in childhood.

It is New Year's Eve. The open pavilion is crowded with people. They shriek and squeal in delight with every new tune and they grind and sway to its rhythm.

Young ladies, each decorated with colours to her best advantage, give the impression of nature unfolding. For the moment they are the reasons I have sailed to the South Seas.

An older, mature lady, cannot resist a tune. A mature beauty, she uses her movements sparingly. She anticipates the music, executes an extra fine jerk, a bump, a grind ... It's like fireworks. "Ahhh's" from people watching on the sidelines fade as the next little wonder is anticipated.

I don't know what I feel exactly, perhaps sadness mixed with satisfaction. I am watching the movements of only one girl and thinking about myself. If our lives are not predetermined, if Marie-José had been, say, my sister, she would have answered "No," when earlier today, this same girl spied me, eyed me, walked up to her and charmingly asked, point blank: "Is he your man?" I cannot avoid looking at her dancing partner—her man—in my eyes a completely undeserving character. I see the flower in her hair, her simple white dress, her perfect body—if there is such a thing, and I become more melancholy, "She chose him after she was going to choose me!"

As they dance she displays her full sensuality—it cannot be anything less—to this ... "substitute."

* * *

The *langoustes* are intact except for being neatly split down the middle, having their insides exposed to my curious eyes. We realize with dismay that our hosts are not going to eat anything but will devote themselves to feeding us and four other guests. My own dilemma increases, for the lady has taken back the small and most harmless-looking *langouste,* which I had selected (I have never eaten *langouste* before), and replaced it with a mature one, with a lump stuck to its underside—a clump of eggs, I find out.

Although it is hard for me to appreciate, I have become the envy of the other guests. Luckily I am able to regard our lady host as a well-meaning mother, a friend, a Polynesian beauty, so I manage to convey, if not outright joy, contentment over my good fortune.

Our hosts seem happier serving the meal than we are eating it, but Polynesian smiles work wonders. Before the evening ends we agree to take Judy, Maxim and their children to visit their relatives at Haka Tea Bay aboard our schooner.

* * *

With a cargo of seven people, we enter a bay between steep massive rocks and lower the anchor where the bottom slopes up to a sandy beach. We are completely landlocked.

Haka Tea Bay might just be the lushest corner on the earth; as I look at the wide freshwater stream flowing from an arcade of trees, digging its bed into the sand of the beach, I cannot think of anything that is missing.

Three days have elapsed and now our boat is being reloaded with the same people plus one extra, as well as a lot of bananas.

At first it was only a big swell and a headwind, but now there are violent rain squalls as well. The conditions for our return trip seem entirely unfavourable. All too familiar with seasickness, I spot several children affected by it. The mother is blaming her own diminishing zest for life on the bananas; she no longer hands them out with the lovely giving gesture of the Polynesians.

The heavy responsibility of caring for other people is a new feeling for me. The children, whom I have the urge to count—six—every time the boat heels sharply under a strong burst of wind, give me increasingly long stares. I am becoming dismayed.

Maxim keeps his family organized on deck (none will go below) and although he can be counted on to help, even he, their father, is not able to convince the children that the boat cannot sail in a straight line, but must first sail out, before it can come back in. The children know where their bay is and look fiercely at me as yet again we tack away from the shore. Until now, I have seen Polynesians either passive or smiling; the young ones that are not too sick are neither. One of them stretches to his full height, and points firmly in the direction of Taiohae Bay. Using several sharp words, he glares at me challengingly. Did I not have a grip on myself, I would have taken this as an order, for better or for worse. But neither this child nor I is master of the elements.

The sun, occasionally blotted out by the squalls passing over us, is a lot brighter, now that we are entering the calm water of Taiohae Bay. The distance between the two bays is a mere six miles, yet it has been six-and-a-half hours since we left Haka Tea!

Happy feelings return now that we are moored and are unloading stalks of bananas together with prawns, boxes, parcels and children whose names I never did get straight.

21

Each day at Taiohae Bay is pleasant; the sky tries to repeat the shimmering blue of the day before. True enough—I have heard of this phenomenon—at least one brief rain shower occurs each day. It has the qualities of a happy event and few seek shelter from the tropical downpour. It is refreshing to be smiled at by faces that glisten with raindrops running down their cheeks and dripping from their noses. When it is all over, sometimes only a few seconds after it has begun, the sky looks as innocent as ever.

When the rain showers don't coincide with our desire for a fresh-water rinse, we can use a man-made shower placed conveniently near the dinghy landing.

Taiohae Bay has a post office and several small stores, where one can buy a stamp, receive a wonderful smile from the lady behind the counter by telling her how beautiful her island is, or, if one prefers, have a cold beer.

"Let's go to Ua Pou," I suggest. "We can stop again at Haka Tea Bay on the way."

*   *   *

I meant to pay strict attention, but I'm forced to admit, judging by the lay of the land, that we have overshot the entrance to Haka Tea Bay, even though we have only sailed for an hour. The entrance is hidden but the reason for sailing past, I suspect, is psychological. Although it is possible for our little schooner to sail from one bay to the other in an hour, we do not want to believe that we have actually done it when it took us over six hours in the opposite direction.

We sort out our confusion and turn the boat around: for a reward a tuna struggles on the fishing line we were bold enough to trail.

The calm waters at the entrance to Haka Tea Bay allow for flights of fancy. We glide past walls of blackish rock until, as proof that we have found the secret entrance, a long rocky spit recedes to reveal an opening through which we may pass into deeper enchantment! The schooner comes to rest inside a coral reef guarding the anchorage.

Daniel seems to be the unofficial chief of the bay. While he roasts a wild goat over the fire, he tells us of a great cascade further inland. It seems a must to see and I instruct Marie-José to get specific directions.

With the sun high, we are off on an expedition to this fabled spot. We have bananas for lunch, but here and there are mangoes in our

22

path, as ready to eat as they will ever be. The trail leads past empty dwellings and some very curious, obviously man-made, pits in the ground. Daniel later explains that the pits were used by his forbears to ferment breadfruit in times of plenty, for use in the lean years. The fermented fruit is called *poi,* so the pits were at one time used for making *poi-poi.*

All along, that sweet smell I have come to associate with the South Seas has been with us. It is hard to believe—as has been suggested— that this smell is given off by rocks and rotting vegetation. I'm still convinced that the living things—those brilliant hibiscus flowers, the fruits just ripening—are responsible.

Our sweet-smelling trail has ended before it has led us to the cascades, and we are puzzled. Daniel had said to follow the trail, which we assumed would lead us to the waterfall.

"Didn't Daniel tell you which way to go when the trail ends?" I ask Marie-José.

"No, he just said to follow the trail." A man on a horse has appeared! We never expected to see a man on a horse, but here he is. Would he know where the cascades are?

"Over there," he says. We are not satisfied with this information. "Over there" is the answer these beautiful people give to many requests for direction. We have sometimes felt stupid not being able to find something we were told was "over there." Having lived in a small area all their lives, they know where everything over there is.

Marie-José interrogates him in French, while I drink in the scene. This man, equipped with sacks and bush knife, is obviously doing copra—gathering and splitting coconuts, extracting the meat from them.

"He will show us," Marie-José says finally. The man leaves his horse and leads the way to a creek, which he indicates we should follow.

We walk along the banks of the creek, but it is easier to keep right in the middle. We can hear the falls now! One more bend, and one more and the creek ends—high walls of rock, the noise of a great falls, but no falls in view. We are standing in a shallow lagoon—we wade forward and the falls are revealed to us—a magnificent sight! I look at Marie-José who appears overcome with feelings of wonder and awe.

Had we not got lost in this picture-book jungle after we left the falls, we would have made it back to the bay a few hours earlier; as it is we are just in time for one of Antoinette's best Polynesian smiles, accompanied by a bowl of fish and breadfruit salad that she and her daughter-in-law have prepared.

All afternoon we have been bitten by the *nou-nous*. They are tiny little flies that attack exposed skin, in our case mostly the ankles. Their tiny nibbles are hardly noticeable but the itching that sets in about twenty hours later is a test of human endurance.

Tonight, with spirits high, a bowl of fish and breadfruit salad, a glass of wine and some leftover bread, we are where we want to be—tomorrow we'll endure the itching.

* * *

"Klaus, take a big one, I have no small one," Daniel is pleading. He startles me by pronouncing the few English words he knows, almost without an accent.

I have asked to buy a stalk of bananas, but he won't hear of it. In reply to my insistence that I will only accept a small stalk, he tells Marie-José that only a week ago he gave three big stalks to another yacht. First he gave them one big one but the people simply said, "There are seven of us on board." So he added two more big ones. Anger and embarrassment rise in me. I wish I had never asked for bananas; I would leave the bay with sweeter memories. But this is how we are: I ask for a small stalk of bananas, and the crew of another yacht asks for more ... Daniel does not approve of greed but he does not judge. He is a Polynesian.

Daniel is standing knee-deep in the surf holding the dinghy steady for us to climb in and get sorted out. The oars are in their locks and I brace myself—he gives his push in unison with my first stroke. Then—the inevitable wave.

* * *

Ua Pou, *Holes with Needles*, cannot be mistaken for another island. The needles point starkly at the sky, threatening to pierce any cloud that come their way. If I was to live in the Marquesas, I would not live on Ua Pou; I would live on one of the other islands so I could look over to Ua Pou and say, "Wow, what an island!"

We are sailing toward it with our large stalk of bananas suspended in the rigging. We enter Haka Hetau Bay, Ua Pou's principal bay, and I visualize what it would be like here in strong winds. The waters in the bay are overly agitated with the light wind that is blowing. We prepare to spend a night in the rolling motion.

We are below, resigned that we cannot make a landing by dinghy, when we hear voices—shrieks and yells. They come from five young ladies standing on the concrete pier, who apparently want us to come ashore.

We are willing to give it another try because if they want us to come ashore they must think it is possible for us to do so. We are near the short concrete pier and the girls are in focus, beautiful, playful and excited; but there is only one word for the landing conditions we are facing—dangerous; or maybe two—very dangerous. The swell often washes over the pier and recedes with a great suction. The girls giggle and laugh and run off to avoid being washed by the sea, though they come right back to continue giving us directions.

I row in again, stern first. They excitedly point at a big wave; they want me to row back out in a hurry! I think I should call it quits, but they motion us to hurry in. This time I'm able to manoeuvre the dinghy to the desired spot. The rope we throw falls short but they grab hold of the oars, Marie-José, the dinghy and me....

An extraordinary scramble brings us to the top of the pier; I have held onto Marie-José, one oar, and the dinghy part of the time. Everybody is soaked and laughing as we carry the dinghy up so that it cannot get washed away.

We are laughing—perhaps because the girls' laughter is contagious. The scramble up the pier was certainly worth a hearty laugh. But I'm wondering why we attempted something so dangerous. Because of five girls?

Absent-mindedly, my gaze rests on a girl with a sturdy body but missing several teeth. She notices me looking and covers her mouth. The girl knows I was wondering about how she had lost so many teeth, but "How are we going to get back?" is uppermost in my mind.

With the ingenious philosophy of now is now and later is later, we follow the girls into the village. Although I am enjoying myself, meeting local inhabitants, buying a straw hat, drinking coconut juice... the few hours would be more pleasant were I not keenly aware that we will have to repeat our great accomplishment in reverse before the day is done.

25

The ocean is malicious. It heaves and washes over the landing with every wave. We had dared to hope it would be calmer by now. Even the girls (only two of the five have come along to help relaunch the dinghy) who are carefree, and whose necks are not at stake, do not think the mole a safe place to launch a dinghy. They look along the rubble dike. We all look along the rubble dike—it is the only alternative.

Two to a side, we carry the dinghy until we become exhausted and our feet are sore. We are willing to try it from here. We watch the waves, not just to judge their size but also to become attuned to their rhythm. Some are spellbinding as they smash into the dike with pandemonium; others are much smaller.

Twenty minutes of wave-watching have gone by and none of the waves has been the right one. A young male native has come to give his advice—he is largely ignored by the ladies. For a moment I become a spectator, too. "Now!" One girl is pulling on the dinghy— she is determined, the moment is here, we are almost in tune. With the dinghy between us we rush down the steep rubble dike; Marie-José and I let go of it early, time is precious, the girls hold it steady; we leap inside, I do a quick stroke with the oars—I can see the wave coming—ah, good, I get in one more stroke. The wave has not yet broken—it passes harmlessly underneath us to crash violently into the rubble.

CHAPTER FIVE

Peaks, Reefs, and Lagoons

After three weeks in this place with a touch of paradise, I cannot come up with a better reason for leaving than the sake of travelling on. This is a place of positive thoughts and magical moments—we have even seen a rainbow trapped against a rock wall so that the end was within our reach.

I'm looking restlessly at the horizon knowing we could sail toward it anytime but not knowing how to explain myself to Marie-José, who is quite willing to stay for a while. I mention our financial situation. "We should prepare ourselves for a return voyage...." It sounds very feeble. But then something very clear and simple emerges: "The winds are right for a passage to Tahiti." Marie-José looks about, knowing this is true. "We'll be staying at many more places," I say encouragingly. I think she is catching the mood and is ready to look at the horizon.

The 700-mile passage that we are setting out on today, January 11, has an exciting ring to it. When I only knew Tahiti as the name of an island in the vast Pacific I was always intrigued that this small island should have acquired such fame and prominence. Now, entering "Tahiti" into the logbook as our next destination, it becomes something tangible.

After three weeks at sheltered anchorages the seas seem big. But they are typical seas caused by a steady trade wind, and the good thing about them is that they don't get any bigger, they stay relative to the steady winds. The little ship falls in with the rhythm of the wave pattern, allowing me to anticipate its motion.

I'm in no mood to complain, though I feel seasick. With high spirits and a comfortable reclining position I suppress it, until a wave of it washes over me as I am called upon, as skipper, to take a sight with the sextant.

* * *

If anyone ever asks me if we make love at sea, on a small boat, I will say, forget it—it's the furthest thing from my mind. Then why is it on my mind? Marie-José's glances at me have until now been mostly analytical, to check the degree of seasickness; but now she is looking at me with astonishment. This makes her look even more attractive. Although she doesn't feel sick, she thinks that the heaving of the little ship is not conducive to lovemaking. But she concludes that if the skipper, for once, feels that good on the heaving ocean, why spoil it for him.

Here is a clear-cut example of how the species survive! They will mate under less than favourable circumstances. I feel a little sheepish, and maybe brave, and somewhat bold, for mingling the motions of lovemaking with the motions of the boat.

* * *

I'm seeing everything in a new way today, having woken with a nasty pain in my groin. I show my mate the swollen lymph nodes, concluding that a tiny little something on the bottom of my foot was originally a puncture. I remember that in warm water bacteria grow fast.

We cannot attempt to sail back to the Marquesas. To beat back against the trades could take more time than I want to guess. Tahiti is perhaps a six-day sail, with the boat practically sailing herself; Marie-José can manage on her own if I give her the course to steer. Tahiti is about three times as far from us in miles as the Marquesas, but being down-wind it's a lot closer. Thus I have made my decision.

Marie-José is taking care of me. No meat or dairy products is one part of her prescription, the administration of Golden Seal root is the other. In a quiet mood, reflecting on the pitfalls in life, I follow instructions.

Marie-José eyes me with new interest every day. She is encouraged when I announce that it isn't getting any worse. A spot on the top of my foot (not the bottom where the wound was) has become very itchy and a mole is forming. The swelling in the groin goes down— Marie-José is triumphant.

We have not been able to draw a straight course from the Marquesas to Tahiti on our Mercator chart. The Tuamotus, or more

28

suspensefully called, "dangerous archipelagos," lie in the way. One has to go around them, or weave one's way through. We have steered a course to take us between the *motu* Takahau, the northernmost of the Tuamotus' maze of coral islands, and an island named Matahiva on the chart. This morning, the seventh day, it is time to look for them.

Coming upon a place suddenly, without having looked for it, is an experience where suspense is replaced by surprise. This morning I have come up on deck with the intention of carefully scanning the horizon and the first thing I see over the tops of the white-caps is a congregation of coconut trees.

Having no charts that show details of these coral formations, it is challenging to go near them. The winds seems stronger today and the tops of the waves are foaming; we seem to move along so swiftly. I have not come to grips with the situation, and yet I find myself looking abaft the beam at the coconut trees. How the palms sway in the wind, their fronds clustered together.

*   *   *

Yesterday we passed the *motu* Takahau; the noon sight I have just worked out places us only fifty miles from Tahiti. It is both a thrilling and an uncomfortable distance to be from the island. We can't possibly do that many miles before nightfall but will do more than that before dawn. As we do not want to arrive at night, we must slow the ship by reducing sail.

One would have to be way off course to miss Tahiti. A shadow in the shape of a great mountain looms ahead, yet we are still forty miles from it.

Under a shower of stars, I tell Marie-José, "I can smell the land." Big Tahiti! We can see its shape and, with the uncertainty of such a dark night, we are approaching its shores—its reefs.

We are only halfway through the night, but the shore lights sprinkled in front of us must surely be lights of Papeete, the capital. I hate to pull Marie-José from her cozy sleep, but we are too close and must turn the schooner around, away from the shores. I recall all the times that the boat went too slow when we wanted it to go faster.

The morning greys as we again point the bow towards Papeete whose location—a gift from the night—was revealed to us by all its lights. The wind, however, is no longer favourable. It causes me some unexpected apprehension as it gusts from ahead of the beam.

Under shortened sails we approach the pass—a curious moment for us. How fascinating the ocean is as it foams over the reef; if only we didn't have to go near there in order to go to Tahiti.

"Listen! Do you hear that?—that's the waves breaking on the reef." How unfair not to have a perfect day for entering the pass. My mind is considering all the things I might do to bring our little ship into harbour....

I'm greatly relieved when I finally have a clear view of the pass. It is actually quite wide and, more significant, clearly marked by buoys.

* * *

When coming into a new place, my attention is always divided between getting a first impression and finding a place to moor. Here, it is all one. Yachts are anchored stern to all the way from the quay in the heart of Papeete, down to the boundless beach; the incredibly long and colourful line of sea-going sailing yachts is easily the most outstanding single feature inside the reef.

The wind is far too strong for us to make the manoeuvre of mooring by taking lines ashore, and we content ourselves with swinging to an anchor at the end of the line.

Later, we take advantage of the early-morning calm to move into a gap in the long line of yachts, dropping our forty-pound plow and securing two stern lines to trees. Immediately next to the trees is a sidewalk and a wide road with a rush of vehicles in both directions. As I stand here, in my swimming shorts, for I have swum the mooring lines ashore, I might look like just another guy, but I am a sponge for the variety of impressions washing over me—the large number of yachts from everywhere, straining at their anchors, their national flags, courtesy flags and burgees fluttering and snapping in the wind, their masts swaying each to its own rule, with halyards drumming to their own rhythm. And on the other side of me, there is the rush of traffic with honks and mutters and screeches and burrs and beautiful Tahitian ladies on mopeds ... I suspect I am even part of this uproariousness, as I stand here, in my swimming shorts.

* * *

I suppose when yachts arrive in large numbers, long waits are normal, but something here is all wrong. The officials don't ask about our voyage or offer us a cigarette.

"Have you a visa? How much money have you?" are the questions, and "You must post a bond!" is the gesture.

How unfair, is my mental reply, after we endured this long passage, lived under the stars, were guided here by the sun and tried to think well about the world.

"All new regulations," they explain. For a two-month stay we are required to come up with a sum of money that amounts to more than we expect to spend in a year. Still, I detect a trace of sympathy in the official. We have time to come up with the money, he explains, but are not allowed to move our boat until we do.

The solution is to find a trusting sailor, with the amount of money we are short, borrow it and.... We have found him. He hopes that the officials don't record serial numbers as he has just received the money back after lending it to somebody else for the same purpose. Not knowing us that well he stays nearby while we demonstrate convincingly that, with his money pooled with our's, we will be able to live in luxury, as seems to be the requirement. I remember Daniel telling us with a grin that five bananas will cost one dollar in Papeete—when he only had big stalks to give away.

But no matter what the officials expect, Tahiti is a striking place. The beauty of the people matches that of the island. Even what could be considered a fat woman is a pleasant sight, as she effortlessly makes her way along the street as though she has oil in her joints.

My mouth is open, but I'm lost for words. A young man, a Canadian who noticed our flag, is asking emphatically, "Where are all the beautiful women that are supposed to be here?" He seems eager to sue someone for false advertising. "When I get home and people ask me if the women here are beautiful, I'll have to say 'No'."

He just can't see it our way. He is travelling fast, by plane, and I guess he has little time for letting, or making, things happen.

The beauties are definitely here. I think that even the fat ones could exchange their company for something as valuable as a rusty nail was in the days of Captain Cook. I do not tell this world traveller of one beauty—not a fat one—who waded into the water by our stern, with a flower in her hair, and a pareu around her which she had to re-adjust, momentarily exposing her full body.

I think what has me lost for words with this fellow Canadian is that he is ugly as sin himself, and I only tolerate him in the hopes that he is beautiful inside.

31

* * *

We take the passage between the barrier reef and the island to Maeva Beach. It is thrilling to navigate amongst the corals in clear sheltered water. Since the channel is well marked, we can view everything, the coral formations, the different colours in the water, the changing shore line, with little apprehension.

Now that we are in the tropics we cannot wait to put on a diving mask and look at the reefs! The day is brilliant as we row the dinghy across the lagoon, anchoring it a healthy distance from where the Pacific waves break. It is quite wondrous how calm it can be on the lagoon side of the reef, with all the pandemonium of the breaking waves on the other. It is even calmer only a few feet below the surface. An array of colours and shapes—fingers, arms, branches, columns, fans—are scattered at random and yet seemingly arranged in their places. There are clams with blue and purple lips like ruffles, and starfish as well. Little fish, very colourful, as befitting the tropics, come right up to me—they seem most interested in my diving mask.

What do I feel, what do I think?

"Like I am in another world," I answer.

To intense sunlight and the roar of the surf, I break water to report to Marie-José what I saw. Marie-José, having had thirteen, mostly unsuccessful, operations on and around her ears, cannot submerge her head without risk. For that matter, she can't swim. I hand her the mask and carefully, only submerging the mask, she looks at the reef from the dinghy.

* * *

In preparation for our onward passage to more of the Society Islands (of which Tahiti is the principle one), we have again taken a spot in the long line of yachts at Papeete's waterfront.

We have cleared with customs, immigration and the harbour master but something about the weather makes us feel like waiting a day.

We are glad of our decision, innocent though it was, for the weather is really deteriorating. The second day it is worse yet. There are now breakers in the pass—heavy rain squalls are hitting the island. Everybody knows of an approaching cyclone! The harbour officials are now insisting that every yacht has at least two anchors down. They suggest that all yachts move into the inner harbour and they offer assistance to the ones without engines. The gay line of yachts is rapidly dissolving.

The approaching storm has thrown us together with a delightful sailor, a single-hander by the name of Rolf. We first saw him at the Immigration Department where his sun-burned face showed an ecstatic smile to officials. Now, in an onshore wind and a heavy chop, we help one another to re-anchor. This suspenseful evening is far from unpleasant in the company of a smiling companion with a gap between his front teeth, which Marie-José knows to be the mark of good luck.

We wake to a rather dull day, though warm and still. Cyclone Diana struck the island of Bora Bora during the night and we are getting the edges of it—the center has already gone past Tahiti the radio announces.

The danger has passed, but the seas are mountainous. It will take a day or two for the pass through the reef to be negotiable. Rolf, too, wants to leave. He feels that tomorrow the pass will be tame enough.

Nevertheless, the pass is still wild enough for an exhilarating trip. The open ocean is more playful than dangerous: up we go, and down we roll. Rolf's sloop, *Resolute,* is coming up astern. We are both sailing by eye for Tahiti's sister island, Moorea, which is only about twenty miles away, although it looks a lot closer.

Even though *Resolute* left one hour after us, she is the first to stand into Tarea Pass leading into Papetoai Bay. We have arrived into the middle of a setting for a perfectly balanced picture. All one has to do is put a frame around it; we anchor in the foreground.

I often wonder why certain things linger in the foreground of our minds. The place where one falls in love is memorable but not necessarily beautiful. Tahiti's waterfront is memorable to me because of a woman with a flower in her hair who waded into the water near our stern lines. I'm searching for what it is that makes one moment more vivid than the rest: a woman who stands out among a thousand others, and this present scene, a teeth-gritting coral reef guarding white beaches, fruit-bearing slender palms and a jagged peak, all topped with a generous formation of clouds in radiant colours. Perhaps it is some quality of bravery or uniqueness.

Rolf is so enjoying himself that he would lose track of time were it not for a feeling of duty to rejoin his family, and his wife's poems that he receives in various ports. He had bought his boat in England and felt obliged to sail it to Australia, his home, single-handed, as his wife gets so violently seasick that she could not attempt the voyage. He would never, however, do another single-handed voyage. I can appreciate that. He told us of being in a long calm, where one day was like the next: a glossy sea, the boat leaving no wake, and the only source of orientation, the glaring sun, becoming meaningless. The mind plays tricks when there is no one to talk to, to compare with, and one must prove one's sanity to oneself. Suspended in the calm his thoughts lost focus: *is today yesterday—or yesterday tomorrow? When is tomorrow?*

But he is, according to his teeth, a lucky person, and he is still smiling broadly. We enjoy his company, so we ask him to stay with us at Moorea for a few extra days.

* * *

It looks as if Rolf will be staying with us a few more days than he agreed to. A new cyclone, Charles, has been born. Rolf has been lucky again, according to our calculations he should be about in Charles' center had he left when he planned to.

I'm lucky too. Rolf is showing me new methods of celestial navigation using a series of calculations which result in a position line on the chart. One such line is already very valuable to a navigator; but a second one crossing the first gives a fix. This method can be used with stars, moon and planets—any time a heavenly body and the horizon are visible.

Until now, due to ignorance, I have been using the noon-sight navigation method where the sun is observed at local noon. If it's cloudy or hazy, the one chance to get a fix for this day is gone.

There are no further cyclone warnings, the days are again typical for the South Seas—brilliant, warm and scented. Our heart-warming friend weighs anchor.

* * *

We left Moorea yesterday, at noon, and sailing through the night has brought us to the island of Huahine. How easy it is: leave one beautiful island, sail through the night under a shower of stars and arrive at another magical place when a new day begins.

Shades of green contrast with the blue of the ocean and the white glitter a distance from the shores show the reef's edges. From the spreaders, half way up the mast, I can clearly see the gap in the reef, which we are about to go through. Again we tie our lines to trees, but here there is no rush-hour traffic.

In a very similar fashion we sail to the two islands next in line that share a common lagoon and barrier reefs, Raiatea and Tahaa. I have now come to appreciate the secure harbours these encircling reefs make and no longer regard them with dread alone.

Bora Bora, this last island in French Polynesia, seems to want to imprint itself in our minds for all time. From a lagoon that shimmers with pastel colours, knife-edged rocks project up and touch the clouds. The encircling reef is complete, save for one break—the pass we will use to enter. We were told that what one sees of Bora Bora is the rim of a volcanic crater. And so it is, two thirds of a rim—one side is left open through which we sail, to anchor inside the crater.

But the bottom of the crater does not prove good holding. We fare no better than another yacht and drag a considerable distance. Topua, a *motu* in the lighter-coloured waters of the lagoon, seems an appealing place to anchor near. There are wild guavas on the *motu* for those who don't find the bush too prickly.

Every island has a character of its own. While all feature reefs, peaks, palms and lagoons, each one has a different arrangement and thereby creates its own atmosphere and flavour. Each island, according to its size and formation, shapes its own clouds.

No matter what the winds are like in and around the islands, five or ten miles off, the trades are usually found, and when abaft the beam, the going is always good. The wind has been billowing out our sails for hours, but Bora Bora, astern of us, is still imprinted on our minds as the perfect South Sea island.

*   *   *

The rhythm goes on and on. The boat heels a little—then rolls back again. The wave has gone underneath us; a new one repeats the pattern.

I want to keep things in perspective! I don't want to think about the very hard beginning of our voyage. I want to enjoy the here and now, the South Sea islands. But having seen our first island, and then many more, it's all a little less magical.

Should there be magic at all? Why not be realistic? They are only islands in a deep wide ocean and we are only a couple of people in a small boat.

Reality or make-believe, we are here sailing with a commanding breeze—if I handle myself carefully I can suppress my seasickness and experience a warm wind caressing my neck and cheek. At night our wake is phosphorescent. Should one sail here without thinking about the universe? Is it better to be here thinking about it than to live a life of preoccupation in a city? Are we here in the fabled South Seas with our tiny ship because we haven't made any fatal mistakes and have persevered.

For days now we have been listening to Radio Rarotonga. The music is delightful, but what are these constant interruptions?

"Vote Cook Island Party, the strong one ..." Hang on a minute, I protest. We didn't come all this way to listen to politics—these are the South Seas! It is obvious the island is not expecting us!

As we stretch our necks to see the land that houses the radio transmitter, the wind boxes the compass. The clouds that are moving in are dark, the rain heavy.

The wind has settled into its new quarter and allows us to continue on our course into shrouds of mist. The commercial radio with the annoying slogan is even of some help. By turning our receiver, and therefore its antenna, I can determine that "Vote Cook Island Party, the strong one ..." is coming directly from abeam. It is time to heave to.

When the skies clear we see the attractive island with a rather unwelcoming harbour entrance. The reef extends out from the shore and the man-made harbour has suffered much damage from Cyclone Charles.

A more significant sight is the big iron hulk a little further down the shore where another harbour used to be. So this is where she ended up, the *Yankee!* I have read somewhere that she has sailed around our little planet seven times, and here she is.

We have come at election time; one simply cannot get anywhere with the officials, at least not very quickly. We have just received our visitor's permit that is good for seven days but it is already our fifth day on the island. It's time to apply for an extension.

Still, if one could put all the illogical things aside, the island can qualify as pleasant. I'm pursuing my favourite pastime of laying in a good supply of fruit. Being cheap and plentiful, this small island boasts a large plant where local fruits are canned, without preservatives.

I am trying to come to terms with the politics of this small island, realizing that they are going through a certain stage of political evolution.

Later we learned that, Sir Albert Henry, leader of "Cook Island Party, the strong one ..." eventually declared himself elected. The New Zealand government subsequently unseated him. After he was stripped of his knighthood by the Queen, he let it be known: "I still have my coconut trees." This is perhaps not an overwhelming philosophical thought, but it demonstrates how resigned a man can be when his dreams are shattered. But then again, if he could rediscover how wondrous a coconut tree is—almost a sure proof of life's abundance, he may have thanked the Queen.

Besides waiting for the outcome of the election, the island's population is waiting for the cargo of a ship anchored offshore. The winds are unfavourable, and the ship risks being driven onto the reef. It puts out to sea again.

*   *   *

The trades are in our sails, Rarotonga is receding steadily. I anticipated that I would have no regrets on leaving, although I still like the appearance of this small island. The people, I'm sure, are as good as any, once they get politics out of their hair.

I'm still laughing about one event on Rarotonga: I invited a couple of locals to come on board around midnight, after we had been to the Banana Court Bar. And so, drinks in hand we made for the harbour and our eight-foot dinghy by which we were to reach our schooner. One fellow was small, but I studied the other with a critical eye. He was big, very big! Still, our dinghy had held four people with freeboard to spare, so why not this small guy, me and this big one? The dinghy did sink, in a more or less level way—we were all in our respective places but with water up to our chests. No one said anything. I finally remembered who was in command and yelled, "Swim to the boat!"

They took it all so calmly, I felt I had overreacted.

I arrived at the schooner with the dinghy in tow and was astonished to see the two of them already sitting in the cockpit.

Marie-José offered them towels, but they declined and took a swig from their cans. "You saved your drinks!" I exclaimed.

It was their turn to look at me in astonishment. "Well, sure, why wouldn't we?" they replied.

We all laughed and the one who had "sunk" the dinghy asked to play my guitar. At two o'clock we decided to look at the island from another angle. The big fellow had worked in New Zealand for many years to get his car and now that he had it, he drove it. We covered every yard of the twenty-two miles of road that lead around the island.

CHAPTER SIX

Island on Its Own

*A*PRIL 16: The wind veered around to the SE for only a short time then went back to N-NW. Many squalls. Thunder and lightning. We keep all sails reefed during night due to prolonged squalls. Heavy spray landing on the decks.

APRIL 17: Beating in very light winds. Skies cloudy. No sight. Drizzling rain.

APRIL 18: No progress.

APRIL 19: No wind at all. No more rain. Clearer skies. From one extreme to the other. Position: 19 degrees 50 minutes south, 163 degrees 41 minutes west. First visible sunset in many days.

APRIL 20: Calm. Sea flat. Went for a dip and short swim. Around 10 o'clock slight breeze from SE—could be trade winds gathering.

* * *

This last rain shower seems to have marked the end of the unsettled weather. With steady trades and a friendly sky we are sinking back into a comfortable and agreeable routine of tending the boat and looking after each other.

Hearing a siren, suddenly, in the middle of the ocean can be hair-raising. Could there be a boat, or—oh, it's our fishing reel. We have forgotten about our fishing line, and we seem to have caught a big one! But where is it? All I'm reeling in is the line. The lure and hook are gone and with them half of the stainless steel leader.

In our wake, I see a long dark shape catching up with us. We can look almost straight down onto a fish, about five feet long with a sword extending from its head. Prompted by curiosity I throw a small herring into the water ahead of it … it is spooked and shoots away.

Knowing that this creature is now burdened with a piece of plastic and some steel in its mouth, or stomach, tarnishes a brilliant day.

* * *

It's our fourteenth day out from Rarotonga and Marie-José is out on deck straining her eyes to see land. I told her that we should be able to see Niue Island in the morning but now, even though it is well after sunrise, no land is in sight.

Although I'm restricted to one position line with only the one morning sunsight, it reveals that we should be no more than twenty miles from the island. Tahiti can be seen from forty miles away on a clear day, and from sixty or more miles away on a very clear day, so where is Niue? We look again … and yes, we are heading towards a very faint line above the horizon.

An hour later we can see that Niue is a very flat island, about 200 feet high all the way across. High peaks, so typical of the French-Polynesian islands, are absent.

The birds are around us now, all diving for fish. We are trailing our line again, this time with a plastic squid for a lure, and one bird makes yet another dive for it. We have often noticed that where there are birds feeding on little fish, big fish also feed. I'm reeling in a fat, metallic-looking tuna who, out of its element, is pounding on our cockpit.

A good following wind makes us confident about anchoring in Alofi Bay before dark. We normally make very slow passage with our thirty-foot schooner, but now the wind and current are pushing us on, and we are closing with the land very fast. By mid-afternoon we have the island on our beam, and now, we only have to sail around to the west side, to Alofi Bay, the port of entry and the normal anchorage for boats visiting Niue. Sitting on deck, we rejoice at sailing in the lee of an island that we did not know existed until we planned our route from Bora Bora a few months ago.

Niue is all on its own, with nothing around it for about 230 miles. We have no detailed chart of this island that measures roughly ten by twelve miles, so we debate whether Alofi Bay is what we are seeing now or is around the next point. A fisherman in an aluminum boat has altered course and comes over. "Hello! Next point Alofi Bay, next point!" are his greetings.

Now, where to anchor? The pilot book mentions anchorage in

100 feet with coral bottom. Only one boat is in the bay, a local fishing boat and it is on a permanent mooring. Even if we did find a spot in about sixty feet of water, it is still not encouraging with a coral bottom. A fisherman in a peculiar canoe has turned his face toward us—"Is this a good spot to anchor?" I ask him.

"Over there."

"Where over there?"

"I show you." He is paddling away, to "over there," moving his craft easily through the water at about four knots. His dugout terminates in slender points at both ends and is decked over except for the mid-section. Amidships, a strip of wood is added to give it more freeboard. Overall it has the appearance of a kayak with an outrigger. (Each canoe, we found out later, is built with the size and weight of the future occupant in mind, so that there are hardly two alike.)

Our guide has come to a stop, as close to the reef as anyone would care to come with a yacht. From the water he has pulled a thick rope. As he holds it up higher, we see a small grown-over float attached to the rope. It is a mooring. We hand down our line.

"Is that strong?"

"Yes, all the yachts tie up here." As the weather is stable, I will wait until tomorrow to have a look at this mooring. Several other natives have come out in their canoes, all very friendly, asking many questions.

"Did you catch a fish?"

This is an area of expertise for them, and I'm a little glad to be able to say, "Yes, we caught a tuna!"

"How big? With what? Where? Where do you come from?" Our little green plastic squid is receiving skeptical looks. "That's a very small line."

"We don't want to catch too big a fish."

"But you can lose your hook."

I know they are right.

An aluminum boat has come out with the doctor and customs officer. They are cheerful and ask a few questions. We are the first yacht to visit the island this season. Now that they have cleared us, they are off duty ... I'm thinking of the half bottle of rum we still have, and of all that canned pineapple juice from Rarotonga.

These happy and dignified people are telling us about their island.

41

Niue is independent and has a population of around 3,000—their native tongue is spoken only on this island. There have been as many as five yachts in the bay all at once, they tell us proudly.

This day has been perfect enough for us, and I think we will always remember it—a glorious sail, a fish, making the anchorage before dark, the best reception anywhere. Now, the setting sun is creating a panorama of colours over the whole western sky. We have all fallen silent—the natives of Niue apparently don't see the sky as ablaze as this too often either.

It was only a half bottle of rum but in the meantime it has got very dark. There are no fees to be paid, we are assured again. The doctor's mild voice delivers an invitation, "It is one of my rare days off tomorrow. I would like to drive you around the island."

*   *   *

I'm astonished. Our boat is in over fifty feet of water and with my mask on I can see every detail on the seabed. It's intriguing to see the boat suspended above me, a long line connecting it with the shelf, which we are moored to. Not far to seaward is a drop-off and another shelf, beyond that, only a deep blue.

The mooring consists of a heap of heavy scrap iron, a length of chain, which is buoyed and reaches to within twenty feet of the surface. The rest is a double rope with another small float. As the rope system from the chain to the surface has many knots, we drop our small anchor about twenty feet from the scrap iron with the rope left coiled up on deck, ready to run out should the anchor come into action.

We meet Dick, the doctor, on land. "We call this the 'backside' of the island," he explains. The road which encircles the island traces the shores before it cuts a little ways inland. We leave the main road and go down a narrow trail, until we reach a dead end. Dick wants to show us a special place.

Hiking down amidst flowering bushes and palms beside a formidable wall of rock, we come to a small creek that emerges from the rock bottom and trickles into a lagoon almost completely enclosed by high rock walls and boulders. Dick says very little, very quietly—the place speaks for itself. Here reigns a solemn coolness on an otherwise hot tropical island.

We pass through villages, forests and plantations. This village here looks slightly familiar ... well, doing a round trip we were bound to come back to Alofi again.

"Many people don't know that we have a hotel here," Dick is saying, proposing to drive there. He must be right: we had not even known of Niue Island until a few months ago, let alone the hotel—just as few people know about the airport that can accommodate passenger jets.

The hotel far is enough off the beaten track but grand enough to have a polished and well-versed manager whom everyone meets. One has the feeling that important business is conducted here, important beers are drunk here. Dick's cousin, Wilfred, is here, and is going to accompany us to a big party at the doctor's house.

As we have been to Rarotonga, Wilfred wants to know if we met his good friend Tangi. Would we know Tangi? Unless there is more than one, then it is the very one that sank our dinghy. "Is he a real big fellow?" Wilfred's face lights up with admiration.

The party is truly getting under way. Dick's sons are producing the sweet sounds of Polynesian music and the lady of the house adds her beautiful voice.

Wilfred has been telling me a great deal of the most interesting, if not hair-raising, accounts of his diving experiences. He stops short and says, "Food, you are going to have some food now." I see fire in his eyes and hear the emotion in his voice. In the next room the cause of his excitement is laid out before us: a delicious feast of a variety of fish in coconut cream and local vegetables. Like good Polynesians, we pass food to our mouths with our hands.

* * *

Captain Cook gave Niue the name "Savage Island" and like many other Niuens, Wilfred is opposed to the name.

"Why did he do that—why? Why?" he demands to know.

History says that Cook never landed on Niue but merely observed it from his ship, and the name "Savage Island" appeared next to a little dot on charts of the South Pacific, with total disregard for the name the inhabitants had already given the island, Niue.

I have no satisfactory answer for Wilfred, for it is likely that it was not Cook's intent to single out one island as being more "savage" than another. I ask the doctor if he knows the answer. When Cook approached this island, Dick offers, his forefathers went down to the shores with their spears, ready to defend their very small land.

Wilfred is even more distressed now because I have told him a historical fact: Captain Cook was eventually killed in the Hawaiian Islands.

"No! No! No!"

He is shaken. Far from being pleased that Cook got what was coming to him after naming Niue Island so unjustly, Wilfred is as indignant as a mother who refuses to believe that one of her perfect children could have committed murder, even in self-defense.

I have suddenly woken up to the fact that Dick had the whole day arranged for us. Marie-José is tired and he is showing her to *our* room.

Almost everybody else has gone to sleep, but Dick, Wilfred and I are passing the guitar back and forth between us. There is a sense of brotherhood in Wilfred's haunting melody, accompanied by Dick, who is singing with the most precise, delicate voice as if to lure away from the universe the mysteries of life. Although I cannot understand the words the melody touches me.

Dick hands me the guitar and I sing about cold winds and snow and find it oddly out of place ... except now that I look up, I see the warmth of their appreciation.

* * *

Unfortunately, Niue is very low on fruit and vegetables due to a great drought last year. People will not sell us any vegetables; share them, they do. We have spied something very unusual in the small store, red, round and delicious-looking, and with great delight we ask if we can buy this small heap of tomatoes. "Not for sale." "Aaah!"—but we can have half of them as a gift. They are the storekeeper's personal supply, and he convinces us that he can spare half of them, and so we accept. He also promises there will be some limes.

Paul, the fisherman who showed us to the mooring, often comes by our boat and we have little talks, but sometimes we just exchange greetings as he goes paddling to his fishing grounds. He is perhaps the most dedicated fisherman and therefore a familiar sight. I see him paddle towards us with deliberation today.

"The island is out of small hooks." This was a statement, not a request. It is up to us to act on it, and among friends, one does the obvious? "We have some that we never use, you can have them."

"I bring you coconuts tomorrow."

"No, no, you don't have to bring us anything. We never use these hooks."

Hah! coconuts for fish hooks; we can't buy coconuts and he can't buy fish hooks.

Three glorious tropical days have gone by and Paul is back: "Sorry, my kids drank all the coconuts."

"That's fine, don't worry, no problem," we reply. He listens thoughtfully, then produces three large cucumbers from inside his canoe and places them gently on the deck.

* * *

We are turning around in the pastor's garden, together with our laundry, but the pastor does not seem to be anywhere about. A few days ago he gave us a ride in his car and said that if we had any laundry, we could do it at his place. Someone is rushing towards us. "The pastor said you would come and do your laundry—I will bring more buckets." Ah, the pastor is a thorough man, how could we think that he had forgotten about us?

We are aware that Niue's water supply is mainly rainwater, caught and stored in various tanks. An uncertain amount can be obtained from deep fissures in the rock. "Use more water," the lady advises. She stands with her hands clasped together as if to control them while they are so close to a chore that they could do so well.

We are halfway through our washing. Two men stride towards us very deliberately and we stop rubbing our laundry. A coconut and a papaya are placed on the ground in front of us; the coconut has the husk removed, a difficult job for an inexperienced person. "For you," says one of the men, both smiling. They turn and walk back exactly the way they came.

Marie-José and I blush a little; we lack experience with such graceful human behaviour. Giving can be anybody's pleasure, but for a Polynesian it is something very fundamental, as necessary, it seems, as breathing.

* * *

It is May 7, a day of excitement. *Fetu Moana*, the ship servicing Niue, is at anchor in the bay. The place is bustling with activity. All the cargo has to be brought ashore by surf boats and trucked away. As the ship has been overdue for more than a month, its arrival comes as a great relief.

the cargo ship has left and a swell has begun to roll into the bay. The wind has swung around to the west, the exposed side of the bay, and white caps are forming on top of the growing swells. We are ashore obtaining clearance to leave in case it gets worse and we have to leave in a hurry. It is getting worse and our ship looks as if she is already leaving. She is riding the waves, spray flying as the bow plunges into the head seas.

Getting into the dinghy from the landing is extremely difficult; we finally board it, and so has a lot of water. Five reasons why this was so difficult are five gigantic papayas that the doctor left under the dinghy for us as a farewell gift. They are now getting washed in sea water. In fact, they are so huge that they are threatening to upset the dinghy.

We have reached our schooner and we must make ready to leave at once. If we wait we may not be able to leave at all. I pull up the anchor and hoist the foresail; the ten-horsepower diesel is warming up.

I give Marie-José the sign to put us on full power ahead. It looks as if we can overcome the swell and so I let go of the mooring. I can't believe that instead of moving ahead of the mooring buoy, we are leaving it in front of us. The wind that was on the bow is now on our starboard side, the wrong side.

With the foresail sheeted in this way, we are being pushed sideways, the shortest distance to the reef. The reef, a familiar sight for the past two and a half weeks, is showing its teeth. "Let out the fores'l!" I yell, tightly gripping the wheel and the engine controls. There is not enough power to make way against the swell and wind but there is enough to turn port side to the wind.

We can afford to be on the port tack, for the reef tapers off to starboard before it re-emerges near the middle of the bay. Let us make an offing before that. We must put up mainsail and jib and keep the engine going under full throttle.

It takes the whole length of the bay to put a safe distance between us and the land, but we can now give the poor motor a break.

The weather out here seems milder than it was in the bay. We look back.

We are still looking back.

46

CHAPTER SEVEN

Tongan Way

*B*eing geographically isolated and its own nation, Niue Island has a special quality. The people on this small island speak a unique language. When we came to its shores from across the sea, a whole nation knew that we had arrived. What made the arrival of "Klaus and Marie-José on a boat with billowed sails" special was the fact that we were asked to stay as long as we liked, without cost. It was so different from being told you have three months, or three weeks, or seven days. The length of our stay was governed by the natural forces, the wind, the very wind that brought us there.

My feeling of loss brought on by our hurried departure from Niue is challenged, however, by my restlessness, which stays with me as loyally as the seasickness. Each place is special ... and still I am restless! I understand better the meaning of the words "drifter" and "wanderer." I am wandering over the oceans of my emotions as I wander around the world.

The sky is all clear now, yet the wind is still all wrong. It will be a matter of time before the trades come back—just a matter of time. In the meantime we are safe, far from land with lots of water under our keel and there is no hurricane. How much like sailors we have become, to think like that—to feel safe with our little ship at sea and fragile near land.

The winds are gradually gathering in the south-east—I'm in the cockpit, nursing the sails, leafing through a magazine. *Whoosh! There it was again!* What is that sound? We are barely making way. A trick of the mind—that's it. *Whoosh*—"Oh, gee!" A tall sailing yacht only about two boat lengths off our starboard beam—motor-sailing on a reciprocal course. A head has popped out of the hatchway; the two of us are staring at each other in total surprise. We are so close that I could toss over the magazine. The distance between us is increasing, but where are our salutes, long overdue now? Here they are, our hands are up and swaying back and forth. I must call Marie-José on deck so that she can share my amazement over this close encounter. The ship, a gleaming white ketch, is flying not one, but two Canadian flags, one from the masthead and another from the backstay.

* * *

We are now very close to the meridian 180 degrees, the international dateline, and I am preoccupied with how this position will effect my navigational calculation. Going from east to west we will lose a day, or move ahead by one on the calendar.

Presently, however, I'm aware of a creaking and straining and, with it, a different heel to the boat. We have got "by the lee"! The wind has passed from our port quarter to our starboard quarter, and the preventer—a line preventing the mainsail boom from slamming across to the other side—is under stress.

I have responded too late and taken too long to untie the steering wheel; the ship is no longer making way and it cannot respond to the rudder. I must get to the mast and bring down the main. It is not at all simple, I'm pulling down on a sail that the wind is willing to stay up. Eventually, everything returns to normal.

* * *

There is no wind on our sixth day at sea, but we have the company of land—we can see the northern end of the Tongan Islands.

As we motor toward Vavau I don't have the time to watch the land as I'm distracted by landing one, two, three little tunas. Marie-José is steering us into a fine harbour called Neiafu. For lack of knowing how to clear with the authorities, we drop anchor near some other yachts.

This morning we are alongside the town dock. It is here, we are told, that we must await clearance. This is a different Polynesia from the one we have been to. The people are not as mellow, perhaps not even as pleasant to look at—but the main difference is in their activities. Some of them rush to get to us. They have things to sell; they have services to offer: do you have laundry? We can arrange for a feast. You like to buy a nice seashell? You like to buy a basket? Do you have this, do you have that...? Aside from not wanting most of the goods or services, I'm reluctant to make any deals before obtaining clearance from Customs and Immigration.

The peddlers step back, the officials parade on board, looking rather stern. It is curious that the heat in our cabin is felt just as much by people who have lived all their lives in the tropics as by us. The health inspector takes the opportunity to ask for books and magazines.

The "yacht chasers" have stepped forward again, pushing for a deal. We buy a basket and a seashell and, we are sorry, we cannot satisfy everyone.

We haven't decided whether or not to go to the feast that is being offered for two dollars. It is to be at a nice beach, not all that far away, perhaps one hour by boat if we care to take a short-cut through a reef-strewn channel. Now that bystanders on the wharf have heard of our intentions, there is an immediate controversy among them. Some are shouting their opinions and advice, but one comes to tell me, quietly and confidentially, not to believe the others, for this passage is definitely too dangerous and too shallow for our boat. But somebody else refutes this. "I live there. I have gone through it many times ..."

I, for one, cannot see why it should be so risky. I have a chart that shows enough water even at low tide, coral heads too, and it is so calm today that one could see them. The one who lives at the other end of the channel has offered to be our pilot. Yes, he definitely wants to be our pilot. I have refused, and he is not pleased. I have decided to do it on our own, in peace and quiet, taking our time.

As we head for this controversial channel, we pass a large rowboat with its waving occupants—they want a tow. We have taken their line and this same would-be pilot, with the qualities of a pirate has leaped aboard, again offering his services. I make him get off our boat back into his own dinghy, where he seems to be master among the large crew; I now invite him officially on board. He looks at me incredulously, but it had to be done this way. He is a small man and fits behind the wheel more comfortably than I.

When we reach the channel I throttle back the power and climb the spreaders so that I can see the water ahead of us more easily. What I see and what I hear makes it hard to evaluate the situation: children are crying in the boat we have in tow, and the men are shaking their heads. "No, no, you can't do it!" someone is saying. The women look resigned for a disaster. I get out the lead and take a sounding. Ten feet! That's more than twice our draft, and the water ahead of us looks about the same in colour; coral heads all over the place, yes, but Sikalau, our pilot, seems to have an eye for spotting them.

While Sikalau is doing all this he even has time to ask us for some used clothes for his family. The idea of asking for Aspirins as well presumably came to him when he momentarily took his eyes off the coral heads and scanned the interior of our cabin.

Sikalau is smiling proudly, "No more rocks now. I live over there; do you have a passport?"

"What!"

A letter of recommendation he means.

"To whom it may concern: Sikalau has piloted our schooner *Sea Helen* of four-and-a-half-feet draft through the channel ..."

Sikalau gives the letter a lengthy look. "Is my name on it?"

The beach is inspiring, the feast is without ceremony but the food, cooked in an umu (earth oven), is well worth the effort we have made.

*　*　*

In Neiafu it has became a daily routine to walk through the small town, partly to buy vegetables and fruit at the market, but also to drink in the local scene. This is such a typical South Seas port, and it has the quality of making one think that the ages roll by without very much changing. The faded signs seem to have always been faded; the buildings have always been in need of repair.

If we stay on board we can expect to be visited by a number of enterprising Tongans—some interesting and some annoying. I do not mind primitive carvings, but I do mind carvings that have no artistic flare or are done without skill.

I was having a nice little nap, a proper little snooze, here in the cockpit, until just now. I was jolted by rapid banging against the hull of our ship. I would not mind being wakened by a Tongan princess wanting to bestow her honour on me, but she would never have woken me like this.

"Hello! You got a cup of tea?"

I get myself up—"You got a cup of tea," says the mouth that moves broadly below a pair of sunglasses.

"No, no tea, I'm sorry."

"You got a cigarette? Can we come aboard? Have you got a cup of tea?" There is a trace of urgency in his voice.

Now I gave this character—white overalls and sunglasses, yes it's the same one—and his companion tea and cigarettes yesterday and I'm not about to become their daily supplier of these. "No tea, no cigarettes. You cannot come aboard."

"You sleeping?"

"I was and you woke me up. Don't come back!" I'm trying to be as abrupt as I dare, without distorting my image of a friendly Polynesia. They are leaving—which is good. I wouldn't have known what to do next.

The man who organized the feast frequently visits. He wants to make sure that we know that if there is anything at all we need, he can help. He is so dark, sly and cunning that we refer to him as the witch doctor. There are certain characters who would have made a sailor feel uneasy in earlier times; now, they serve the purpose of providing a less than pleasant taste of human nature, a glimpse of the coarser side of paradise. I don't know how my tactics would have worked in the past, but I have made it a policy to be brief with the arrogant types, welcoming to the friendly ones.

Here comes the couple that seldom fails to see us at least once a day, and they are so amiable that I wondered what happened to them yesterday. They do things in a more Polynesian style, approaching with dignity. A wondrous Tongan custard apple is now rocking on our deck—the lady is smiling shyly. Their boat is loaded with basket work and carvings—and, of course, they know we'll like at least one of the items. Another fruit, of a different variety, is being added to the one on our decks. Again, we show our appreciation by praising these fine fruits. I have rolled myself a cigarette and I pass the tin to the man in the boat so he can roll himself one too. I don't have to ask, they all like to smoke.

There is a rather nice straw shopping bag that would make a present for someone we know ... The lady holds it up. It's usually five dollars but we can get it for four. Since her husband is a carver it is not inappropriate to suggest a good wood chisel in exchange. The man's eyes light up, though the lady is left holding the bag. But they work as a team. She would like the money—he won't let go of the chisel and would also need a stone to sharpen it with.

Few words are said—no one is in a hurry—a deal is eventually going to be made. It's only a matter of making it the best possible

51

one. I bring out all my small change—seventy cents. "Here, you can have the wood chisel and seventy cents for the bag!" Well it's not quite the right deal for the lady who, after all, made the bag. Marie-José has been below and is back with a short nightgown she never wears. For my part I feel that if we give them the wood chisel, the seventy cents and the nightgown, they should throw in a small woven tray that normally sells for one dollar. The lady gives the gown a sidelong glance.

"What would I do with the nightgown?"

Well, everyone is asking us for old T-shirts and now we can't get rid of a beautiful new nightgown! "You wear it!" I am ready to finalize the deal: "Okay, no tray. You take the chisel, the seventy cents and the gown for the bag."

The bag is handed over. They know they have the best possible deal. The tray, too, is handed up, over the bowed head of the lady. They have beaten us in the game and I think they feel a little sheepish. "I know you like the tray." He must have married her for being so shy and modest.

Now that we have the tray, Marie-José feels that the score is slightly uneven and asks them to wait. She comes back with half of the bread she baked in the morning. Marie-José hands it over with a grin. The hand that has accepted the gift has returned, holding some more fruit. This is now a free-for-all giving game so I may as well give the man the small tin which has a little tobacco left in it.

We are all laughing, sharing the universal joy of this bartering game. We all know that we have run out of things to give.

In these low latitudes, night rushes in behind the setting sun; it is the close of another day, though the persistent yells from the shore are more like crude waking calls. We assume this noise is not directed at us, but, nevertheless, I must investigate. Binoculars gather the light and I can see a figure standing on the shore, no longer yelling, but waving. Now that I'm in our dinghy and the yelling has ceased, I conclude that it was directed at us, though I am puzzled.

At a healthy distance from the beach I relax my oars: "What do you want?"

"I want to come aboard." That simple a reason, he wants to come aboard! I want to allow people their little desires, but not at my expense "Are you alone?"

"Yes." He looks slightly to his left and right.

"Why do you want to come aboard?"

"I want to talk."

Christ! What a time to want to talk. I don't want to appear indecisive; I must be resolute. "Come on then."

I cannot imagine what we will talk about, but I guess we'll brew a cup of tea; subjects can always be found. Marie-José and I look at this self-appointed night visitor in wonder; he conducts himself as if he has had a long-standing invitation. He is indeed talking—about the world, and his world is the island. Yachts like ours seem to be fragments of the outside world wheeling past him and he wants a part of it.

He is a young school teacher revealing his aspirations, his place in the community, and judging his community. He talks about his Tongan life—his love who has married someone else. He recites his own poetry, he sings the song he wrote. Marie-José hands him a jar of honey. The desperation in his face seems to fade. He expresses his desire to sit on our decks again, some other time.

A Tongan carving, a Tiki of course, has finally found its way into our cabin. A friend, Johnny Moa, has been so good-natured that we thought we would buy one of his carvings. The man's character is reflected in his work. Because we have a small boat, he has made his price small, he tells us gracefully, as if trying to keep things in the right proportion in his Tongan world.

He tells us about the kava house, an important place for him, and he invites us to go there with him on Friday evening.

"What's the kava house?" I ask.

With gusto he answers, "It's where all the Tongans drink kava." Judging by the way he says this he must mean everybody who is somebody.

The way to the kava house is by water for it is on Pangai Motu. The old outboard motor seems in harmony with the well-mannered man and the heavy wooden hull. Johnny, getting on in his years, is looking fit and trim and dressed for the occasion and we feel slightly honoured.

I try not to let our landing on the beach of Pangai Motu go by without absorbing the scenery. I have time to let the new impressions mingle with the old before Johnny takes us up to the house. It is simple and yet so majestic. The air is pleasant, the surroundings are still, and Johnny is about to make things happen.

I would like to describe Johnny's niece in a word—"beautiful"— even though it is banal. She is striking. What a child of our planet! I dare to look at her often and she looks at me. Is there some bond between us?

The women are raised to act shyly. They look on from a distance while the man and the visitors sit on a mat on the floor, drinking lemonade that they have served. Marie-José is not entirely comfortable with this arrangement: "Everybody sit down ..."

"No! Tongan way!" Johnny has cut in with finality. The women do not respond to Marie-José's gesture to join us.

When I look at this aging Tongan, I'm convinced that enthusiasm can make a person ageless. Johnny looks exquisitely fit, announcing that we will now go to the kava house. Still thinking about his niece, I'm also curious about this kava house "where all the Tongans drink kava."

There are more people about, exchanging greetings with Johnny. We arrive at the kava house, a large building with windows without panes. It is divided into unfurnished rooms. Our host relishes his arrival with us. A woven mat is rolled out on the floor and, even though nobody else has a pillow, Marie-José and I are each given one.

Our purpose in the kava house is obvious. A pitcher of kava is emptied into the huge four-legged wooden bowl that stands in the middle of the mat. The mat is different shades of brown; the bowl is brown, the walls are brown, as are the people. The colour of the liquid blends with the surroundings, looking but not tasting like muddy water.

People have started to join us. A new reality takes hold as I feel a wreath of fresh flowers placed around my neck. It's unlikely that such things are done for all the numerous visitors to the islands, but here in the kava house, it happened to us. Johnny looks sheepish, so we know that he had something to do with this. He has apparently also ordered a cake. The presence of Johnny's niece as one of the maids serving the kava is just another reason why I want to bathe in this evening.

Despite my blissful state, I have caught on that kava has to be bought before it is brought. I think the bowl is now down to where it can hold a couple of extra pitchers, so I will get the waitress's attention. The brew is dispensed to the individuals on our mat one at the time, in a half coconut shell.

Kava, made from a root and non-alcoholic, is considered a man's drink. Marie-José is allowed small quantities because she is a visitor even though she would not mind having the coconut shell filled when her turn to drink comes around. The kava tastes strange—but not all that bad when one is bedecked with a wreath of flowers. In another room, on another mat, somebody is playing the guitar and people are singing. Johnny is poised. When the guitar stops, he breaks into song with a moving favourite that draws the people together.

I have noticed Johnny staggering a little as he walked out to relieve himself, more and more often now. I like the evening: the air outside has changed, it is crisp and fresh, but I am feeling fatigued. Whether or not I'm staggering is not for me to judge. Marie-José, too, is very tired ... I gently suggest to Johnny that we should be getting back to our boat. The smiling old man has anticipated this for a youth is on the spot to take us back. I believe Johnny feels he has consumed too much of a man's drink to do it himself.

I'm confronted by our ship's clock: 4 o'clock, it says—4 o'clock!

* * *

I wonder now if it is true that nothing in Tonga has come very close to my heart and therefore I have no regrets in leaving the place. My state of mind confirms it: though we have only just started to sail clear of land, we are already trailing a lure with the hope of catching a fish. When I feel emotionally sensitive, I do not lure a fish onto a hook; I want the creatures of the sea to be my friends and I want to find out why I am like I am.

The line has gone taut, and I'm delighted that we are going to have another one of these small tunas. I'm reeling in ... ohhh, shoot!... the knob slipped out of my fingers—the reel spun so fast ... oh, brother! My knuckles—three of them are bleeding.

It's a fat tuna in our cockpit. With a savage mind—thinking of what it has done to me and not taking into account what I was doing to him—I have clubbed it with a force uncalled for.

Infection sets in quickly in the tropics; I want to attend to my wounds—one of the knuckles is quite swollen now.

CHAPTER EIGHT

Fiji

*A*round the Fijian Islands, the reefs are much more dangerous than the other islands we have visited. Until now we have seen coral reefs encircling islands in a well-defined manner, but the reefs here reach out like tongues from the land and many are lurking just below the surface. It's good to have charts, to know where to look for them!

Three days of sailing from Vavau has brought into view the first of the outlying Fijian Islands, the Lau Group. We are to take the Oneata Passage through them, but it is late afternoon and I simply cannot be sure that we are heading for the right gap. Scanning from the spreader bars, halfway up the mast, I think I can identify the huge Mbukatatunou Reef several miles to the north of the passage. Still, I think we will wait until I get a fix.

It is twilight and I'm measuring the altitude of the stars Sirius, Canopus and Hadar. The position lines I have worked out and plotted on the chart have made a very small triangle. It is our fix, but it is now quite dark, and we think of the snug comfort of our bunks in preference to a tiring night-watch through the unknown and the uncertain. We will heave to for the night by standing the schooner under very short sail into the slight onshore current.

In the morning we are still in the same relative position to the islands. Now it is time to head for Oneata Passage! I'm standing on the spreader bars looking for the reef that is said to lie in the entrance but I cannot detect it. However, several peaks and contours are as indicated on the chart and we proceed.

The day passes, darkness is falling again; Labemba Island is to starboard, shrouded by the dark. Now we are on our own. The night becomes dark and cloudy, and a little stormy. We cannot leave the wheel for a minute. I know that with the wind at our back there will be no leeway, perhaps little drift, and a good compass course should see us through. By dead reckoning I have deduced that we have passed the island of Vanua Vatu to starboard, and Naratu Reef to port. The names of these places play strangely in my mind. It is pitch black and we are sailing through "the Lau Group," hoping that we'll make it through.

My eyes are not nearly so tired with this first daylight for I see Moalu Island to starboard—just where I wanted it to be. Ngau Island, next in line, has appeared as well.

With islands coming into view, one after another during the day, it is easy to ascertain our position and progress—but once more night is upon us and we must steer through the dark. Great showers of rain are pouring down; the wind, however, has remained about the same and so I have great confidence in our course.

This squally night has not ended, but the lights of Suva harbour are visible and they lift the weariness from me.

I have not yet analysed, nor overcome, the shivery feeling I get when I see a stranded or sunken ship. Very near the entrance to Suva harbour are not only beacons indicating the edges of the reef, but also a large stranded fishing vessel.

Having guided our ship through islands and reefs for two dark pandemonious nights, the wind now dies, just outside of Suva harbour, allowing us to enter a gay world on a smooth sea.

*   *   *

Suva is one of the crossroads in the Pacific and small ocean-going yachts gather in large numbers. There is a forest of masts, stepped onto an assortment of floating vessels, competing with the straight lines of city buildings.

Propped up on one elbow in *Sea Helen*'s cockpit my eyes follow the skipper of a new arrival who, with a fancy captain's cap and a trim smile, stands at the helm of his ship—an average sloop that he weaves through the crowded anchorage. It reminds me of the contradiction between how we see other people, how we like to see ourselves, and how we would like the world to see us.

Visiting the museum in Suva and seeing the war clubs and other instruments for the destruction of living beings, I look with new wonder at the gentle Fijians. I stop to look at myself: I consider myself gentle and respectful of life, but I know I can resort to violence if threatened by someone.

Volcanoes erupt and from their violence beautiful islands are created. People make war, but still they are no less beautiful, once the violence is over. War is a tragedy but we are consoled by this realization.

I'm happy to have discovered the gentle spirit in the kinky-curly-haired islanders. It would be difficult, if not impossible, to know where we would be and what we would be doing now, were we not here in Fiji. Perhaps there was never a choice; perhaps we live by predestination. For the moment, however, I'll accept my fate gracefully, and even cherish it a little. Sitting cross-legged on the floor of a one-room house, we are invited to reach out for a breakfast of prawns, fish, tapioca, and taro. We went to sleep on the floor after a night of singing, dancing and drinking kava and we now feel wonderfully fit, after only a few hours sleep—the world appears so new.

The prawns and the fish taste good—everything else too.

And to drink in the gentleness of these people....

How natural all this is.

Life is made complex by all the things we want; it becomes simple when we want the few things that we really need.

*　　*　　*

We are in a valley that can only be reached by a narrow and sometimes steep trail. Our visit here has been recorded in the minds of the residents, three or four families, as the first visit by "white people." One man asked his niece why he had not been told of our arrival right away—he would have come in from his plantation at once. He apologized. I cannot help make my own notation that I have never before been the first white visitor in a settlement. The people here think it is an honour for them, but it is a greater honour for us.

We are back for a second visit. One family in particular, a couple with one son, has adopted us. Already, as we are coming down the trail, which is very muddy this time from the rain, young Joe shyly but firmly welcomes us. Arthur and Lina have smiling open faces. Several weeks have elapsed since our historic visit and there is lots to talk about.

Being a realist, I didn't think that muddy feet should be problem; yet, as I look into the happy faces of our hosts, I know that the mud must be got rid of and I'm wondering how this can be done. I have the sensation of something cool and wet around my feet, and I look down and see Joe proceeding to wash them.

Joe's sensitivity is extraordinary. I have correctly located the little shack where one deposits the waste from our bodies, and I hear his voice outside saying, "Klaus—do you need water?" It is the same as saying if you do number two, and not just number one, you will need it. He has a bowl ready. I am touched.

I take a few steps towards the river, and Joe offers to show me around. He points out his favourite swimming hole. As we linger here, I try to remember when I was his age. Joe asks his questions sparingly—about my home, Canada. He doesn't ask anything from me; he doesn't want to know how much money I make—he wants me to tell him about the world. He speaks softly as he gazes at his familiar swimming hole. The river is like the ocean—Joe is looking at the horizon, trying to see what lies beyond and I'm aware that to him I'm the skipper of a little sailing ship who has come to his land from very far away.

Later, Joe is sitting by the door stroking a chicken that I never noticed him catch. At an almost invisible sign from his father, he strides off with the contented bird.

The kitchen is separate from the one-room house and so we didn't know that lunch was being prepared. It is like magic to see half of the floor become decked with cooked food—including chicken.

The muddy trails lead us to the family's plantation. Arthur is proud of his crop. As he explains each plant, his beautiful "Missus," as he calls her, is the model of modesty, with the air of someone quite self-assured also. My question: "What kind of plant is this?" has again triggered Arthur's bush knife, and we have a demonstration and a sample. Papayas as well as cocoa pods can be conveniently plucked from their plants. Arthur has pulled a small tree out of the ground and here are tapiocas, a potato-like root that we have eaten several times already. The stem, or trunk, of this plant is cut into one-foot lengths and these are stuck back into the ground. They will grow more tapioca.

Joe looks at his father for a second time; we have come to a coconut palm. Yes, is the signal, go and get one. Joe has a little trouble keeping his lava-lava (wrap-around) from arranging itself in an unfashionable manner and he interrupts, with a smile, his vertical walk up the palm.

The prize crop is the plant from which the kava is made. While everything else grows relatively fast, this plant takes a minimum of three years to mature—for good kava anyway. Arthur smiles as his hand reaches under the healthy specimen of a leaf of the maturing plant. Did we not already know about kava, we should misread Arthur's display of great pride: kava is Fiji's national drink. Serving it involves a whole ceremony, a ceremony that was performed in our honour and that will always be vivid in my memory.

The kava, like in Tonga, is mixed, with critical judgment, in a legged wooden kava bowl. A youth has been chosen to do the offering. On one knee, his arms stretched out, his hands delicately holding a half coconut shell full of the brown liquid, his eyes, deep in their sockets, are steady and solemnly on mine. It is a moment of purity. He has to do it just right in front of the elders; this is perhaps his first opportunity to perform this act for a stranger. One of us is the bride, I'm tempted to think. The hands at the end of my outstretched arms are holding the bowl, the youth has clapped. I'm taking the empty bowl from my lips—he has clapped again, several times this time—the rest of the people in the room have joined in. It was then my turn to clap, twice, but I did not know this at the time.

It is perhaps a law of nature that anything that takes a long time to grow, or make, lasts for a long time. Inside the house, the lady prepares tea with loving concentration and disregard for time. But the time is not wasted as we deepen our awareness of the surroundings. We sip the tea and the moments last.

With curiosity, I concentrate on Arthur wrapping a sliver of tobacco in newspaper; but I'm also aware that his missus, Lina, has left the room and not returned for some time. I offer Arthur some real cigarette-rolling paper, he tries it, but it doesn't taste the same; it is newspaper that does the trick.

Lina has returned from the store with two bottles of beer which were bought in our honour. From our point of view this was not necessary, and we feel somewhat confused, almost disappointed. And yet, Arthur gets great pleasure from pouring out the beer for us. "I made the money, I bought the beer—now you drink and enjoy," is written all over our host's face. I don't think Arthur earned the money for these two large beers that easily, but he seems to value what he is getting for his labour. It is as if giving us something from our way of life tells us that he knows more than just life in the bush.

The earth has been turning, and it will most likely not stop. We want to make it back to our boat before it has turned to where it will block the sun's rays and leave us on a dark trail. I sigh at the amount of various fruits and vegetables that we are to take along. Arthur dismisses it, conveying that two boys would carry everything for us; one of them is Joe.

Joe has elected to take a slightly different route from the one that we know. It leads us past a little house, a little house with an old lady; every fairy tale has a core of reality to it. The old lady's voice is croaking, "Moce." It does not at all sound like "Bula," which means hello. Joe is whispering, "She says good-bye."

* * *

At the Suva market, where the quantities of produce are witness to the fertility of the land, I try to determine if I have seen this young lady before. She is looking at me with a promise of friendliness in her eyes. Yes, she reminds of a girl at the party in the valley, the one who asked me for so many dances. I'm happy to see her again, although I see that an older woman hovering behind her does not approve of me. Not knowing the local customs, I feel vulnerable. The girl seems less concerned, she wants to stay close. I am caught between day and night.

Today I realize, in earnest, that the young ladies and the very mature ones are a world apart. This girl is actually quite beautiful, despite the slightly dirty T-shirt. I will brave a few more moments—time enough to tell myself that she is quite beautiful "... say hello to all the people in the village for me. Maybe we will be back one day."

I have left her behind. Looking back, I see she is still smiling—the old lady has stopped in her tracks—her face is slightly flushed. She gave me the feeling that she would have done anything, anything to be with me. I feel sad. If it hadn't been for that old hag, I might have put my arm around her, or held her hand, to make both of us feel that we walk on common ground—as children of the universe.

* * *

The days have melted into one another making a lump of three months. We are harbouring a secret hope for smooth seas and fair winds, as we make our first efforts to ready the ship again for the onward journey.

All is quiet at the anchorage; was I so involved in the chores on

61

deck? Where is Marie-José? It does not take more than a turn of the head to confirm that she is not on deck. A peek through the hatchway does not reveal a five-foot-four-inch body, either standing or sitting inside our compact cabin. What a cruel shock! Marie-José is gone.

At a time like this I wish there were more places on our boat to look, but our boat is so small. A search for a person on board ends with a glance here and a glance there. My god, did she...? She can't swim! "Marie-José! Marie-José!"

"Klaus, I'm in the water."

"Where?!"

"I'm here in the water." My god, I can't see her! She sounds so far away.

"Where are you?!" Jesus, she can't swim! I know I'm racing around the deck—I will dive in if only I can catch so much as a glimpse.

Hell, she might be under by now. I wish we were anchored in clearer water; I would be able to see then, maybe even to the bottom.

"Marie-José!"

"I'm here!"

Again it sounded so far away. She can't be under the water if she can call. Hang on baby, hang on. Why can't I see her? "I'm in the toilet." I heard toilet—I heard that. My look into the cabin is impulsive.... She is standing there, Marie-José. First things first, she hasn't yet pulled up her pants and is laughingly tugging at them.

"Aw! Gee! It sounded like 'I'm in the water!'"

"No, I said 'I'm in the washroom.'"

"In the washroom!" I am deflated. I just couldn't think of our toilet bowl (the head), sandwiched between two bulkheads, as a washroom. I'm watching her pull up the bleached pants; I have the urge to go back on deck to look and see if people on neighbouring yachts have been alerted by my commotion ... Sheepishly I'm looking from yacht to yacht but not a soul appears concerned; that's surprising! And I have seen in myself now the frailty of the human mind to imagination.

*   *   *

To complete the laying-in of ship's stores, we have to visit the butcher. In the heart of Suva we walk into a shop that we have visited three or four times a week for the past three months, with secret smiles on our faces. We know that, according to human nature, the butcher should be surprised by our order. This most friendly man is on the spot to attend to us. Because we have grown so fond of him, we regard the cast in his eyes more as a virtue than a deformity, and Marie-José and I refer to it as the "silver look."

"Seven pounds of beef please," I say, with a smile, reflecting the smile on the other side of the counter. The butcher gives his classic contented nod and turns; stops in his tracks, and turns back again. "Seven pieces," he says, to convince himself that he has not heard wrong.

"No, seven pounds," I repeat reassuringly.

He walks off looking over his shoulder, "seven pounds" still on his lips. While he cuts the meat at his chopping block, he keeps looking over to us, smiling broadly and inquisitively. He is holding up piece after piece and we keep encouraging him to cut some more until it makes up seven pounds. He has begun to think it funny, if not incomprehensible. Marie-José and I are now almost roaring with laughter. It is catching—the butcher is beginning to have a good time too.

Over the past three months, this good man has served us impeccably. Until now the routine has always been the same: we would ask for two very small slices of beef, which he would cut from a chunk that he first held up for our approval. The two tiny slices, when masterly separated, were also held up for final approval, then wrapped and provided with a moderate price tag. Now, with his slightly "silver look," which is perhaps responsible for the tilt of his head, he is still in doubt as to whether we really wanted that much. But we take the package from him, and there is nothing left to do—but smile some more.

CHAPTER NINE

Pine Trees
and Palm Trees

*O*ur departure day is a glorious one; it is good to have a commanding breeze with which to head our ship through the pass. As we look back we wonder about what we'll remember of our stay in Fiji. While the Fijians live in quiet contentment, I believe that deep inside they realize that they don't know why they are on this planet or where everything is going.

I look at the hills where I know the valley of Arthur and Joe lies. A picture of a light-blue plastic radio appears in my mind. Arthur showed it off to us while telling us he knew it was a cheap model. In Suva, a duty-free port, tourists are falling over each other to obtain the latest in electronics, and Arthur had his share of the booty which he wanted me to appreciate too.

Alternately looking at the paling landscape and the new horizon, we are entering Mbangar Pass with the island of Mbangar to port. It is here that Fiji's fire walkers perform their feat of walking on hot stones. It does not seem important, however, to be eyewitness to this demonstration or to come home with photographs, so we sail on. With distance increasing, the Fijian islands fade until darkness provides the final curtain.

This new day, the seas are noticeably higher; any leftover melancholies are overshadowed by my wish to get rid of my nausea. On top of the deckhouse I struggle with the sextant to obtain a fair shot of the sun's angle in order to determine if we are following our course, one that is to take us to the second largest island in the Pacific Ocean, New Caledonia.

The sea dictates the rhythm—an easier one now—so with confidence we let the days run together. Sailing like all voyaging, requires time for waiting.

"I don't know if I like it on a boat," a nice lady once confided in me. "I like to feel that I accomplish something every day. At home I have a studio, and I can't have that on the boat."

"Why think so materially," I remember answering, as if I had a deep insight into the subject. "If you have a new thought every day, you accomplish something." Now I know that it was a hasty response. What is the difference between a boat and a studio in material terms? In fact, it's a subtle difference: isn't she also waiting in her studio to have a new inspiration or to complete a painting? And when it's complete, isn't that the end of a voyage? Isn't a voyage a work of art—a line one is tracing on the world?

When I was nineteen, I wanted a car and went out and got one. I was vaguely aware of myself in the car in a traffic jam, but my strongest impression was of the dashboard! It seems odd that it could have been that way. I wonder if this is the case with the boat? I wanted a boat and finally got one. But in the car I lost myself in the dashboard; on the boat I am aware of myself on the planet ... I try to justify being on a boat by reasoning that my experience on the boat is more valuable. But perhaps the experience in the car made this awareness possible ...

Wait a minute ... how did land get to be there—over on our port bow? Hunter Island would be the only land in the vicinity but we were not supposed to see it—we were to pass far to the north of it. Even as I grab the sextant for a sight, I accept that we have probably drifted too far south, and this is Hunter Island.

*　*　*

They are albatrosses—I know that now. They are birds with a five-foot wingspan that sweep the ocean, often only avoiding a collision with a wave top by an apparent stroke of luck. They live in the air and pluck their prey from the sea, consuming it in a single swallow.

There is a white bird with a straw-like projection from its tail that circles over us with curiosity. It keeps returning in loops, gleaming in the sunlight. Marie-José is confident that the bird is reacting to the sound of her voice: "Hello birdie. How are you? You are beautiful!" The bird is almost certainly seeing Marie-José for it banks into turns to align its bird eye with her.

Over our starboard bow I suddenly see the form of a ship. "A small cargo ship ..." I pronounce the discovery to Marie-José, wondering at how we hadn't seen it sooner. "Oh no! it's a real large one!" I

65

modify my hasty comment as I look through the binoculars. Its bow points directly toward us now; that's strange, it wasn't when I first saw it. What's he doing? It's coming closer fast.

The big letters on the side of the huge steel wall that read "Gearbulk" momentarily scatter my apprehensive thoughts, but have no meaning. The name *Eagle Arrow* is painted in smaller letters on the bow. Boy, is he ever close! A figure all in white has appeared high up on the superstructure. Well, I suppose he wants to say hello; it is a lonely sea, isn't it? I give him a big wave. He is waving too— but what's this? He has a flag! I don't know all the flags but I know this one—red and yellow divided diagonally. "Look it up in the book," I urge Marie-José, "quick!" I know what it means though, it means man overboard! Yes, that's what the book says, "Man overboard." The officer is signalling with the flag again, he does it so perfectly it's unmistakable. We don't even have a flag to answer with—and no radio. I give him a negative wave, with two arms; but waving two arms could mean that I require assistance; so I must only use one arm; now it looks like a salute … I realize that I don't know how to give a negative wave. Still, I feel that he understood. I think there is a basic understanding among seamen: if I had picked up a survivor I would have been able to let him know one way or another.

The ship now veers away, seemingly retracing an old course. I'm still excited but the emotion is mixed with sadness and despair. The ocean is calm—perhaps they will find him—they can see a long way from the bridge of a large ship…. I give orders to look for a man overboard.

Life is funny! It really shouldn't matter which way one is going, so long as one is not in danger and has the basic necessities of life. Still, it's like a game of chance: one can gain or lose, depending on the direction one takes. We don't know what we miss by choosing one direction over another. Is this where wisdom comes in—knowing which direction to go in? But surely it's not unwise to look for a drowning man. There is nothing unwise about spending a little extra time at sea.

We are no longer following our course, the one to New Caledonia, and now that the excitement and sadness have ebbed away, we feel uncomfortable not going in the direction we consider the "right one." The feeble wind with which we have been tacking has disappeared, leaving our sails limp. I marvel at this natural solution to our dilemma. We don't really know where to search and yet we are reluctant to leave the scene. It is, I believe, the first time that I look favourably upon a complete calm in mid-ocean.

With no wind, the sun pours down on us thickly; the blue ocean, as far as the eye can see, just lies there.

I think about the world—our boat in the blue element—a man overboard—his predicament. To be or to be lucky? Was predestination at work here? Surely not free will.

Night, even with its mysteries, feels like a pillow for my thoughts.

*   *   *

Darkness is slipping away again, releasing our thoughts to the flutter of a brand new day—the ocean is full of ripples and wavelets are building up.

Our deep melancholy of yesterday is shelved. One cannot keep something in focus once one has gone on to something else.

In response to the anticipation of our next landfall, we start a new set of activities. Our position has to be found again by celestial means so that a new course can be plotted. I must also try to make a more careful allowance for currents; it will require frequent checks.

After reading the "Havanah Passage" information I struggle to remain outwardly calm. The pilot book gives the most discouraging two pages of instructions concerning the passage: "Ships batten down and proceed at high speed...." I think of our small engine that can barely head the boat into a two-foot swell or a ten-knot wind. Havanah Passage is the way we have planned to go!

I try to be objective: first of all, the pilot book always mentions the worst; a small boat can drift in from a deep channel without being in immediate danger. Besides, it might just be an extra fine day when we get there!

The wind is light again and as we drift along we see some dorados. We have come to appreciate the fine meat of these fish but our lure is moving through the water too slowly and they are not fooled by it.

I like fine days at sea. With gentle winds, ripples on our bow, a slight gurgling behind the rudder, we feel unrestricted; our conversation is livelier. We pass the binoculars back and forth to get a closer look at a fish that keeps coming to the surface, poking at a piece of wood—picking off marine growth.

*   *   *

We watch some dark clouds that are fine examples of those accompanying a squall. Twice so far we have lowered our sails as a precaution against a sudden strike, only to have it pass us by; this time we will keep the working sails up and wait.

The line of ominous clouds seems to roll a lot closer than the others have done, but still, I think it will miss ... actually I'm not sure now—it's coming close really fast.

Neither Marie-José nor I say anything as we brace ourselves while the ship lies on her ear. Marie-José has noticed the water running through the galley porthole and climbs into the cabin to close it. I have gained enough footing to release the sheet of the mainsail which, together with the lessening of the first gust, allows the schooner to right to a manageable angle. Now, like a whipped horse, the little ship takes off.

With the seas still smooth from a long period of light winds, the ride is not unpleasant—rather exhilarating I would say.

I have finished reducing our sail area to a fully reefed main and jib, and we are galloping over much rougher terrain.

"Oh no, not now!" The fishing rod is bent and jittering. One can trail a line for days, even weeks during calm weather, and never have a strike; but let it get miserable and blowing so that one doesn't know what to do first, throw up or reef the sails, and you will have a big fish on the line. It is, of course, the deep-sea fish we tried to catch earlier, a dorado; Polynesians call it "Mahi Mahi"—they often eat it raw with lemon juice.

I glance at our other fishing line, a hand line—it, too, has a fish on it. I have landed one fish and I'm trying to shake this other one off the hook. Despite an oncoming nausea, I recount all the times I have lost a fish because it wiggled off the hook just when I was going to heave it aboard.

It is getting dark. Marie-José is cleaning the fish; my thoughts are somewhere else. My worst fears—being in a storm when approaching land—have materialized! Havanah Passage is out of the question; but then, we are not there yet. "One thing is certain, we have to steer carefully all night."

It was just a local squall after all. It is midnight. I am certain that the winds are steadily decreasing—the skies are definitely clearing. There is a full moon tonight, and look how bright everything is getting. What a stroke of luck. Some early navigators would have said, "The gods are good to us." I can say it too—I know what it means.

*   *   *

"Klaus—Klaus," I dimly hear my name called as I lie in my bunk. "I see a light."

Marie-José, my good helmsman, reports a light at 0300 hours. Navigational lights are beautiful if one can identify them. But I have skimped on coastal charts for New Caledonia and so I can't be sure which light we are seeing. But I have an idea. If the light is the one I think it is, then we have travelled a lot faster than anticipated; perhaps there was a current in our favour.

Not heeding a warning that moonlight does not give a true horizon, I measure the angles of two stars and the full moon itself and proceed to work out the position lines on the chart. The lines make a very small triangle and I know where we are: almost level with Havanah Passage.

It is morning. We observe the pass through the binoculars; the weather has become so fine that it can probably not be improved upon; a light wind will be at our back going in.

We can see now what we are in for: it is not a gap in a visible reef, but one that leads over shelves and between sunken reefs, as well as exposed ones. There is a stretch of disturbed water outside the reef-strewn area; it has disturbed me, too. I remind myself that we are going in the right way and not making a drastic mistake. We must start the little engine to be sure of better manoeuvreability.

Marie-José is at the wheel, I'm high up on the spreader bars. It is mostly the tail wind that allows us to make steady progress through the pass. The surface of the water has a different appearance in various places; depths and shallows, tides, ocean currents and wind are the ingredients for such conditions, and none of them stay the same. "I wouldn't like to be here in rough weather," I think involuntarily. Marie-José is having a hard time with the wheel. I yell encouraging words down to her. We have already gone past the most critical place.

It is a relief to be "in" and to have behind us a passage that the pilot book regards worthy of two pages.

*   *   *

I treasure the sensitivity I feel toward the land after many days at sea: I look keenly at its colours—the shapes it holds against the sky; I cannot ignore how the ocean laps up against it. Our anchor has found

69

bottom; it is our first physical contact with the land for several weeks.

What is it about a tall, arched church window that makes me feel humble? What is it about a landscape that challenges the mind to form an impression?

"Red mud—sticky red mud!" I exclaim as we retrieve our anchor from the bottom of a little bay that we had chosen for the night.

But red mud rivulets running along our decks suddenly seem in line with the odd combination of pine trees and palm trees grouped together along the shores. They stretch up the low hills that are weighed down by a tropical blue sky.

CHAPTER TEN

The Southernmost Coral

*I*f it is true that Adam and Eve were kicked out of paradise, then this is largely responsible for our short stay in New Caledonia. The often asked question, "How do you finance the trip?" has never been satisfactorily answered by us. Man invented money, and it is this trivial phenomenon, unworthy of mention in paradise, that has prompted us to plot a course for Australia where, we have decided arbitrarily, a solution will come.

For love of islands we are planning to make a stop at Lord Howe—according to the chart, a tiny patch of land about four hundred miles east of Australia's capital, Sydney. With a pencil sketch of it and a discouraging, "You won't make Lord Howe. The winds are not favourable!" from another yacht, we are motoring out of Noumea Harbour on this magnificent but windless afternoon.

When New Caledonia's capital, Noumea, was called Port de France, a lighthouse intended for Fort de France in Martinique (an island on the other side of the globe), was shipped to it by mistake. It is fitting somehow that this huge lighthouse placed on a small sandy island immediately inside Bulari Pass presents itself in such a conspicuous way—white, gleaming and reaching into the sky. This majestic building comes into view very slowly, relative to our progress of two miles per hour. It is the fastest the little engine can force the fat hull through the water and into a light head wind that has sprung up.

The late afternoon suggests approaching darkness, and we want to forego the experience of rolling in the swell outside the reef. Accepting the option to think like mariners, we see nothing wrong with anchoring over one of the many shelves inside the reef while nature is so peaceful, so tame. Within close proximity of the light-house that is standing there because of a mistake, we let our small

71

anchor drop into the coral gardens; we will worry about retrieving it in the morning.

A wreck on the reef presents its silhouette against the sun-reddened sky; the stars and planets glow overhead, promising a calm night. I'm pleased with my decision to have anchored.

It is good to feel calm, to be content for a time—even if we don't have answers to the many questions in our minds. Somehow I feel that the calmness of this moment reflects its tranquil beauty through us.

I have come to a simple conclusion: the earth is violent. It's beautiful and peaceful and life-sustaining, yes, but it was created with violence and remains so: volcanoes erupt, landmasses disappear, rivers overflow, the ocean—well yes, the ocean can be angry. And elsewhere in the universe: our own sun erupts into sunspots; stars are said to blow up ... All this is violent ... Perhaps we don't want to call it that because seemingly good things come out of it, but it is all nevertheless turmoil. And so why should there not be turmoil inside us? How could it be otherwise when the universe sets the precedent? Except for tonight, and other nights like tonight. We don't understand magic.

*   *   *

Plenty of wind changes—light winds and strong winds—beating for part of one day and reaching for part of another—no shortage of grey clouds; we are literally working our way towards Lord Howe Island. But nothing can take away our complacence; a really nice day, one that allows us to spread our full sails to the wind, helps view the next grey sky with less hostility.

We are in good shape—and even if we don't make Lord Howe Island, it won't matter; we can head straight for mainland Australia. There is a feeling in my bones though that I sometimes trust. I'm in a whistling mood, but not actually whistling, not because of superstition, but because a trace of the old seasickness reminds me that I am a fragile rubber-legged creature climbing out on a limb.

*   *   *

No matter how many landfalls I make, I will never cease to marvel when a small island appears at the place and time that I expect it to, according to my navigation. How much more mysterious it must have been for the early sailors who did not have our navigational aids!

Lord Howe looked like a nice island—from what we saw of it; as though the hump of land has been revealed to us in error, it disappears in a haze being pushed ahead of a squall. "Ah, too late! I have already seen the island, I know it's there!" So we will run for a while, but we'll be back. First, however, I will pull in this fish. I'm pleased, it is small, supper for two; and it won't be any trouble at all.

I don't know why I was so greedy to throw the lure and line back in for more, but I did, and I have another fish on the line. I don't like it. This fish is big, for a dorado it is very big—the line is so taut I wouldn't blame it if it broke.

Nature is like that, allowing you to believe that everything is fine and made to order ... You catch a little fish suited to your frying pan; you equate the smallness of the fish with its willingness to be fried ... Then this! You have a monster on the line, tugging and jumping. Take this! And you have to change your thinking.

All this violence at the end of the line—and the line is attached to the boat. Didn't I think peacefully about violence just a few days ago? Yet it is I who put the hook in the water, looking for food. But now that the food and I are playing tug-o'-war on a thin braided line, I can't help feeling the pulse of nature; nature is breathing down my neck.

I'm falling to pieces, I'm feeling sorry for the fish! It's struggling so hard; it's so mad. Hell, mad! Didn't it take the lure because it was going to snap up another prey, another little life, a tidbit, something it does maybe hundreds of times in a day. Now it is caught and if I get it in, we will eat it. It's the food chain, that's the term—eat and be eaten. I have to change my thinking.

No creature really allows itself to be consumed willingly; it just happens, like an unfortunate accident. Call it predestination, if you like. Humans don't like to think that they are part of such a vicious cycle, but aren't there worms in the ground? Eskimos acknowledge the process: they used to leave their old people behind to be eaten by the bear they were hunting. Even if this is not actually true (I have never been witness to it), the idea is conceivable.

I'm still pulling on the line; there is line all over the aft deck. I have it nearly alongside. The fish has turned on its side; the time has come, the colourful creature is looking at me, eye to eye. I hear a slight tearing sound—it was me, putting the gaff into him. I'm heaving ...

Marie-José's eyes are wide, confirming my own perception.

Wishing to put an end to the scene, I clubbed the fish with a force that would have slain a dragon—except that it keeps on wiggling and jumping; it doesn't really fit into our cockpit. "It's only the nerves," I console Marie-José. "It doesn't feel anything now."

Finally, the fish is still, it doesn't change colours any more; Marie-José is now willing to look at it as potential for our preserving jars.

There have been a few birds around before, but now … birds, birds all around! They started to cry with the first piece of scrap I threw overboard. It makes for an odd scene: the boat driven before the wind, clouds moving swiftly by, red blood all over a green deck, and birds crying, screeching and diving into the frothy sea.

I don't want my boat to be a slaughterhouse—we are Klaus and Marie-José, we are not killers. But wasn't I laughing a bit just now? Was it just a reaction to all the pandemonium or is it the joy of winning?

Between frequent lunges I make after the fish which is constantly threatening to slide away from me on a slanted deck, I glance at the sky and am convinced that it is looking friendlier.

* * *

It is a new day. Lord Howe Island has come back into view. From our foredeck I'm observing the pass into the harbour through binoculars.

The ocean floor has become very visible—we are entering the pass through the reef. The harbour master is standing by in a launch, asking to know our draft and motioning us to follow him. He is directing us to a mooring in close proximity to the coral reef. I'm hesitant to moor that close, but I can also see that the mooring is close to the reef for lack of sufficiently deep water elsewhere. We will have the option of moving into the less exposed "boat pool" but only at high tide and after we are cleared by customs and health authorities.

The local doctor and the customs officer are rolling with us while they fill in their forms and sip the coffee Marie-José has made.

First, I was amazed; then, I was amused; now, I don't know what. Never before have we had to go through so much paper work. The forms keep on coming. Never before have I been wrong so often in so short a time: every time I think that's it, that's the last form, it isn't.

The officer is pleasant and polite and he does all the writing, so it isn't that; in fact we are special: ours is the first yacht to officially enter Australia at Lord Howe Island. Lord Howe was proclaimed a port of entry only two weeks ago. I watch the officer unfold sheets of paper, turn them over, insert carbon leaves ... and I feel a little pleased at *Sea Helen* making a little history.

All things come to an end and so have the entry procedures. I realize now that we have been treated exactly like a big ship; there are no short forms for little ships.

* * *

We look back at Lord Howe Island. It has a lagoon—it boasts the southernmost coral—it has highlands and lowlands—it has fish in its waters and there are birds in its skies that are a constantly changing drama. It's a pleasant sight.

I'm not saying that I was unhappy at this island, but I have come to regard fruit as a symbol of fruitfulness, fertility. At Lord Howe I did not see any fruit except at the grocer's who has them flown in. Perhaps the sadness I feel comes from the conclusion that this island does not sustain its people.

Having begun to think of our planet as an island in a vast incomprehensible space, people of Lord Howe seemed overly protective, unnecessarily possessive and unusually uninspirational.

In Polynesia, at Niue Island anyhow, the people walked up to us with shining eyes, eager and proud to share the fruit that they grow for themselves, or just because a traveller found his way to their island in a vast sea. And when they sing it is a sweet yet painful acknowledgement that we are tiny dots on a small planet in a vast space; it is a whole philosophy.

I was not about to forget the two old ladies at Lord Howe who did invite us for a cold beer one afternoon. They were two brave little old ladies, spirits fit for the universe! And now I'll do something for them: I'll drop the label "little old ladies." That's how I choose to remember Lord Howe Island—we met two brave ladies.

CHAPTER ELEVEN

Culture Shock
and Southerly Busters

*T*he wind is light and at our backs, as is Lord Howe Island. The ocean is so quiet that below decks it almost feels as if we are still anchored in the lagoon. We appreciate a quiet sail—one that allows us to see ourselves skipping across the ocean. Time might be moving just as fast but thoughts can linger.

We consider it a fairly short stretch, these four hundred miles to the Australian coast. Three days from Lord Howe, an array of angular shapes catches the eye. Sydney's man-arranged projections are far more conspicuous than the softer contours of the land.

There is no intricate way to enter Port Jackson, as Sydney harbour is known. We saw the edges of a continent from the deep sea, steered on over the continental shelf—noticeable because of a different wave pattern—and now, having drawn level with the land, we are practically inside the harbour.

We are looking at a heavily travelled expanse of water with Sydney Harbour Bridge and the Opera House at the far end. There is little time to sort out our feelings for the skies are unleashing a rain squall that demands a hurly-burly sail to the anchorage.

*   *   *

"Culture shock" is the term that seems to describe this new experience: the fast life is so irrational, almost incomprehensible, it does not seem to add anything; it does not open any horizons. How reversed things are. When we first arrived in the islands, it was us who were impatient with the slow pace of life—with the fruit sellers who saw no sense in selling anything without smiling at length and savouring every event in the most, to us, peculiar way.

Slowly we have fallen in with the island way of life and have made it our own. To buy twenty cents worth of vegetables, we would take time to inspect them from all angles and to allow any random thoughts to run their course. How a heap of vegetables could come into sharp focus; the soul reflected in the seller's eyes that were so elated to see us! We knew our presence was accepted.

We had learned to live this new way—to meet things directly, to be alive to what we were experiencing. Moored in a tranquil lagoon, one could study the curve of the mooring rope leading to a palm tree or to a bollard on the town wharf. One would then contemplate the slant of the palm or the angle of the wharf ... the sensation of one's foot on a peculiar boulder is only the beginning ...

But here in Lavender Bay, almost under the shadow of the great arc of Sydney Harbour Bridge, our little schooner rocks and rolls unrhythmically to waves created by an old ferry that circles us at regular intervals and by other craft coming and going at random.

In Sydney, the grocer will not do himself the favour of selling and living at the same time. His idea of living is to collect money feverishly then to spend it on trivial pleasures or material things.

What we like best about Sydney is that our friend Rolf, whom we met in Tahiti, lives here. His presence and his hospitality are a match for a sunny day.

We appreciate Rolf recounting moments of his single-handed voyage from England to Australia, for it confirms our own experience of joy, frustration and fear, and helps us understand the process of viewing the world from the decks of a small ship.

* * *

The many weeks that we have anchored *Sea Helen* in Pittwater, an area twenty miles north of Sydney where tongues of the ocean reach deeply into the land, have been pleasant. It is time to have our steel schooner sand-blasted and repainted. Port Stephens, seventy miles up the coast, has emerged as the obvious place to have this done.

An unfavourable north-east wind is blowing, however, so we will beat up close to the Barrenjoey Head, a point of land standing prominently at the entrance to Pittwater, and wait behind it in a nook just hidden from the open sea, for the southerly that will take us up the coast.

I'm awake because of the uneasy stirring of the schooner and the grating sound of the anchor chain. I stagger up the companionway, still drugged with sleep, because this is perhaps something more than a change in the tidal stream. My head is filled with a symphony of

77

mournful whistling that makes my scalp tingle, and I imagine that this is our initiation to the "Southerly Buster," the wind that comes out of nowhere and of which people have warned us numerous times.

Distances are hard to judge at night and I suppress my fear that we have moved closer to the dark rocks. There is comfort in the fact that our heavy ground tackle has always held us, but I go forward and check if the anchor cable is hard or soft. I'm holding the chain and can feel the tremor that the anchor transmits as it drags over the ground. I now see that the shore has definitely come a lot closer. Details of the rock formations have jumped into focus—I'm contemplating where we will drag ashore. But I'm thinking more clearly ... the engine will help to hold us off; I'm screaming over the fury of a heavy gust for Marie-José to engage the propeller and keep the nose into the wind. I storm forward again, attaching a length of chain and a coil of rope to the Danforth and drop it over. The anchor grabs instantly, as if something has snatched it up; my relief is secondary to my puzzlement.

The heavy gusts have blown themselves out. The closeness of a pulsing jagged line of froth marking where the sea ends and rocks begin, urges me to move away while our luck still holds.

The skipper of a trimaran anchored nearby has rowed over to offer his help. He, too, put down a Danforth for a second anchor and it is holding him well. "Since you are holding so well now," he suggests, "why don't you stay where you are?" Although his advice is appreciated I would move out if the Danforth would allow itself to be weighed, but it doesn't.

I'm awake, this time because of the daylight. I thought so much about how the Danforth held so instantly and would not come up again—until I fell asleep in my bunk—that I have eliminated all but one possibility ... I'm on the foredeck looking into ten feet of water and I see what I expect: a dark line running across the sandy bottom. I'm under the water, grinning about how things happen—or don't happen: only the very tip of one fluke of the Danforth is caught on a huge steel cable.

* * *

We are facing the open sea, but a light north-easter is replacing the south wind. For the sake of going on to Port Stephens, I have decided to beat into it for the time being.

It is evening and we have gained ten miles.

Later in the evening I have reason to wish that we stayed at Pittwater: I'm struggling to lower the foresail and a tearing sound from the mainsail informs me that another gale has made its grand entrance.

We have stayed on the off-shore tack for most of the night but now we bring the schooner about. We have no illusions: sailing ships like ours do not point well in a boisterous sea. We will not be surprised if we have gained only a few miles or even drifted back to Barrenjoey Head.

We see land again and recognize it—it is the man-made structures of Sydney. What a shock! Thirty hours of sailing, stern first, to Sydney! Had we wanted to go there, it would have taken about three hours, down-wind.

We are in Port Jackson, patching the mainsail and already the south wind is stirring. We must take advantage of it if we are ever going to get to Port Stephens. Within the hour it is howling; it is the Southerly Buster! Now we know what people mean when they describe the choppy seas over the continental shelf. It is no comfort to know that they have not exaggerated.

The wild sleigh-ride lasts throughout the night and only the fact that it is hurrying us towards our destination keeps our spirits high.

It stops, almost as suddenly as it began—we quickly spread all of our canvas to a dying Buster. We are within sight of the lighthouse on Point Stephens but the south wind has taken its leave, saying, "Sorry, that's the best I can do for you." I agree: we should have hoisted more sail sooner.

I have noticed before how lighthouses can take on a particular character, depending on their location and shape, as well as on our state of mind. Some appear wretched and miserable or even hostile. Point Stephens' light is a friendly one. It seems pleased with its location high up on a grassy vantage point. Somehow the conditions make it possible for us to proceed under engine, and presently the white tower is on our beam. I am grateful to it for its inspiration and for waving us on. Late in the afternoon, with the first gusts of the north-easter straying through our rigging, the lighthouse gives us a wink and we slip into Port Stephens.

CHAPTER TWELVE

Mutton Birds and Mutton Bird Gales

*T*he answer a mountaineer gave to the question, "Why did you climb that mountain?" was, "Because the mountain is there!" This answer, coming from a simple mind or from a genius, provides a true insight into human nature. But sometimes we forget that when we reach the peak, we must come back down.

In reality, it is probably a combination of factors that makes us do things—that make us decide what we do. Being an unfavourable time to sail north along Australia's coast, we decide to visit friends who are living on Philip Island to the south.

The sameness of the Australian coast makes it hard to recognize specific points of land. We know we are passing Wollongong, Jervis Bay, Ulladulla, Kiama, Eden ... because of flashing navigational lights at night, or because of our celestial fixes.

A fix shows us to be at the south-west corner of the Australian continent—so we turn into Bass Strait.

Rolf, who is twice the sailor of either of us (and who doesn't get seasick) was concerned when we told him where we planned to sail. His strong reaction to the name "Bass Strait" gave credibility to tales of horror we had heard.

It is night and we are about halfway into Bass Strait. The wind, like a page in a book, has turned from north-east to south-east. The light on Cliffy Island is flashing. The light on Wilsons Promontory has a special significance—it marks the southernmost point of the Australian mainland. A mist moves in and gives the lights a halo. Rain drums on our cabin roof—there is a snorting sound through our rigging, a "shoowooshing" by our stern! Both the Cliffy Island and Wilsons Promontory lights have disappeared.

We steer by compass—with the wind over the quarter. Wilsons

Promontory light has reappeared in the frightening guise of a wounded eye; we see the cliffs close at hand! Marie-José is concerned. We are moving swiftly—we are past the cliffs.

Morning is misty, morning is.... What a tale I will have to tell of a little ship rounding Australia's southernmost point on a dark and stormy night:

I have given Marie-José the wheel and gone below to check the charts again, to make sure I take the best possible action. I pull the hatch shut behind me to keep out the spray.

A noise far louder than any other I have heard in any storm ... why should such a horrific noise be associated with our boat? I open the hatch. My eyes confirm what my ears have already understood—a wave has completely washed over us! I pull the hatch shut again. "Sorry, got to keep the water out—I'm right here," I yell to Marie-José.

I open the hatch again and look at her. My heart is breaking: Marie-José's expression is worse than fear, it is more like that of a beaten dog. Her eyes are vacant; I know she is beyond complaining.

"Sorry baby, sorry—we won't make the anchorage now. But I know exactly where we are, we have room to run with it."

"It pushed me, like this ... I hugged the wheel." She demonstrates with jerky movements.

"Yes baby—it's because we've been beam on; it's good now. We'll run with it; we have room to do it. I'll get everything ready for the sea anchor, then we'll go below."

"Where's the dinghy?" I blurt out and then regret the harsh tone in my voice.

Marie-José jerks her head in my direction and points, "Oh Klaus, it's going to fall over the side."

"Oh, it's still on the deck." I leap forward to where it is rocking, right side up, on the edge of the deck.

The jib has to come down! Ah, too late, it has torn off its hanks; it didn't wait for me. To see the jib flying out crazily, only attached by the halyard and the foot, imparts a sense of hopelessness.

Now for the sea anchor! The thought of the sea anchor gives me hope. We have used it before and been comforted. Marie-José has willingly shifted her position several times to give me maximum room. I have tied two car tires together and weighed them down with

81

a length of chain. I let them stream out astern on one of our nylon lines. "Now baby, I'll tie the wheel, then we'll go below. You go ahead now, I'll be right in." She is uncertain about leaving me out alone. "I'll unhook you when you are inside," I coax her. She takes the line of my safety harness into her hands and gives a couple of tugs, reminding me of the vacant look in her eyes after the big wave. I must stay on deck to tie the wheel and to see that the schooner is lying to, the way I want her.

"I'm coming in!" She is by the companionway, still in her wet clothes. I feel her tugging at my clothes; she doesn't let go, she pulls me down, away from the ocean that is like a giant washing machine.

We both know we are in a mess, but I'm not going to say it out loud. Instead I will say something surprising but equally true: "You know something baby, I'm not seasick." She is looking at me with curiosity; she is always worried that I will be immobilized by seasickness, so I say it again: "I don't feel sick, I'm good."

Twice, dawn follows night and the gale rages on. The inside of the cabin encloses our life—what have we let ourselves in for?

It is depressing in the dark bunk; will it ever brighten? We may come out of this victorious—is that what we wanted? We don't know.

I had a thought; but it has slipped away ...

"When I was young I didn't believe in heaven or hell," Marie-José is saying. She has broken the silence of a lull in the wind. "I remember before I was born. I don't believe in heaven or in hell," she states firmly. It is howling again.

If she is willing to speak above the silence then I am willing to think above the noise. She didn't say that she didn't believe in anything, only that she didn't believe in heaven or hell. What would early mariners have felt in this situation? Fear? I don't think it's possible to know. Our lives have been so different ... we believe different things. Try as we may, we cannot experience another person's life ... how we feel is a function of our surroundings and conditioning: when the waves are big and I'm seasick, I feel humble and small; when the ocean is calm and tame and surprisingly familiar, I am arrogant.

I have a romantic streak; I like to think about the days when ships sought their way across the oceans, to find another world—not to take it, or destroy it, just to find it. The reality is different from our fantasies. So I have a dilemma about space exploration. Still I cheer on the astronauts who lift off in their spaceships from the 'round earth.'

The astronaut in space doesn't seem to have a better vantage point. One claims there's a God, and another that there isn't? They make these statements without knowing whether there is one or not. Some people say God is simply nature, but nature is not just animals and plants and volcanoes ... humans are certainly part of nature, so is the atom, and so is the atom bomb. These are not new thoughts for me but they are useful now.

I have opened the hatch to look. Somehow, likely due to wishful thinking, I expected the storm to have run its course in unison with my thoughts, but this is not the case. Two tiny blue patches in the sky, however, compensate for the salt spray I'm taking in my face. I report these tiny patches to Marie-José. "Tomorrow, tomorrow it will be better," I gesture with contentment, for I believe it is true.

I climb back into my bunk, to think about more blue patches into the sky, but a pestering problem occupies the space. Our detailed charts ended where the gale began and we have been drifting for two days into an area for which we have only a general chart. A detailed coastal chart would have provided the information to ascertain our position near land; the chart we have will make it difficult.

I am acutely aware that we don't have this detailed chart because I didn't want to spend the money. I reasoned, not entirely irrationally, that since we have detailed charts up to Wilsons Promontory we could just plot a simple course to Phillip Island, probably easily recognizable, and then use eyeball-navigation. So simple, and a few dollars saved.

*   *   *

Finally, it is calm and sunny—it is good to be 'in,' damaged sails and all. A small open boat is steering towards us.

"Where are you going?"

Where are we going today? "Oh, just around Phillip Island." I scribe a half circle with my finger, but he seems perplexed. "To Newhaven, that's just around this island." He looks like a nice sort of fellow—I can't understand why conversation with him is so difficult; he came here to talk, didn't he?

"Newhaven is forty miles from here—this is Port Phillip Bay." He is beginning to lose interest in us. "Yes, and this is Phillip Island," I reply weakly. Could this fellow's behaviour be connected with the way we arrived at this anchorage. I'm willing to give him the benefit of the doubt. I get the chart.

"Here, where do you think we are?"

His finger goes to Port Phillip Bay. "Phillip Island is here in Westernport Bay," his finger moves along to the east on the chart.

I think I'm waking to a bad dream! If this man is right, which I'm now willing to accept, then it is clear why so many things didn't make sense when we came in here. Looking at the vague detail of the chart again, I am intrigued by the similarities between the entrance to Port Phillip Bay and the western entrance to Westernport Bay.

After the gale, we intended to enter Westernport Bay by its west entrance since it was closer to us than its east entrance ... (I had to remind myself that Phillip Island was in Westernport Bay, Port Phillip Bay is the bay west of it, just below Australia's second largest city, Melbourne). My sun sight didn't work out but we sighted a freighter and assumed that it had come out of Port Phillip Bay, since that's where Melbourne is. We headed east but could not locate Point Grant, the west side of Phillip Island. Concluding that we had gone too far we headed back west.

There is a point—and a light ... that must be it! When we were near enough for the final approach, Marie-José didn't like it one bit.

"The waves are breaking!" she yelled back to me from the bow.

"Yeah, but it's all deep water. Look it's like that all the way across. This is the entrance," I responded confidently.

The ship, under engine, and driven by a light tail-wind, easily made it past the first two lines of breaking waves, which I took to be the "bar" commonly found across bays and river mouths. We moved ahead very slowly: although the water kept rushing past us, land bearings remained unchanged.

With increasing darkness it got wilder. It was comforting to have the range lights on shore to go by, and I pointed them out to Marie-José to prove that we were in the middle of the channel. But even so, a wave-top leaped over our deck.

"Klaus, I'm scared!"

It was clear to me then that we were caught in the tidal stream. I held Marie-José close, explaining that we should not turn around for we would get caught once more in the waves breaking behind us; it was bound to get calmer further in. "We can move to one side of the channel, drop anchor and wait for the tide to turn," I suggested as an alternative.

"No!" she said, even more alarmed.

I didn't want to anchor either. "We are not losing any ground," I offered, rather than saying we were not gaining any. We were locked in. Under full sail and a revving engine, we were stationary while a turbulent sea swept underneath us. I tasted the bitterness of so much continued hardship, so much bad luck, which we were not the authors of.

After about two hours and many tears we started to gain ground. The more we gained the calmer it became and the faster we went. Now, we had only to move along the range lights, turn to starboard, make Phillip Island and drop anchor. This part of the trip went quite well.

Fate is a curious affair. Had this friendly young man not wanted to know where we were going, I would have proceeded to sail around Phillip Island this sunny morning, which is not Phillip Island on this, or any other, sunny morning.

Now we know: it's called "The Rip," the place where we shed tears, where we felt the wrath of—we dared not speculate what— where we hung in a limbo of bitterness, and frustration and fear.

Now we know this phenomenon, the Rip, can be logically explained: with a change of tide, waters from a thirty-mile bay have to squeeze through a bottle neck. (Westernport Bay, the bay we believed we entered, is a lot smaller and has two entrances making for a weaker tidal stream.)

My immediate concern now is that Peter, the messenger who enlightened us, is wondering whether we are in control of our faculties, and if all people that cross oceans on thirty-foot boats are mad! Carefully I demonstrate that we are fully aware of our mistake, a big error on our part!

What should we make of our error on this beautiful tranquil day? To be thankful, to be humble, to be glad we learned a lesson? Or to be annoyed over four or five cracks in the dinghy and some torn sails. The *right* response is to declare a two-day layover, announced with conviction.

"We'll stay for two days?" Marie-José has asked expectantly, massaging her left breast beneath which her heart beats unevenly (she has been afflicted by a heart condition since childhood). Only by knowing that we will not be going "out" today or tomorrow, can she coax her heart into beating a better rhythm.

We have apparently anchored off a place named Sorrento, so we will pick up our hook and drop it again, closer to the beach.

* * *

There are no breakers. Through binoculars, I'm keeping a keen eye on the area where three days ago we spent long horrifying moments. There is no Rip now, just a sluggish stirring of the ocean surface. It is no accident that our exit coincides with a slack tidal stream.

We have nursed the ship along in gentle breezes for twenty hours, moving forty miles east along Australia's south coast. We are standing off the eastern entrance to Westernport Bay on a midday so tranquil that the conditions appear harmless and manageable. Our sails hang limp in the shadow of Phillip Island's southernmost point and only the noise of the engine pierces the stillness around us. Soon we will see our good friends again. We can see the bridge that Yvonne mentioned connecting the island to the mainland. The weather is so cooperative that I'm more curious than concerned about a supposedly difficult entrance to Newhaven.

We had phoned Dave and Yvonne from Sorrento to let them know that one overnight trip should see us off Phillip Island. Yvonne, after enquiring, "Where were you the last few days—we had a real bad gale," and, "How are you...!" called in a local fisherman to give us instructions on how to negotiate the obstacles between us and Newhaven. The fisherman was a meticulous instructor, but the only practical information I gained was that it was not straightforward. It appeared to be a case of, "it's-easy-if-you-know-it."

A solitary boat is speeding across the water towards *Sea Helen*. The powerful outboard motor grinds restlessly in idle as her skipper, obviously a man of action, satisfies himself that we are Klaus and Marie-José from Canada who know Dave and Yvonne. My gaze falls on a clutter of scuba diving gear as I listen to more directions on how to get to Newhaven—sandbars, a point, a buoy, range markers, a green can, a bridge, black rocks ... no, they are not going back in just now, they are going to dive for abalone.

86

With clear instructions under our belts, it is easy to follow the channel and we are elated at having reached the bridge. We put our trust in an old weather-beaten face to help us sort out the markers beyond the bridge. The figure beckons and points directions as it stands, manipulating the tiller of a smart wooden boat.

Certain people, due to their nature and stature, evoke a sense of fondness in us. This agiled-bodied man, who has guided us through the rocks and mud flats and deposited us at the corner of the pier where Dave and Yvonne's smiling faces shine down on us, has done just this.

We come to appreciate him more in the days that follow when we invite him aboard for coffee, or watch him throw fish to the pelicans parading on the water, or when we chance to meet him or seek him out. George Mapleson is his name ("old George" between Dave, Yvonne and us), self-appointed guardian of sailors.

*   *   *

A rare mixture of thoughts occupy my mind this evening. Yvonne is a gentle being, Dave a sensitive person, Marie-José has a love, if not a passion, for all birds, and I have never felt happy killing a fish. Nevertheless the four of us are content to feast on mutton birds this evening, on board the schooner. We do not want to think of ourselves as hypocrites—we are quietly trying to deal with our contradictions.

The taste of the dark meat is out of this world. "A lot of grease had to be run off," Yvonne is saying. She explains that mutton birds can only get airborne in a strong wind; fishermen, who brought the birds for her, walk up to them, grab them and wring their necks. I look at Yvonne to see if her involvement in this massacre detracts from her delicacy, her bloom.

Somehow, among other feelings and sensations, including a slight annoyance over the heeling and bumping of the boat due to the ebb which makes us concerned about our wine glasses, I feel privileged to be offered fare that is part of the diet of the elite people who live in this area. Although this delicate and educated friend has deliberately requested the execution of these birds to give us a flavour of her world, her beauty is not diminished. I am slightly spellbound.

Eating this local delicacy guides my thoughts towards this unique and sunny land, home to animals found nowhere else on the globe, and reptiles unchanged since prehistoric times; but also to a bleak landscape where escaped convicts perished from want of food, where aborigines survived for eons in harmony with nature.

I have not asked George whether he regularly feasts on mutton birds, so when he discusses them, I prick up my ears! He emphasizes that they die by the thousands, being smashed against the cliffs by the very gale-force winds they need to become airborne. I experience a sense of dread when George says that this is the time of year when the birds begin their migratory flight; they are waiting for the gales: the "Mutton Bird Gales." It sounds ominous, coming from him—the guardian of sailors. It is equivalent to saying: "Sailors beware of the mutton bird gales!"

*   *   *

Today, April 12, we are halfheartedly commencing our return journey—a retreat from Bass Strait as it is impressed on my mind. George is standing by to pilot us through the tricky part.

We have reached the point where the abalone diver gave us instructions and the day resembles the day of our arrival, bright and tranquil. George turned at the end of the channel; ahead of us lies Bass Strait, calm, almost glossy. Slowly, we move further into it; features of the landscape become unrecognizable.

This second day the wind is still so feeble that it is mostly the engine that is responsible for our progress. We will seek anchorage at Wilsons Promontory which we should be able to make before nightfall at our present rate of progress.

Where does this little bird that does not have the energy to keep up with us come from? It flutters frantically by our transom; it has fallen astern by a few more feet and is desperately trying to regain the lost ground. I slow the already slow-moving boat some more, but the bird's energy fails and, accompanied by a sigh from Marie-José, it plummets to the water. We circle around it and I scoop it up out of the water with my hand.

Here is a golden opportunity to review our concept of selfishness. We went out of our way for the welfare of the bird. But with either a more erudite or a more primitive attitude, we might have ignored it and reasoned its death would be in the nature of things.

As it was, we saved it to satisfy our consciences—an act of selfishness, even if a noble one. Selfishness borders on the paradoxical. Altruism is its close companion so there seems to be no such thing as unselfishness.

Had we control of our destiny, we would have arrived at the anchorage before dark. The light has already faded suddenly and we are only just passing a small island, a few miles beyond which there is an indentation in the mainland that will provide sheltered anchorage. It has also got a lot cooler. Marie-José has not changed her sitting position in the cockpit, for the weary bird has sought shelter behind her back, making little bird noises.

We have found our way into the bay, and let the anchor chain rattle down. Total silence reigns. The night is so calm that our thoughts seem to take on a presence. They are questions, reflections, an inner searching—and a little contentment, too. The fate of the little bird seems sealed; it is almost without life, on this clear night.

I believe that thoughts, too, die; sometimes they fade first. They are born on nights like tonight and are swept away by the gold on the horizon at dawn, or even by an ominous storm cloud. No doubt dead thoughts can be remembered, the way that we remember physical bodies that have long since turned to dust. We may mention a dead person's name, even look at their photograph, but we cannot sit beside them, see them or touch them. We can visit their bones and a new thought may arise, and old ones remembered.

* * *

It is morning. The bones of some dead thoughts rattle in my brain as I make long sweeps to row Marie-José and the bird ashore. I have the feeling that this is a sacred moment. We have found a beautiful spot under a tree and the sunlight broke through just as the bird died.

How Marie-José would have liked to see it flutter away ... but a brilliant day and a gentle place cannot prevent the inevitable. "It was probably the end of the bird's life cycle," I offer Marie-José. Either way, it makes for a sad moment.

* * *

When we sail close to shore, for instance towards the tip of Wilsons Promontory in order to round it, as we are doing, we must concentrate on navigation. Thoughts of wine, women and song, or death, or the meaning of the universe, may enter, but they are not allowed to develop. After all, it is the safety of the ship we sail on that must take priority. A navigator, however, is inclined to take note of the landscape: Wilsons Promontory is rocky, has bays with beaches, is wooded, flanked by small islands, is cliffy. There are sheer cliffs at the very tip which are high and formidable. A lighthouse stands atop them accompanied by some red-roofed buildings. It was this tower's powerful light that screamed at us through sheets of rain that dark and stormy night. With lazily rolling decks, we retrace our former course past Cliffy Island, now easily recognizable for it truly represents its name.

Lacking the effects of a commanding breeze, we have been stumbling for three days towards the limits of Bass Strait; I'm keenly aware of an imminent weather change. To the uninitiated, the sky would not look threatening, but there is a new smell in the air, and one's hair ruffles in a different way. Were there leaves on the ground, they would scatter in all directions.

The boat is in irons. I'm dousing the main. A gust of wind—then another … The foreboom held by its preventer answers with a creak. The foresail slams back—a flutter—a crack—I look at it in time to see the white Dacron dissolve into blue sky.

Had it not been our foresail, it might have been magic. Marie-José pokes her head out of the galley, inquiring about this sound like the tearing of fabric. I hate to be the bearer of bad news, but I say what I must. "Foresail." A tragedy is softened by a casually spoken word. Marie-José innocently turns her head to look for herself. A new gale has curtsied to us in a most reckless manner.

I don't think one can force oneself to be inwardly calm. But I'm lowering the gaff, lashing the boom, tying the gaff to the boom and tucking in the pieces of Dacron tenderly with inner calmness. The gale could have happened sooner; but it held off until we were almost off the shelf, the most treacherous part of the Bass Strait. In fact, the wind has swung to the south-west, endeavouring to send us out the rest of the way in a hurry. I think about Old George and mutton birds. I let them linger, for ahead of us is only ocean.

It is easy to have calm thoughts in calm moments. It has been nine days and my nerves are almost raw! We have reefed our remaining sails, streamed our car tires; and have been left wallowing among heaps of seas when the wind suddenly abated, only to start anew from another direction; we streamed the car tires again when it blew in reverse and tried to regain ground when it blew the way we wanted to go, only to be boarded by a wave. When there was wind, there was too much of it; when there wasn't too much of it, there was none. Now I try to start the engine and it won't start because it is flooded with sea water.

Had I not taken an apprenticeship in mechanics it might not have occurred to me that the engine is flooded, and what the salt water will do to its components. The engine has to be dismantled, but it is hard to see how this captain, with sweat on his forehead from motion sickness, is going to do it.

Marie-José has screamed at me, "Are we going to make it?" I swear, had we a radiophone, I would call somebody. What would I say? "This is *Sea Helen, Sea Helen, Sea Helen*—we have flooded engine and torn sails—request assistance, over ..."

In our minds though the words are different: "This is KLAUS and MARIE-JOSÉ—we want to get off, we have had enough!" In some ways we are worse off than in our other gale and in some ways we are better off: we have a useless engine and no foresail, but we are in open ocean and not in the Bass Strait—somehow a real consolation.

Somewhat ungracefully and over a long period of time (fifteen days since Phillip Island), we have now made our way a few hundred miles up the coast; we are, in fact, in the vicinity of a huge natural harbour named Jervis Bay. The opening to it seems very generous and by coincidence, the weather is a little more reasonable, allowing us to hoist our fragile jib and mainsail.

With the feelings of having one's name picked out of a hat among hundreds, we see Jervis Bay unfolding before us with nothing to stop us from entering. Light steady breezes are our crutches as we limp through the opening.

It isn't the most spectacular landscape, rather flat and typical of the sameness which makes Australia's coast hard to navigate visually; but it has the distinction of welcoming a couple of woebegone sailors. Having battled the elements, it is now clear to me that the elements are not our enemies. They just are, and we try to survive their harsh face until they again turn the gentle one towards us. We are not victorious after a gale; triumphant maybe, because we have a new point of view.

Despite a bad engine, torn sails, lost stern lantern, broken hatch, and all—insights like that make me calm. I'm aware that meanwhile our visas have expired (one thinks about these things) and there will be a battle with the authorities in Sydney; but not even expired visas can ruffle my calmness.

*   *   *

Some bloke, we are making assumptions here, has actually stolen our good oar! The dinghy had to be left somewhere so that we could go, find, buy, gather materials, for our repairs ... and then, upon our return, not two oars, just one. But what does this matter in light of the hospitality we received, the friends we made, the relatives we were taken to be? A Mr. Gehrig, who has so far traced almost every 'Gehrig' in the land to his family tree, heard of another Gehrig in Jervis Bay, took his dog and headed for the beach. I thought his interrogation concerning my name a bit harsh, but it was only because he was anxious to take us into his home.

"You better come to the house for coffee," he said when I confirmed that I was a Gehrig. He did not ask if we would like to come.

During our stay in Jervis Bay every Gehrig family event includes us. If there is a lull in the barbecues, sightseeing tours or evenings at home with a bottle of "plunk," one of us shoulders the cockatoo, named Charlie, and we all wander along the beach, maybe scooping up a bucket of sea shells for an extra source of calcium for the "chooks"; in addition we are making steady progress in repairing the schooner. And besides, when the word of our missing oar gets around we are given another one. It is two sizes above the requirements, but nothing a saw and a plane can't set right. She's right, mate!

CHAPTER THIRTEEN

The Battle

*I*t isn't fair, it's two against one. The customs officer, however, is not a hardened warrior. "We can't just keep giving you three months and three months," he says good-naturedly.

Few problems have an easier solution than this one. "If you gave me a permit for a longer period, then I wouldn't have to keep asking for extensions," I point out.

"We can only give you what Immigration gives you," he says. He is apparently being frank with me, but I don't know if he sees this strategy as regrettable or a dilemma. There is certainly no point in telling me what he cannot give, when in fact it all depends on what Immigration gives.

I have shocked the immigration officer by telling him that he does not represent the feelings of Australian people, for, surely, they would not want us to put to sea without first acquiring a new suit of sails.

He surprises me by repeating that we have to show proof of our departure within fourteen days. I'm going to win this battle because I'm rationally furious: to be told that it was my mistake ... that I should have foreseen ...

My voice starts from low down: "I'm sure you have made many mistakes in your life—I'm not asking you for anything unreasonable; hell, you're treating me like a criminal!" My voice has considerably increased in volume.

"No, I'm not!"

"Yes, you are! I came to you with my problem, I asked you for a short work permit and you tell me to leave within fourteen days."

"You overstayed your visa! Have you been working?" Now that isn't fair! We tried to get an extension for our visas in Melbourne but were told to wait until we returned to Sydney. We were also told it wouldn't matter if our visas expired (my worry) before we got to Sydney. And I wrote a courtesy letter to the Immigration Department, from Jervis Bay, informing them of our whereabouts and our difficulties. "Did you receive my letter?"

He is fumbling with the folder that he is armed with.

"Yes."

"Then you know," I reply with a high-pitched voice, hoping to demonstrate that I'm at a loss to understand why my letter has been ignored. "Were we working!" I reply again to this repeated question that I regard more as an accusation. "How could we have been working when we were out there battling the seas?" (I do not say we were out there "surviving the harsh face of the elements"; it would not mean a thing to this bloke). "I'm asking you for a work-permit." I have placed the stress on "asking" in order to set the record straight.

"You are not allowed to work!" he repeats. A computer could give a more varied response. He wants to leave—call it quits; he's going back to his desk. But I want to tell him more; I want him to know the way I feel: "Come back here! The world is not like that! One cannot foresee everything...."

In the meantime, a queue has formed on my side of the counter; this is not surprising since things haven't exactly been moving along. I deserve an audience for these words of torment. Apparently, though, nobody in the queue shares my problem, nobody cheers. "It's all one world!" I blurt out my most important argument, for the sand in the hourglass has run out.

Now, on an impulse, I ask for the name of his boss. People who make decisions should speak for them. Even though there is no sand left in this bloke's hourglass I'm at the head of a long queue. I'm writing. "And what is your name?" ... I write it down, too. "I'll need them for further correspondence," I say flatly, calling an end to this round.

He is young, a little bewildered, and I believe that were it solely up to him he would satisfy my little request, but he is going by the book and by his boss, but against his conscience.

* * *

I have begun to tell people that there is more to cruising than hoisting sails. The fact that in Australia's largest city I could now find my way to the customs building blindfolded tells me that I'm spending too

94

much time there. It seems that *Sea Helen* is providing the main justification for their existence.

A clerk whom I have never seen before—they even have reinforcements—is manning the familiar counter. I look past him to see if there is somebody I know ... but he wants to help me.

I'm frugal with words these days. I give him one name bellowing it out so that it could even be heard above the roar of the elements, befitting the courageous little ship, "*Sea Helen!*"

I marvel. The clerk instantly recognizes the name. Swift as the wind he produces the customs officer assigned to my case.

Having brought the customs officer up to date on the progress with the Immigration Department I begin to feel compassion for his dilemma. The Immigration Department insists that we leave the country, even if it means leaving our boat behind. As far as Customs is concerned this is a turn for the worse. They would rather have it the other way around. It is more problematical for them to have a foreign boat in the harbour—duty unpaid—with the owners away. This officer is rooting for us to get new visas from the Immigration Department, to make things simpler; I'm on his side.

Rolf's and Vicky's snug little apartment has become a place to lick our wounds. Rolf's own encounters with officials make ours look pale. On one occasion he declared he would sink his boat rather than capitulate, but my favourite story is the one involving a Christmas present.

He called at the Galapagos Islands and was given twenty-four hours in which to fill up with water. "I also need food," he insisted and was granted forty-eight hours. But after an influential resident befriended him, he was allowed eight days—more than he wanted. Five days later he went to inform the harbour master he was leaving only to be told, to his dismay, that he owed fifty dollars docking fees. Rolf put thirty dollars—all the cash he had on him—on the table. The harbour master insisted on fifty.

It was strictly a deadlock. In the Galapagos Islands however, the navy has the last word and it was then that the commander came by. The harbour master stated his case and Rolf stated his. The commander took Rolf's thirty dollars in payment for docking fees and then promptly handed it back to him saying it was, "a Christmas present" providing he left at once. It was the day before Christmas.

*   *   *

The top man in a department seems to have it the easiest: at the Immigration Department the top man is not concerned about the legality of my request. He uses his valuable time to tell me that he respects me for what I am doing and wishes that he could do it too.

Well, I respect him too. I even treat him to a few highlights of our voyage. Even though time has run out, mutual respect between people can solve even the most difficult problems. Our new visas entitle us to a new cruising permit from Customs. They hand it over, with smiles. It is agreed, however, that before our cruising permit expires—a mere two months—we will definitely sail from Australia. In order to keep to our agreement, we will undertake a voyage that I would rather avoid, except, at this point, I find it easier to face the elements than to battle the authorities. We will sail to New Zealand, 1200 miles across the Tasman Sea.

Of course, a visa is required for New Zealand.... I'm searching the phone book for the address of the New Zealand consulate. What a life!

CHAPTER FOURTEEN

Twelve Hundred Miles Across the Tasman Sea

*U*npleasant memories of a passage seem to drift away, like clouds after a storm.

"Land ho!"

"What?" Marie-José asks from her bunk.

It seemed the right thing to say after looking through the binoculars, and convincing myself that it is one of three little islands about thirty-two miles north-west of New Zealand, named the Three Kings.

Sixteen days have passed since we left Sydney. Our new sails billow out beautifully when the breezes are stiff; when the wind threatens to become too strong, we reef them early; when the wind is too feeble to keep them filled, we take them down to save them from the dreadful flapping. We opened our bottle of mead (honey wine) on the day we recorded ninety-five miles from noon to noon.

"Land ho!" I repeat for Marie-José. The land is just a smudge on the horizon. While we rejoice at the long-awaited sight, we are belabouring a very heavy swell. Crests foam and gurgle by our transom. We find ourselves in vast valleys, or lingering on the ridge of moving mountains that hold us closer to the blue sky.

So this is the heavy "overfall" that results from the ocean going over the shelf. I am glad that I have read about it and can explain it to Marie-José.

The great swells have subsided again. It is night and we are becalmed north of the Three Kings.

In the morning, the wind gathers into a decent breeze from the north-east sending us towards New Zealand's east coast. North Cape is visible to starboard, but it is already being swallowed by the approaching night. We let the compass rose guide us through the dark; the wind, having built in strength, sends us along swiftly towards our destination—the Bay of Islands.

* * *

The tranquil Kerikeri River wipes away all traces of uneasiness: it is narrow in places but well marked. The branches of trees hang low so that we can reach out and touch them; there are rocks and sandbanks, too. At the village of Kerikeri, a basin separates the navigable river from a mere mountain stream. More than a hundred years ago, the Maori people organized raids and war parties from this very spot.

I spend a great deal of time here sitting on our cabin top peeling oranges—and eating them. I am indulging in the local produce of this idyllic place.

* * *

We are not at all tired of the Bay of Islands but we want to sail to Auckland, New Zealand's largest city, just to look. Deep Water Cove is on the way and we put in for the sheer luxury of it: there is a waterfall. The cove is deep and small, and the waterfall is not at all obvious. Although we have found it, it is to small to stand under. Soap in hand and towels draped around us, we look at what is undeniably falling water, but a trickle, not a waterfall.

Had I not brought soap and towel I might think nothing of it. However, with expectations of a roaring freshwater shower from which we would come out pink and refreshed, we follow the trickle. There are only a couple of difficult places—most of the way up is like an uneven flight of steps.

Here you have it! Had the waterfall met our expectations we would never have known the luxury of bathing in a sparkling rock pool.

At Tutukaka, a day's run from Auckland, we come back to the *Sea Helen* from shore and find a cucumber and some tomatoes on the deck. Finding good honest vegetables on the decks of a humble little ship is equivalent to finding Christmas presents under the tree when one is a child.

Bugs, Marie-José has bugs in her hair! They are flat, white and semi-transparent and on a fine-toothed comb they make swimming-like movements. Out of curiosity, I pull the comb through my hair. There is one—and another. This is ultimate proof that things are not as we thought they were. In all likelihood the lice come from the rock pool, at Deep Water Cove, that was above our expectations.

* * *

Going into a large commercial harbour with a small boat makes one think differently. The water is usually silty and grimy; there are structures in need of repairs, wharfs askew, equipment obsolete, buildings badly arranged and often old. But for someone who has never seen it before, it is all brand new.

The limited area set aside in Auckland harbour for non-commercial craft, at the old Marsden Wharf, is chock-a-block with yachts. Only the poorest of all places, the bottom end of the U-shaped wharf where one has to present beam to the swell, is available to little *Sea Helen*. An off-shore wind, which is favourable from a berthing point of view, blows masses of city dust onto our decks. One other boat shares this unfortunate spot with us: it has a noisy generator that runs for most of the day, starting at breakfast time.

But all is not black. "Klaus! José!" What great sounds! The greeting comes from Murray Lister whom we met at Niue Island where he was an officer on the supply ship *Fetu Moana*. He lives in Nelson on the south island at the other end of Cook Strait. His wife, too, would be happy to have us. A master mariner, with years in the sea-rescue service, he is available to help navigate our schooner. And when we get there, Murray pulls out his trump card—we can make money by picking apples.

Murray is disappointed over my decision not to accept his invitation. We know that we would fare well in Nelson with Murray looking after us. In fact, each of the opportunities he offered were difficult to turn down, quite apart from the pleasure of his own company.

Why on earth, then, don't we accept? Were our boat capable of reasonable speed in unfavourable conditions, I would probaby say yes, even though we would not have much time for picking apples—our sailing itinerary is largely governed by seasons. There is a reason why so many yachts congregate in New Zealand between October and March. During this season—the cyclone season—prudent sailors either find a place near the equator that is not affected by cyclones, or move far to the south beyond where the tropical storms will travel.

In just a few weeks, two months at the most, it will be time to head back to the tropics. I can imagine a confrontation with Immigration and Customs if we have to remain in New Zealand because we missed the safe sailing season.

Murray, not finding a "waterfall" where he expected one, is trying to understand our situation. He looks at our sextant and makes some adjustments which will be a great help to me later.

*   *   *

We are on our way back to the Bay of Islands, passing between Kawau Island and Flat Rock. This rock is a flat slab, exposed by only a few feet. There is a light atop a conical structure and another small cone beside it. I can't help thinking of it as a monument, something associated with a great accomplishment, a revered person, or an important event. The schooner is driven on by a good following breeze—I look back at the "monument" but I don't want to come too close to it; I don't want to come too close to any rock in the heaving ocean, even though it draws me, like a true monument.

Black markers, in New Zealand waters, must be left to starboard when inbound from the sea. One black marker stands at the entrance to Whangateau Harbour on a protruding point of the eastern shore and there is a second one on isolated rocks a few hundred feet beyond. The pilot book says to leave them both to starboard upon entering. Our sails are down and we are carefully motoring towards the entrance.

Things don't look right! There does not seem to be enough water between the rocks and the western shore, a sandy peninsula. Marie-José thinks there is a lot more water between the point and the rocks and suggests that we go through there, but it would mean ignoring the meticulously compiled pilot book, and the colour of the marker; not an easy thing to do. Surely, if the entrance was between the two black markers, the pilot book would have said so. Ahead of the isolated rocks, very low in the water, bobs a small red float, such as fishermen use. Why is it there? Just one more oddity.

It is obvious to Marie-José that the only deep water is between the two black markers—pilot book or no pilot book—in fact, she would be happy to turn around and forget about entering this harbour.

However, I don't want to lose my faith in human logic. Surely, somebody would have taken a brush and painted the marker on the rocks red, were it meant to be left to port.

A heavy ground swell makes us surf; it felt as if we touched bottom—the seas are breaking on the sand ahead of us—it is too shallow. The wind is blowing offshore—I counted on it—and we are backing off; but the wind is also pushing our bow off to starboard. We are in between the little red float and the rocks. Total chaos! We hit bottom. I take the wheel. Marie-José yells out, "There is a rock in front!" The wheel wrenches in my hand—there is a definite thump, now a scrape as we slide off a second rock. Finally we have ended up where Marie-José thought we should have been in the first place, in between the rocks and the point.

I decide to enter by leaving the rocks to port. Immediately after we pass the point, we have to make a sharp turn to starboard into the north-bound channel; we are taken aback, the place is mostly sandbanks. A few boats are moored at the end of the channel, including a fifty-foot sailboat which is aground. Thinking that there will be a more generous anchorage in the south arm, which the pilot book describes as the main part of the harbour, I stand on the bow and point directions for Marie-José, but she does not follow them because we are aground.

We are astonished at so little water. We take it lightly, it is quite calm in here. I row an anchor into the channel and drop it. We float free with the incoming tide. There is no swinging room, so we set a second anchor and stay where we are.

Now that we have settled into this confined anchorage, we may even stay a second day. The owner of the large sailboat has shown up. The deep channel is indeed between the two black markers, he confirms. He smiles knowingly, "... has been so for years." The red float has been placed there recently to mark the advancing sandbank.

It frequently happens that we share an anchorage with another yacht and never exchange a word with her crew; a salute maybe or a little wave, if someone happens to show him or herself on deck. Yet, certain people wouldn't dream of missing the opportunity to meet us. It may be our boat, or the flag; yes, quite often the flag, I'm sure. Or it may be my beard; someone seeing it might anticipate having a yarn with an old salt.

In any case, the Hairies, Pat and Slim—who introduce themselves after anchoring next to us—wonder if we could help them drink some of the Greek beer that they have so much of.

I have never had Greek beer before. I'm interested—besides, the

Hairies have a nice old wooden boat with patchy sails. We can find nothing wrong with the Greek beer; in fact, we find nothing wrong with the Hairies.

*   *   *

It's been two weeks since we fought our way back to the Bay of Islands against a nasty chop raised by a south-wester. *Sea Helen*'s bottom has been freed from barnacles and provided with a new, inexpensive, coat of anti-fouling, at the Russell Boating Club. We have answered to the call of the Kerikeri river ... now it is time to move with the seasons.

We have a choice: if we want to obtain clearance papers from Customs (a paper sure to be asked for at the next foreign port of call) we can get them in the Bay of Islands for a fee (the expenses incurred by an officer driving from Whangarei) or, if we don't want to pay the fee, we can sail to Whangarei and get them there. We don't want to pay the fee. With money not easily earned along the way, money saved is money to spend elsewhere.

We do not consider Deep Water Cove as superb an anchorage as its name implies, but we decide to anchor in its south-east corner, anticipating a glorious morning sail to Whangarei. But preconceived ideas only work out half of the time at best. Neither Marie-José nor I sleep very much, listening to gusts of wind that roll down on us from the hills.

I hear a distinct crunch, and feel a tremor run through me. I hope this is not a grounding, which is trying to ignore the obvious. Looking over the stern I see that the rudder is still under water; I sense a rock ledge under our transom. Marie-José wants to know if she should start the engine?

"Start the engine!"

I engage the propeller. I have not given the engine a chance to warm up and it is spewing clouds of smoke. I know what the next gust of wind might do to us will be irreversible. We are not hard aground ... we have moved off. I hand the wheel to Marie-José: "Keep moving ahead while I pull up the anchor!"

"Stop!" The anchor will not come up. There is no way that we can stay where we are. "Let the boat fall back towards the reef and then move ahead at a different angle! That's it, the anchor has broken out!"

We move over to the north side of the cove where a yacht, a black sloop, has apparently anchored during the night. Only the lead line can help us find the sandy patch indicated on the chart; the sloop does not seem to be well on it. For peace of mind it is necessary to sound out the area more extensively, to be sure that we do not drop the anchor too close to the edge of the shelf. Finally, we let go the anchor and pay out lots of scope ... we back down on it hard. We are holding.

It is getting light and rather than climbing back into our bunks we decide to have breakfast. I look out at the sky—I reach for the horn and blow it. I blow it again and again. I will try to blow harder! Finally, figures appear on the deck of the black sloop. Their boat is moving towards some rocks at considerable speed. The putter of an engine is audible above the howling of the wind and the sloop moves ahead, re-anchoring near its former position. Her crew, apparently finding no pleasure on deck, has gone below. But the graceful sloop is gliding towards the rocks again ... I reach for the horn. This time the crew reports on deck after only two blasts—they recognize the sound.

Our anchor seems well set for, despite the fact that the gusts are now more frequent and stronger than ever, we are holding. But we will take the precaution of reefing all our sails, so that if we are forced to put to sea, we will present a small sail area to the wind; it is easier to shake out a reef than to put one in.

In the meantime, the sloop has dragged for the third time, given up and left. A power cruiser has arrived, but its anchor, too, cannot take hold of the ocean bottom.

I decide to review our anchoring tactics for greater peace of mind: I'm convinced that we have the best possible anchor spot in the cove; our heavy plow anchor has held us through some severe gusts and therefore we can assume that it is well set. To give a well-set anchor less strain we let out extra scope. Then we set a second anchor.

We have partially slept through another night. The gusts persist— they are actually bullets of air shooting down from the mountains. When a lull following a gust is noticeably long, I suspect that the next one is gathering strength for a greater assault.

"Ah, what a beautiful day!" I say this now and then when it is really miserable, laughing inwardly. I'm reminded of a woman who used to say this about any day, regardless of the weather. Having no expectations of something better, and accepting bad weather grace-fully, can support this incongruous remark. I can't concentrate on the artistic cloud formations when I'm also aware of the ship straining against her anchor cable.

My eyes watch the shadows as I lie in my bunk, wondering if one could ever get used to the sound of these violent gusts. So far I have arrived at the point where my heart doesn't thump quite as hard. I can predict with accuracy when the boat will snub its anchor cable and how hard ...

Another night has passed for there is brightness in the cabin ... it is so quiet. Is it quiet? What's missing? No gusts.

It must be late in the morning. I don't stir in my bunk. I watch the sunlight dance and twinkle in the cabin, telling Marie-José about the absence of wind, as if I'm the only one capable of realizing it.

I look out: what a beautiful morning—and we are in it. We are just a little pressed to obtain our clearance in Whangarei so that we can sail on in good time; but we shall stay in Deep Water Cove one more day, for the same reason that I stayed in my bunk to watch the sunlight dance and twinkle.

Once More
to New Caledonia

A large truck has pulled up to the wharf. On its flat deck is one solitary carton. I suspect who it is for, but I will let the driver ask the name of our boat. It is official, the carton is for us. I feel slightly embarrassed—the truck is so big and the carton so small.

Our ship's stores until now have always included one or two bottles of liquor at the regular store price. In Whangarei it is very easy for yachts to take a case on in bond, providing one is outward-bound. Liquor is, of course, not life-sustaining and therefore not absolutely necessary. However, we regard such juices of the earth as desirable. A case of this luxury bought duty free amounts to a real saving in the long run.

We are facing the ocean from the mouth of the Whangarei River, which seems more eager to receive than to spit out. For the moment the swells are rushing at us, giving us a feeling of inadequacy, but our course in just a short while will be off the wind.

"Our course is 340 degrees," I announce, for both of us. I'm letting the bow fall away from the wind to catch that reading on the compass. It is now a lofty, graceful ride.

The ship swooshes and whooshes and heaves with the rhythm of the sea and the two of us are gathered in the cockpit under a patchy sky. We have not chosen such a bad day to begin this passage.

The smudge that was New Zealand has vanished—nothing stands on the horizon. There is no question, we have grown a little quieter—the waves are a little bigger, the decks are heeling a little more. The schooner, although not equipped with a self-steering apparatus, can be made to stay on course by trimming her sails and tying the wheel, but during dark and squally hours, such as we are now experiencing, we take short two-hour watches. I reef the mainsail and change the genoa—the most difficult sail to handle on a black night—for the jib.

It is my second watch of the night. Marie-José's head appears once more in the hatchway; she is gratefully signing off to spend her two hours in the lee bunk. I wish her a nice sleep ... "And don't worry about the time. I may let you sleep longer." I soothe her because I know the worry of oversleeping and the concern for one's partner out in the cockpit that makes falling asleep difficult. The one going on watch must demonstrate convincingly that he is in good form, and willing to take spray in the face; not necessarily that he is thrilled, but pleased to be at the helm and not sick of sailing or sick in body.

I brace myself against the occasional unrhythmic wave, absentmindedly listening to the rush of the sea. The world and I may be real or imaginary, either way, I'm sick.

The weather has deteriorated. It is on the verge of getting worse without actually doing so; we are probably on the periphery of a weather system. I find the ocean intrusive when it climbs over the lee rails.

The seas are perhaps noisier than on other nights. The hatch must be kept closed, for after every lull in the wind there inevitably follows a new gust accompanied by driving rain. It is dark, and just a little stormy. The pale-grey clouds look torn and a new black mass has appeared by the time I look up a second time.

I stand up and step out of the cockpit onto the side deck, the windward deck, and reach for the rope—I want to straighten it out.

What great loneliness! How incredible! Without knowing it, I have been flicked over the rail and into ... I'm in the sea! Not on our boat, our safe little ship!

But the safety harness, which I donned, largely for mental comfort, is holding me to the side of the boat.

My life! Time!

I have come to my senses: I must yell for Marie-José to come out of her sleep and stop the boat. I'm yelling—but Marie-José is not coming—my God, she may not hear me, she may be sleeping on her one good ear! I'm yelling my head off for my Marie-José to stop sleeping. That's it! She's sleeping on her good ear. I can't yell any harder. I think I have begun to panic. I'm on the windward side, the high side; how peculiar to even have gone over the high side against the wind.

My senses are more acute: I'm obviously still attached to the boat.

I should stop this silly yelling and use my own helping hands.

I'm back! Getting back on board was almost like falling over in reverse order. I was not conscious of the movements. I remember the rope of the safety harness in front of my nose and the windward rail lowering itself—my hand clamped fast to the rail ... The rest must have been a joint effort between myself and the rail. What might have been only seconds was measured in subjective units of time—relative to my predicament.

It is satisfying, even exhilarating, to be aware of both feet firmly planted on the decks of the schooner, inclined at an angle, in rather bad weather.

I have stood here on the windward deck for some moments now, experiencing the heeling ship as a safe little island, "safe" so long as one stays with it ... wordlessly I greet the dark and stormy sky.

Marie-José has appeared in the companionway, doubtful that she has actually heard screams of urgency.

"In the water," she repeats. She looks in wonder and concern, but unable to do anything since I am, after all, standing here.

"Yes, I stood up to grab a rope and was thrown overboard; but I came back," I rephrase what I have already told her.

I'm certainly not sleepy, I will finish my watch, I insist.

It is cozy huddled by the wheel, watching the clouds mold into exquisite shapes, pondering the peculiar noises of the sea. The ship rolls on, through the dark and vast spaces. Man may see himself in all sorts of ways and roles; occasionally he is forced to see himself as he is: humble in the face of greater forces.

* * *

"I don't care what anybody says, it's blowing a gale!" Marie-José blurts out. From the time we took the genoa down, which was eight days ago, until now, we have carried many combinations of sails but never a full set. Now the storm jib, which we acquired with the idea that "it will be a comfort to know we have it, but hopefully we will never need to use it," is up. We have no wind-speed indicator, but our kerosene running lights no longer stay lit, and I guess Marie-José is right, it's blowing a gale. For more comfort and because we have no desire to arrive at New Caledonia's barrier reef accompanied by a raging gale, we stream the sea anchor.

"When I'm sailing I look terrible, bleah! I don't look after myself,

107

my hair is all greasy and I stink—I'm miserable." Marie-José repeats the exact words that Joni, another sailor, once said.

"Yeah, and my ambitions and desires, my aspirations, I don't care about them—I feel awful," I add, laughing about Joni's unpretentious self-confession.

Do we stink? Are we miserable? Not all that much—actually we are not in such bad shape. I have involuntarily slid down an inch or two on the mattress—a wave has smashed into our transom. "If only the gale stops by the time we reach New Caledonia—we are only 260 miles from its shores now."

Eventually the winds weaken and the skies clear; we can look at the world and ourselves in a new light. The sail area is increased, we shake out one reef after another. Now the wind has become so weak that the the genoa replaces the jib. Well, we are not complaining!

* * *

"The fish have arrived!" I notify Marie-José as a school of dorados, also called "dolphin fish," swim beside the boat. They seem to seek out a boat and stay with it for a while, the way dolphins do. I keep trying to lure one of them onto a hook, but we only catch them when we are moving swiftly, in a gale. A strong craving for fresh protein couldn't achieve anything either; or could it? There is one, that keeps very close to the hull. It darts off, but then returns to the same spot. I reach for our three-foot long gaff—one might actually just, well, gaff it. There it swims off—and here it's coming back again ... I poke the gaff down and turn my eyes away. I don't remember pulling the gaff up, but now that I'm aware again, I see it is a live gaff in my hand.

In my heart I am not a fisherman. I was hoping, I am almost sure, that I'd miss. This explains, in part, the mournful exclamation I offer the world, "Aaaah! I got it!"

* * *

The most easily-seen lighthouse I know has come into view. We are a little way downwind from it so we must sheet in the sails in order to tack up to it, wishing to use Boulari Pass again. We beat towards the reef until its edges are uncomfortably close, then out again until the foaming breakers seem far away—then back again—finally, into Boulari Pass. The wind is blowing straight out of the pass and the boat insists on hobby-horsing as it nearly comes to a stop: "You have to keep the wind in the sails all the time," Marie-José advises, rubbing shoulders with me at the wheel.

108

"Hey! I'm the one who usually says that," I say.

Now that we are safely inside, the lagoon instills a very different attitude. Laughter can be heard on board the little *Sea Helen* as we proceed to restore soul and body: the soul with a feeling of security and anticipation, the body by stripping off all clothes, washing it with soap, and placing its naked form in the wondrous water of the lagoon.

CHAPTER SIXTEEN

Two Bottles of Rum
and Twelve Liters of Wine

*T*wo bottles of rum and twelve litres of wine for a farewell present is not necessarily proof of a friendship, but we are very touched. We have stayed a lot longer in New Caledonia this time, and the friends we made make it a lot harder to leave.

The cold I came down with a few days ago is at its worst, though the day is otherwise fine. We are at the market to buy oranges. For this tall man from Martinique the marketplace is obviously the centre of cultural exchange, and he greets us with a prolonged handshake. I reevaluate my own handshake—it was rather hesitant; I have, after all, the bug in me, and probably on me.

"We have the 'flu," Marie-José tells everyone.

"Oranges are better than mandarins ... Lemons are very good for a cold ..." the fruit sellers within earshot advise us. Our acquaintance from Martinique agrees with them, with a weak smile as he now knows he was perhaps too hasty in shaking hands. One surprising piece of advice for a cure comes from the orange seller, "It is good to smoke Indonesian cigarettes," he claims, offering me one.

It is definitely a "giving" sort of a day. It started with the fellow giving me his hand to shake, then the cigarette. Afterwards, when we delivered some scrimshaw work to a curio shop (one way we make money), the shopkeeper gave me five little whale's teeth on top of my fee. Serge handed Marie-José a shell fossil when we stopped by his antique shop to say hello; a lady who came in to buy a Buddha figure was given a free saucer which she seemed more happy about than the Buddha. "But it's authentic," she exclaimed—Serge shrugged his shoulders. And now that Jack and Makalita have given us lunch in their homey little apartment—not worrying about my 'flu because they had it before us—Marie-José gives them the doily that she brought the cake in, because it looks beautiful on their homemade coffee table.

On the day before our departure, we look around Noumea for things we think we need. Bernard has popped back onto the scene. His head is under the hood of a car that sits in the middle of the street. Having already given us two bottles of rum and twelve litres of wine thinking that he would not be around for our departure, he is now unexpectedly back in Noumea.

"You come for a meal at my place tonight," he insists, climbing back into his dust-covered car which he has just driven for hours over rough terrain. "Helen will do the cooking."

Helen, a beauty from the nearby Wallis Islands, is indeed doing the cooking. An older gentleman, introduced as the Mayor of Hyengien, adds colour to the scene.

Bernard speaks good English, Marie-José can speak good French. I know a few words in French, and Helen and the Mayor know a few words in English. It is an evening of laughter and good-natured fun with moments that we all find hilarious. One bottle of wine is declared unfit for human consumption and consequently poured, without protest from anyone but myself, into the kitchen sink. The replacement is agreed by everyone to be excellent. Because I can't recognize a bad wine, I offer to sing a song.

The morning scene has the quality of an aftermath. The very same people are assembled in the little apartment—we left to sleep on board our schooner, but Bernard insisted that we all return for breakfast. My comment about the very strong coffee convinces him that he has achieved what he set out to do: make very strong coffee. And the truly enormous cup is like a soup bowl with a handle, except that it is fine enough to actually be a coffee cup. The coffee is at least twice as strong as normal, the cup holds three times the amount of a regular cup … that makes six cups of coffee …

Marie-José, an avid coffee drinker, wallows in her good fortune; but I wonder whether I can finish this large cup of strong coffee without doing myself serious damage.

Bernard's ardent eyes are upon us; he has a great insight into what sailors about to embark on a long voyage need: "Helen will go with you to the market for fresh produce." The idea, I suspect, is that Helen will dare anyone to quote us anything but the lowest local prices. Helen, radiant in a pink dress, acknowledges with a smile. The Mayor is off to the Legislative Assembly and Bernard will meet us later.

Bernard is a curiously pleasant specimen: his strong build and character deter anyone from doing him wrong; but he has a deep sensitivity which makes him aware of our aspirations and apprehensions in sailing our little ship around the globe.

The day has begun well—it is grand and the trip to the market, actually a fair distance, seems too short. Under Helen's supervision we are buying bananas and coconuts and oranges.

This prominent heap of oranges is managed with gusto by a stout little lady who seems to have had as good a night as we did. "You are leaving today?" she repeats, while adding more oranges to what we have bought. "Where are you from?" She asks as an afterthought, while her hands rest amongst the oranges.

"Canada."

"Oh, Canada! I might go to Canada one day." Forgetting her business objectives, she shuffles more fruit into our bag. "Try some of these," she says, embarrassed by our gratitude. Like a victor she holds two grapefruit over her head, then crowns the contents of our shopping bag with them.

Helen, like the rest of us, finds this hilarious. She is bent double, turning herself away, snorting and stomping her feet. I swear it is not the free fruit we received; it is the way the lady did it. We are now all roaring with laughter, drawing the attention of others in the market place, giving the market lady a feeling of achievement.

*   *   *

Sneaky Bernard went to the market before breakfast. Opening the trunk of his car, he asks us to look inside. We glance sidelong into a box that he indicates is ours and realize that he has spent a considerable amount of money—the box contains more than fruit and vegetables.

"That's too much, you shouldn't have done this," Marie-José tells him something similar in French. He shrugs his shoulders as if he is only an innocent bystander and can't do anything about it. Helen's beautiful grin is of no help.

Though the moment is awkward, we let it linger—handshakes and kisses put the final seal to our departure.

We have to be on our way—voyagers driven by our aspirations and dreams—for reasons just as vague.

We are making for Dumbea Pass—a pass through reefs nearest in line with our destined course—with the aid of a chart I manufactured myself by transferring all the relevant information from the pilot book onto a sheet of paper.

It was the Mayor who told us not to forget to throw twenty francs into the pass as we go through.

"Why?" I asked with the curiosity of a child.

"Why? For good wind, of course!" he answered, seriously. We are about halfway into the pass, my hand is gathering all the coins in my pocket. They amount to only eighteen francs.

"Eighteen is almost twenty," I say to Marie-José, handing her the coins. She throws them quickly, not making a show of it. I wonder whether she has serious concerns about us short changing the pass or whether she is annoyed by this ritual. "Anyway, we have already got very good wind," I say in good humour.

The pass is perhaps no more than a single mile behind us and the wind has freshened considerably. The genoa is replaced by the jib; and now, at least for comfort, the main must also come down.

We are better than halfway to Australia but ever since we threw the eighteen francs into Dumbea Pass, the wind has been an unpleasantly mixed bag, nothing really fearsome but annoying enough to make one wonder what sailors' dreams are made of. Long periods of shifting winds coupled with squalls make for angry seas: the boat plunges into a trough, coming almost to a stop—it shudders, a wave licks up the side of the hull.... "Marie-José going into fits—talking of drowning," I enter into the logbook.

CHAPTER SEVENTEEN

The Great Barrier Reef

"*I* knew it! I just knew it!" My fist comes down on the cabin table. Marie-José switches her glance from my face to my fist which I'm about to bring down a second time.

The customs and agriculture officers both look bewildered. They are extremely friendly people and, apparently, of fine character. I am reconsidering if they deserve to be subjected to my outburst—even though it is my table we are all gathered around. "You didn't get another visa?" the young customs officer asked inquisitively while studying our passports.

After the battle we went through in Sydney, wouldn't we make sure that all was in order before returning to Australia? Yes, we would! At the Australian Embassy in New Caledonia I made such strange efforts to ensure that the officer and I understood each other, she probably thought me odd: I would shake my head in agreement, turn away as though to leave, then turn toward her, look deeply into her eyes and ask the same questions again.

Her patient response was always the same, "You don't require a visa when travelling by yacht. We never give visas to people who travel with their own yacht." Ordinarily her answer would have been a relief, for not needing a visa meant no fuss and bother.

"But we needed one the first time," I replied, searching for the missing clues to the mystery story.

Her answer was emphatic: "You should never have had the first one." I decided to call it quits. I thanked her and told her that I believed her.

Now, I'm looking at the customs officer doubling as the immigration officer, with despondency.

He looks at me questioningly, "How much time do you need?" I suspect he is hoping I will not asked for too much. "Well, three months to sail up into the Great Barrier Reef—but then we should have a little extra so we don't run short—four months would be enough for sure."

He hesitates at the "four months," preferring to give us the customary three. But if as a customs officer he can give us the same amount of time as the immigration officer, then there should be no problem, since he is both. "Three will probably do it," I fill in. "We want to sail north as fast as possible to catch the season for the Indian Ocean crossing, but just in case...."

The agriculture officer who has been watching, suddenly displays the true Australian spirit. "Come on, give them four months!" he says, in a loud voice, not unlike that of my earlier outburst. The customs officer forces a smile. Hurrah! He does it; he brings the stamp down on the passport. We all laugh as if marking the happy outcome of a conspiracy.

This all takes place in Gladstone, a designated port of entry. Two factors—the endless round of playing to man-made rules, and the limited number of places that a small sailing ship can pull into—have brought us here. The people are called Australians, and the patch of land they live on, or "own" is called Australia. They treat the land, provided to them by Nature and their forefathers—who took it from someone else—like an ant hill, knocking a society into shape the best way they know how.

They are suspicious of people like us because they suspect each other, and so they post guards. They let us look around if they approve of our appearance, but first we must crawl past the guards who register our arrival on paper. Universal realities, like the phase of the moon, or the angle of the sun, are reduced to "time of arrival" by a guard writing on a piece of paper. The more paper, the better.

Gladstone is our entry point to The Great Barrier Reef that stretches innocently for well over a thousand miles, roughly parallel to Australia's east coast. It begins as isolated clumps of rock at Gladstone, and, as one travels further north, becomes more closely knit until eventually it is an almost unbroken chain near the top of the continent.

We feel we need a strategy, and decide to get inside the reef where it starts, at Gladstone, and stay there all the way up to where we can round Australia. Although I have no axe to grind with majestic ocean swells, knowing what it is like to sail in the sheltered waters behind a reef makes this scheme very attractive.

With the entry procedures behind us we can take a fresh and legal look around. We are free to think anything we want, so we think "harbour master." Although Gladstone is a large commercial harbour, sheltered and convenient anchorage for small ships is limited and confined to Auckland Creek. We are dismayed that there are boats moored in every conceivable spot—they are all on permanent moorings. A sign on the wharf dares anyone to stay for a purpose other than entering, loading or unloading.

The harbour master maintains his pleasant expression while informing us that there are no vacant moorings. It is useless to speculate how much we would have to pay for a mooring. But it is a very sunny, lofty sort of a day and it does not seem right to be discouraged, despite the fact that my philosophy that "there is always room for one more" is threatened.

"... I'll give him a call ..." I missed some of the harbour master's words. He points out a large steel work boat on a pile mooring. He will phone the owner and advise him that we are tying alongside. My face lights up as does the face of the harbour master. He is pleased that we are pleased. We are doubly pleased because he can't charge us; a mooring can only be rented once.

Life on the pile mooring alongside the big work boat is pleasant. The owner of the vessel is happy to meet us and encourages us to stay for as long as we wish; we cannot ask for more.

* * *

One day while anchored at Suva, Fiji, we smiled at a small sailboat (twenty-six feet long) making its way into the anchorage. Her skipper was the only person on board, his arm hanging over the main boom, his bare foot manipulating the tiller. Wearing a straw hat, his "lava-lava" exposed his rich belly to the tropical airs' caresses. The vane of his self-steering gear—a sure sign of a modern single-hander—was so large that I mistook it at first for a small mizzen sail. The mast of the sloop appeared crooked to the eye. Marie-José and I were quick to label him a "South Sea bum"; we meant it respectfully—we had a good idea of what it had taken him to be in the South Seas.

Eventually we exchanged greetings with this character because we shared the same dinghy landing. He was not anxious to strike up a conversation, but then he was not opposed to it either. His name was Heinrich. The steering vane was his own design, the spar was crooked because he had been dismasted by a whale.

Here, in the streets of Gladstone, a man in workman's overalls smiles broadly. It is Heinrich. After ten years of sailing one and a half times around the globe, he settled in Australia, in Gladstone. We suggest supper on board our boat; Heinrich has in mind a barbecue in the backyard of the house he rents. We will do both.

We gather at the hospital, to visit another sailor that we met in the "islands" who also lives in Gladstone and has just given birth to a tiny human being.

There is not that much to Gladstone, no awe-inspiring landscape, no daring and enchanting city architecture, and worst of all, no ladies with flowers in their hair walking with generously lubricated joints. But we meet still more cruising folk, people that we knew in Sydney. Thank goodness they are only passing through. For a moment I was afraid that Gladstone is "it," without being able to explain why.

Such rendezvous, aside from the pleasure they can bring, have a very practical side. One can exchange books, charts and valuable information.

There is one nagging thought—we have to get going, we must meet the seasons! With every day that passes it becomes a more pressing thought. Determined to slip our mooring lines with the next favourable wind, we are bent over the charts planning the route. This is going to be unlike other voyages we have done; this time we will have land on one side and reefs on the other, for more than one thousand miles. There will be no beating or running out to sea when we are not sure of our position, nor will there be unlimited sea room where the boat can look after herself in a storm.

Studying the charts where an arm of the ocean reaches behind a large piece of land, the Narrows, we discover the words "Cattle Crossing." It means that at low tide one can drive cattle across this channel and at high tide one can sail through it. It presents a considerable shortcut.

Today, we slip our mooring lines, for it is as good a day as we are ever going to get.

We motor across the harbour and into the Narrows. At the cattle crossing, we slow the boat and hold our breath. Once across we speed up again in order to keep pace with the tides that have already begun to turn. The channel broadens and deepens; it seems a good spot to anchor for the night.

Days go by but our progress is too slow. The season may well move on without us. It is blowing discouragingly from the wrong quarter and we remain anchored for another day. To make up for the delay, we promise to start sailing early tomorrow, at 0400 hours.

I have always felt that there are some special insights to be gained from an early-morning rising, when the dew covering everything is an assurance that one is in time to witness the unveiling of a day; if only one could wipe the sleep from one's eyes. It is 0600 hours instead of 0400 hours and we are only just getting under way.

*   *   *

We are entering Port Clinton and I'm thinking, "What about our letters?" Australia is indeed sparsely populated! We assumed that Port Clinton has a post office, and we asked Rolf and Vicky in Sydney to forward our mail there. There is not only no post office, or a general store doubling as one, but also no building of any kind, no human beings and no boats. My eyes are on a huge sea turtle as it hurries to dive.

Before us, we see thousands of very small crabs with blue backs marching over the sand flats exposed by the receding tide. They break up into groups as I drag the dinghy through their midst. Do they know where they are going?

Marie-José and I head for an unusually wild, wonderful looking beach.

*   *   *

How can one enjoy the sight of one's little ship in a seascape and ourselves strolling over the sand, through the mangroves, when the winds are blowing the wrong way? The thought that winds are bound to change helps. The further north we go the steadier they should be blowing from the south-east—and it will be more tropical; clear water, white sand, palms. Besides, no one says that we have to enjoy everything we see or do, or are obliged to do, like putting into Island Head Creek.

Two more days pass at anchor, but now the wind is up—it truly is—we must be off, even though it is already late in the afternoon. But

118

our plan has changed: we will not stop at Middle Percy Island but sail overnight to Mackay Harbour, further north.

Even against the night sky, we can distinguish dark clouds being driven along, forced into new shapes and torn apart as if something is in the making. The ocean beneath is greatly disturbed—it heaps up and foams, as if it, too, is in the making; and we must guide our little ship the best we can.

It is the south-east wind that we hoped for, but we never asked for so much of it. There are no great ocean swells, but in their place is something worse—a short steep sea. They are short waves that place themselves vertically behind our transom; one cannot imagine how a ship like ours could go against them, if it had to.

Morning is breaking and Mackay Harbour is forgotten. We no longer wish to go there. The way the wind and the tide conspire, the way we are being tossed about by this dreadful ocean, Scawfell Island seems a quicker route to our salvation.

I'm soaked with melancholy. The constantly unfavourable weather, the merciless seas, and then Scawfell, and island with only three coconut trees, have gradually ground us down. I'm actually tempted to envy the sailors who stick to home waters—they can stop at any time. I don't know what we will do! We are far from home with our boat. Shortage of money is a nagging problem; distances seem so great; we have treacherous waters to cross; it'll take years to encircle the globe—time has already slipped by; what about the people we called friends, the place we called home?

"We got away from it all!"—funny how this phrase comes to mind. I wanted to *go to it all*, see more, see a new world, not get away.

It is said that the sea is a lonely place. I have been lonely before, in big cities, even while with friends. One isn't lonely when one is in love … but love can make one blind to other realities. I can *see* now that I am alone in my thoughts. The next time somebody asks me, "Where is your home?" I will say, "This planet here—which a small boat can sail around—this is my home."

Only one of the three palms has coconuts under its fronds. The promise of a taste of clear water from a green nut is enough to make me do the climb. I pry off their husks and laugh: the nuts that emerge are so very, very small.

As we sail from Scawfell Island, the wind, for once, is truly reasonable. What a difference. *Sea Helen* gracefully makes the forty-two miles to Shaw Island. A flashy tourist ship slows down beside us to give everyone a chance to take our picture—we have to wave several times.

It isn't far to Shute Harbour, the nerve centre of the Whitsunday area. This is a big name because, I presume, Whitsunday is just about as good as it gets along this coast.

We are entering the harbour, busily confirming with the chart that, yes, wherever a boat isn't anchored the spot is too shallow. An open aluminum boat is pursuing us. The world is mad! In a place where someone might give his jib or a spare halyard for a mooring, this fellow wants us to use one for free! "I can see you are cruising," he says, clarifying his position. Perhaps the world is sane!

With lighter spirits, possibly due to meeting someone who recognizes weary travellers when he sees them—and also because of good winds—we make for Magnetic Island (I watch the compass carefully). We push on to Hazard Bay (I keep a keen lookout for hazards).

Birthdays are valuable occasions, molding our lives. We stay over in Hazard Bay, in spite of good wind, so that I can hand Marie-José her new T-shirt (wrapped up) with the boat on an even keel.

Bright and early, with our sails billowed out by a fine breeze, there is a fish on the line—a Spanish mackerel. It is our day.

The morning was great but now the wind is dying; it has already died. The still air increases the weight of the sun pouring down on us. Even after years of cruising we still haven't made up our minds as to which is worse—the sails filling and emptying with air as the boat rolls stationary, or listening to the noisy patter of the engine knowing that we are gaining only two or three miles in every hour. We opt for the noise of the engine.

Usually we end up with a headache after prolonged motoring, and raw nerves when wallowing with no forward motion. But now we are recovering from a temporary paralysis—we are trembling. They have gone, these two jet planes that flew over us at an extremely low altitude. They have passed by, but too close for comfort. I really have the impression that, were they to fly any lower, the noise could stop a man's heart.

* * *

Night is different. We turn off the engine and I keep watch in the cockpit. Marie-José is below; there is a fishing vessel to starboard—

the boat rolls in submission to the shallow swells. The hours are long. I have already picked out all the constellations I know; the ones I don't know, it seems, I will never learn. I will be alert as soon as the wind comes back....

Crash!—Crash!—I'm trying to collect myself, which is hard to do. "We hit something! Reef! We hit a reef!" I have the strange feeling that I'm not fully awake—I feel an awful nausea.

It is as if I have been hit by an imaginary club and I'm trying to shake it off. Ah, I'm regaining my senses: it can't be a reef; there is no wind and I estimated our position before nightfall to be a minimum of eight miles from the nearest reef.

I'm curious. Our masts are still standing, I notice with satisfaction. A ghostly ship, a fishing vessel! ... Good grief, it has just crossed our bow! Don't these vessels often tow a multitude of gear? Is there going to be a nightmarish entanglement? But I was lucky I did not hit my head on the main boom, jumping up like that.

The ship has slowed down; it is turning, heading back towards us. Marie-José is suspicious that the ship's automatic pilot is out of control and with a mind of its own is guiding the ship to ram us again.

"No, don't worry now. They are coming to talk to us."

The boat is very near and we feel uneasy having this thing that has just hit us so close.

"Did you hit us?" I hail.

"Well, yes...."

"Say again!"

"Yes, we lost one of our outrigger booms—must have had a rusty wire!" A voice, female this time, answers. I can see three crew members on board, two male and the other female. The men's voices don't carry well; the woman's scratchy country voice comes through loud and clear, and for our benefit repeats everything faithfully.

"Didn't you see us?" I want to know.

"No, we ..."

"Did you have it on automatic pilot?"

"Yes," is the reluctant answer. "Do you have any damage?"

"I have to look!" We seem to be in one piece. There is no big dent in the side of the hull. I know we have been hit, but I just can't see where.

"What's your ... port ...?"

"What?"

121

"What's your next port of call?" the scratchy country voice repeats.
"Cairns!"
"What's the name of your boat?"
"*Sea Helen*! What's the name of your boat?"
"*Pacific Pearl!* Well, if there is no damage ... we must get going—good night!"
"Goodnight."
More annoying than the suspicion that we probably do have damage somewhere, is the mundane salutation, "Goodnight."
The most important rigging screw is easily the one of the forestay. I can see with daylight that the half-inch turnbuckle has a sharp kink in it. Straightening it will certainly cause metal fatigue. We will fix it at Maurilyan Harbour.

*　　*　　*

Sobered to the fact that the weather will not cooperate, we suppress the urge to wait for ideal sailing days, and let a smart wind, mixed with drizzle, drive us towards Cairns.
From there we go on to Cooktown and the Endeavour river. We have already passed headlands and reefs and the morning grey is only just beginning.
We have found the deepest hole in the Endeavour river, so deep that we touch bottom only slightly at low tide.
Marie-José likes it in Cooktown: I'm glad, she needed a lift—and I needed to see her spirits lifted. It is a community where nothing is very new. Although buildings have been kept in good repair, everything is reminiscent of earlier times.
An old-timer is bending down by the side of the road: "Somebody lost a little dress," he is saying. With both hands he holds up a tiny dress. He seems happy to have stumbled upon something. He smiles excitedly, or is it knowingly? With utmost care he places the tiny garment on top of a fence post.
Our feet feel good on the ground, and the sun warm on our backs. Our ship rides contentedly at anchor in the river. A cairn stands where the famous Captain Cook is believed to have beached the *Endeavour*. It is a sleepy sort of a place.
We decide that we need a freshwater shower. Inside the lobby of a hotel that is reminiscent of an old western there is a man's body. It comes to life when we step inside.
"Hi, we would like to take showers." His phoney smile has

122

vanished; his face looks cold. I offer to pay for the shower, we understand it is not free—his face remains cold, he stands his ground.

Apparently it is not the peak of the tourist season, or else the tourists failed to come. A small trailer park is not even half full. The lady in the office, who does not look unkind, answers "No." I have the money out, I make her understand that I do not understand. "We used to rent showers, but not any more."

But our hearts are set on a wonderful, soothing, cool shower, so we walk to the town wharf, around some old sheds ... Ah! didn't I know it? there is a green snake winding its way along the wharf. All we have to do is turn on the faucet. Naturally, we brought our own soap. Unfortunately the wharf is not entirely deserted. At one end is a human form, half-lying, presumably resting. But, why not be bold? We strip to our bathing suits—"Who goes first?" Now a little soap, and some happy shrieks appropriate to such pleasure.

Now a rub with the towel ... "Turn off the water!"—but we are brand new people, at least on the surface; we are ready to smile at the world.

The figure on the wharf smiles at us now. He appears harmless— I'm usually a good judge of people. We tell him that it is a nice day— he agrees. They would not sell us a shower in town, we explain—it seems to coincide with his own predicament. His name is Len, and he has been around Australia seven times. He looks none too good; it is just as well that the days are mild and one can get free vitamins from the sun.

Marie-José and I are going back to the boat for lunch. We can see that Len needs lunch more than we needed a shower, which he needs too. "Len, would you like to have lunch with us?" He accepts in principle, but feels that it will be better if he brings his "gear" along.

I have always had images of hobos with cooking pots hanging from their belts and other sacred items wrapped in a bandana at the end of a stick (in Australia it would be called a "billy" or a "swag"). But Len is different; he has all his "gear" in a plastic garbage bag, except for one blanket that he carries under his arm.

It is a little walk to our dinghy and I'm slightly worried about Len's gear: some of it is threatening to slip through one the holes in the plastic bag. These bags are really not ideal for carrying one's treasures.

Whatever Len is or is not, he is courteous and will not have Marie-

José help with the dinghy while he is around to do the work. Len eats his lunch dutifully and declines a second helping; he is careful not to ask for anything else—he does, however, accept what Marie-José has chosen for him to take along, for later. Len's 'holey' garbage bag reminds me of the time in Fiji when we had a woven plastic sack fouled in the propeller, stopping the engine dead. We kept the sack because it was still perfectly sound, even after we pulled it away from the propeller. Having survived such rigorous testing, it deserved to be saved for future use. Len approves of it as I hold it up triumphantly; somehow I'm reminded of the little dress.

* * *

According to the radio, the persistent high winds are unseasonable and a fisherman in a small boat ahead of us reflects that there are often weeks of twelve-to-fifteen knot winds at this time of year. I want to believe him, for it is the sort of wind I have in mind. The captain of a large prawn dragger maintains a no-nonsense attitude: he thinks only a cynic would want to wait for milder weather when in fact the weather is normal.

That makes one mild-mannered fisherman and the radio who believe the weather is unseasonable, against one cocksure prawn-dragger captain, who knows it is normal.

The trade winds that blow from the south-east are definitely seasonal, and they are the winds we want. The high-pressure systems moving across the bottom of Australia are really the ones in question: the air in a high pressure system spirals outward in a counter-clockwise direction in the Southern Hemisphere. The periphery winds reach the Great Barrier Reef area from a south-easterly direction, joining forces with the trades, forcing sailors to acknowledge the real world.

It is reasonable to assume that there should be periods of lighter winds between high pressure systems, but the days conspire to prove the arrogant prawn-dragger captain right.

I ready to leave in unfavourable conditions; there is a will, but there is simply no way: the schooner, heeling crazily, is facing a tumbling swell. She follows her beam end rather than her head. A great paw of wind was lying in wait for us and swiped us the moment we nosed out from behind the protective headland. The tumbling swells are claws tearing at us and stopping us from getting away.

We only need to get out a little way, less than half of a mile, after which we can bring the wind on a better quarter; yet the goal seems unreachable. Off to port is a massive sandbank, and even if we get past it, there is still the point of land. If we don't make it past either one, we are trapped in a cul-de-sac. The nearer we get to the sandbank, the more turbulent a sea we will have to overcome; the sandbank looks horribly near—let alone the point ... I'm no longer undecided. I put the helm up. The schooner races back into the river and a comfortable feeling comes over me—I'm positive we would not have made it.

There would have been a way, according to the cocksure prawn-dragger captain. We could have fallen off a lot more and made it past the sandbank, is his loud-mouthed opinion (he was watching us). Well, maybe he is not as bad as his opinion is loud; he is just an ordinary person. He may know his home waters well, but it is unlikely that he has ever sailed a schooner-rigged thirty-footer.

Two more days have passed and it is a lot milder. Reviewing our strategy for a retreat, we again head the ship towards the ocean swells. This time the waves slide under us, reluctantly, allowing for moderate headway. Already we can put the helm up and free the sheets—the schooner responds, making bigger leaps with every wave that lunges at her.

* * *

The night, anchored in the lee of Cape Flattery, is a restless one, and equally restless is the next night behind Bewick Island; we hope that the Flinders Island group will provide quiet anchorage.

There are islands which somehow discourage close attention. They are little humps, or big humps, possibly with a poor anchorage in their lee and maybe with a nasty rock to watch for here and there.

The Flinders Islands are different, like sculptured shapes against the evening sky which one is anxious to rediscover in the morning. We glance at them from time to time lest we fail to notice something important about them. A perennial well surrounded by lush green plants and the taste of wild passion fruit leave indelible impressions. We would stay another day perchance to stumble across the answer to the mystery of life, with the help of these extraordinary surroundings, but just now the wind is blowing beautifully, beckoning us to catch a ride.

The reefs are now everywhere. Anxiously looking for a beacon, a small island, a coral cay on the foaming edge of a reef ... we dutifully make our course changes.

Burkitt Island has come into view and our attention is focused on a large sailing yacht on its side in the foreground of sand and shrubs. We observe with awe the expanse of the table reef on which the island is built. A small sea plane, a fishing vessel anchored in the lee of the island and people scurrying around the shores indicates a salvage operation. I have already noticed on the chart that Burkitt Island is one of the few places bordering the recommended ship's channel that does not have a light or a reef beacon to warn a weary traveller.

We choose to anchor behind Hannah Island for the night. We hoist the sails early in the morning to sail still further north. Today we are always on edge. Frequent rain squalls often obliterate reef beacons and small islands; the insidious reefs that can be spotted under a clear sky no longer announce their presence. The shallow water is indistinguishable; the foaming edges, like a barbed-wire fence between the deep ocean and the coral, are swallowed up by sheets of rain. The compass card, pointing stubbornly, mysteriously indicates directions, but I'm keenly aware that it will not warn us of ocean currents, our own leeway or that we have reached a point where a course change is crucial.

Had I been praying, it would seem that my prayers keep being answered. Just when our doubts about our position become too great, it clears sufficiently between showers, allowing us a glimpse of a beacon or a headland long enough to get a new bearing. "Thank heaven," I write into the logbook, "that it always clears a little between squalls."

Why would someone have named this Night Island? Because they anchored there for the night, as we will do, or was it that they had to get past it on a dark night? We steer towards the lower end of Night Island in order to anchor in its lee. By the appearance of the dark masses rolling towards us I can tell that this squall is going to release more rain and wind than the previous one. Marie-José is below, changing clothes; Night Island is near at hand. I give its southern tip a healthy berth: the visible shores are "so" far away, and the coral reef possibly extends out "so" far, and so we should be fine; allowing too wide a margin can get us into trouble with the other reef to the south.

126

The rain is upon us, the mainsail is down and the engine running. A clump of mangrove trees stands in the water to starboard. The mangroves have disappeared; they were so near; it makes me feel cut off.

The rain pours over me "by the buckets"—a phrase that I have always regarded, even as a child, as an overstatement. It is fitting to say that it is "raining curtains," for a curtain has been drawn between us and the rest of the world.

I do not mind the rain—in the tropics, where the air is warm, one looks at it differently. I'm pleased that the wind has not increased drastically and I want to encourage Marie-José to stay below unless she is in a mood to take yet another shower. I'm laughing. I wonder how much harder it can possibly rain.

The boat has broken the rhythm of its motion; it has climbed slightly higher out of the water—a dull thump! "We hit! Marie-José, we hit something!"

But we cannot see bottom. I know that we have given Night Island an adequate berth, so have we travelled so fast that we are upon the reef jutting out from the mainland? Oh my God! In this case, we should turn around—the boat is still moving ahead. Or can it be that we have come too close to the reef south of Night Island? It doesn't make sense; nothing makes sense!

I tug at the sails frantically to bring them down. I curse the gaff of the foresail for getting caught up. Furious about my confusion, I look for an explanation in the chart that is spread out on the cabin table. I have left Marie-José at the wheel and find myself unable to provide her with a course to steer. The chart is thoroughly soaked with the water streaming off my body; it doesn't provide any clarity.

The squall has stopped; it is beginning to clear. The first shimmers have appeared in the water—the heavens break open and the sun pours down on us. Night Island is suddenly here again, in close proximity. How colourful is the coral that looks up at me. It is all around and therefore I am still confused as to which way to go. I climb to the spreaders ... I see the deep water, "Head that way, we might get out!"

My visions of being aground on the reef are fading. We are moving closer to the deep water. I have simply not given the reef coming out from under Night Island a wide enough berth.

Our night behind Night Island was all right, but the weather continues in the fashion of yesterday. Still, we will head for Restoration Island. It is obvious that if we only sail on ideal or close-to-ideal days, we will run out of time.

Marie-José has made it a point to be on deck during every squall. "I better be out because you always run into a reef when I'm inside," she comments.

There is nothing that Restoration Island restores in us except the conviction that there are indeed few anchorages along the Great Barrier Reef that are not 'roly.'

All our perceptions are mixed with excitement at nearing the top of Australia. Haggerston Island, our twenty-third anchorage since Gladstone, and possibly our second-last before we will reach the Torres Strait, has a distinctly different appearance from any other we have seen. It is a rich splash of green, a cluster of coconut palms.

It is typical of the Great Barrier Reef that when one finally finds an island with coconut trees on it, one has to anchor over a mile away, at the edge of the reef. Rowing our eight-foot pram in a stiff breeze across the reef to the island is a test of endurance. I try to row with a rhythm and a stubborn concentration; missing one stroke means that I have to make up for it with ten more. The thought that "the closer we come to the shore the calmer it will be," spurs me on.

We are nearing the wild beauty of the white beach; the waves have become shallow and the corals, ever more unblinking, gaze up at us from a transparent sea. The dinghy must be guided through a mild surf—we wait for the rasping of the sand under the bottom, then we jump out to drag it up the beach. The sun burns on our backs; we rest our eyes on the comfortable green of the palm fronds.

Our boat looks so vulnerable rolling all alone at the other end of the reef; but in order to relish the moment, we must dispel thoughts of our little ship suddenly dragging anchor and leaving without us. The island is very small and we need not be content to see only part of it; we can walk around and see it all. I look for the shortest palm with the most delicious-looking drinking nuts under its fronds; I'm also willing to tackle one of medium height if its fruit look mouth-watering enough.

When attempting to climb this marvellous plant, it is best to harmonize one's strength with a sense of balance; a good measure of determination helps. The hands reach around the trunk while the legs, with the balls of the feet against the trunk, push the body away and up. Slanted trees are ideal, but straight and vertical ones are better than none.

There are plenty of brown nuts on the ground; it is just a matter of choosing the ones that promise the most delight.

We have drunk as much cool coconut water as we can hold, swum in the luxurious ocean, and paraded our naked bodies on the ravishing shore. The dinghy is loaded with fifteen green and brown nuts, as we shove it through the surf.

Even though the wind is behind us, the dinghy does not ride the waves well. It is dangerously low in the water—the nuts are big and heavy and they take up room and restrict our movements. Waves curl by the transom and threaten to climb inside. I consider dumping the nuts, at least some of them, but I can't decide on the moment. Nuts are not abundant around here—the ones we have chosen, hand-picked, are so magnificent, they would be a comfort to have on board. I'm fighting off the idea that our dinghy, with us in it, might get swamped because of greed for coconuts. I'm not greedy, we didn't take that many nuts; they just look like a lot in our little dinghy.

Our schooner seems within reach—Marie-José must move closer to me to give the stern more freeboard. "Don't forget to get on board without delay, the moment we come alongside. Leave the nuts, I'll hand them up!"

The schooner is pitching and rolling almost from gunwale to gunwale. I'm a little elated, Marie-José has seized the perfect moment for boarding. The coconuts are rolling all over the deck. "The cockpit, put them in the cockpit." With our system of hoisting the dinghy on board with a halyard, it unavoidably crashes heavily into the hull a few times before I can wrestle it into its place on the side deck. We are, of course, staying for the night.

* * *

The foresail is up, the engine is running, Marie-José is at the helm, and I am collecting myself on the foredeck. The anchor is a long way down and the foredeck, on which I have to stand to retrieve it, is pitching dreadfully. Marie-José is moving ahead. The anchor rope is not slackening sufficiently. I hold up a circling finger, a sign which we agree means more power. The rope is up, the first link of the seventy-five feet of chain has appeared over the roller. The anchor has broken out, and I work with determination to get it stowed. All is ready. "Let her fall away!" With the wind striking the sail from abaft the beam, the boat takes off; ten horses could not pull us back, certainly not our ten-horsepower motor.

Marie-José does not have a good feeling about anchoring at Bushy Island which we are still twenty miles away from. It would be very unsheltered, something might happen; maybe we should sail on through the night. I'm taken slightly by surprise. Bushy Island is our last chance to anchor before entering the Torres Strait.

I have no qualms about being regarded as a wizard at navigation, but the shock of the thought of sailing at night in these waters takes time to dissipate. I speculate how the world ahead will appear and how we might fare in it, in the dark.

We are preparing for a night sail; what is intuition for? I have a plan: we reduce sail to reduce our speed to three knots or less. According to the laws of mathematics, this will let us arrive at the most critical spot in the morning.

It has taken the wind a half-hour to shatter my plan. The wind has increased, and our speed under short sail is what it was before. Bushy Island, a clump of bushes, is showing to port; it is not appealing. If the anchorage at Haggerston Island was difficult, at Bushy Island it would be impossible.

It is the last of the daylight. Marie-José is preparing supper; I'm steering a careful compass course and I'm stealing frequent glances at a developing mackerel sky laced with unnerving jetstream clouds.

Later, we are crouched around the wheel in the cockpit, in the dark. Marie-José has spoken what I'm thinking: "We are caught!" There is really only one key to finding our way through the reefs during the dark hours—the strategically placed lights. I look for them with stubborn intensity. Cairnecross light has disappeared, yet Waybom Reef light is not visible. The lights are twenty-five miles apart and, according to the charts, each is visible for fourteen miles.

The tide tables, the current tables, the charts, the time, the wind direction … I check them all with a hunger for new information. I go over the plan in my head one more time.

"We must bring Waybom Reef light on our beam and make our turn to port, taking up our new course; but not too soon; yet not too late as there'll be a reef further on. When Albany Rock light becomes visible I take a bearing off it and make a course correction if necessary. Guessing our distance from Albany Rock light we must turn to starboard when we are within two miles, sooner rather than later, as the wind will set us towards it anyway. Adolphus Island, being high and large, should show up as we head for its western tip; there'll be a reef with a visible rock to starboard halfway to Adolphus Island. Once we get in the lee of of Adolphus Island it should be quiet. The tide rips! I hope they are not as bad as the chart indicates."

A light is blinking on our port bow—Waybom Reef light. Our angle in relation to it is changing quickly—it is bearing west. I want to turn now; no, I want to wait. "Now!" It feels somewhat like turning a corner too fast; the sea is boisterous.

Albany Rock light shows itself faintly; I'm almost happy about it. The seas are breaking; are they breaking because of the reef? There are more lights ... it's a ship! It is aligning itself with the channel to travel in the opposite direction. We can't decide; I can't decide ... I'm hoping that a big ship, with all its sophistication, knows exactly which part of the channel it is in, as opposed to us who know it only approximately. The ship has not decided: it's showing us the green light, now the red, now both, red again—"Starboard!" I want to show red, too, I think it is the best way. A massive dark wall is sliding past us. I have the feeling that the skipper was acutely aware of our position.

I'm disappointed that I'm not able to see Adolphus Island. The moon, competing with the clouds, illuminates Albany Rock area but does little for Adolphus Island.

We must now be within two miles of Albany Rock—we must turn now! We are turning; but maybe we should not turn the full number of degrees, just in case.

"I got it!" I yell back to Marie-José from the bow. I detected a new dark shape through the binoculars, lost it, and found it again in an even clearer form. "Let's go a little more to port, then we'll be just fine."

I am severely jolted by a large conical rock standing on our starboard beam—it is supposed to be there, except that I did not see it coming; we are perhaps a little close to it, but then ... we are more or less past.

For hours now, Marie-José has been doing a great job at the helm. I encourage her to relax. I even offer to steer for a while, now that we have a clear stretch ahead of us. She prefers that I remain forward, spying through the binoculars and double-checking the lights.

It is hard to see what the sea really looks like but easy to hear. It is the sound of the tumbling waves; the moon occasionally shows the froth of a wave as it builds up and curls.

Adolphus Island is now close by; behind the near point is a generous bay, our anchorage. A few more tumbling waves, the boat is lurching less—now the same sounds die, there is quiet, we are in the lee of Adolphus Island.

I'm pacified and elated; but the bay does not correspond to the chart—something white to port could be sand or a cliff, or a reef ... I'm swinging the lead ... four fathoms—now only one. "Back up! Back up!" Aground!

The wind is on our side and we move off. My eyes are so tired, I don't want to strain them any more. I let the anchor go at nine fathoms.

The "something white" are boats, one of them has turned on a light. Now the bay makes sense! the boats are where we should have anchored. But we'll stay where we are; it is good here too.

Marie-José is sitting in the cockpit with her head down; I think that she is suffering from depression after such a strenuous sail. I look down to see her face ... a big grin, a smile, turns towards me—"You did it! A masterpiece of navigation!" which is what we always say, even if things don't go according to plan, just so long as we make it to our destination.

CHAPTER EIGHTEEN

Time in Between

I'm leaning back drinking in the sun. I went to sleep knowing that when I wake up we wouldn't sail anywhere today, and maybe not the next day either. Now, with the sun already high, I can't seem to fully open my eyes. I could easily crawl back into my bunk, but I find that I can get comfortable with my eyes half shut, leaning back my mind. According to Marie-José's tinkling on the stove, there should soon be a cup of coffee.

I'm quite confident that I'm not hooked on coffee, but I want it. I want the little something, the aroma, the cup in my hand.

* * *

We wander over the jagged rocks of Adolphus Island—an indentation, a sandy beach draws us towards it. I have long out-grown the notion that a lonely spot to ourselves is what we always want, for we have had many of these spots to ourselves. This beach certainly compares favourably with others in the world, but I suspect that my desire to make love is to make more of it, rather than being able to see more in it. I watch Marie-José wading carefully into the turquoise water. She can float a little on her back but she still has not mastered the technique of swimming.

We retrace our steps, and find supper in the form of black-lipped oysters. The razor sharp edges of the shells inflict cuts on my fingers before I learn to pry them off the rocks.

As the gentle tropical airs spill around me, I look forward to a quiet evening. The burning in my fingertips from the salt water penetrating the razor-like cuts suspends me between two realities.

* * *

How would we feel if there was another Great Barrier Reef to sail along? Well, there isn't. Marie-José, who has become very proficient at reading sea charts, translating their symbols and abbreviations into danger or favourable circumstances, is wonderfully calm as we sail the ship through the Torres Strait and its islands. Having played our cards well we arrive at Thursday Island with no hard feelings towards the world. We do not even complain that there is no open market-place, although we expected one. In one of the few stores, I pick up a single tomato wrapped in clear plastic, and look in wonderment at the price tag—I put it back.

Marie-José and I are sitting on a bench in front of the store. We are discussing the white bread they sell that has few nutrients and a high price tag. I explain to the man sharing on the bench with us—Marie-José understands his name is Leroy, but I'm not so sure—that we prefer dark bread, like rye or whole wheat. To change the subject of bread—perhaps he doesn't think it's worth considering—our fellow bench-sitter asks, "Where are you from?"

I tell him, and I tell him my name is Klaus.

"Thank you, Mister Klaus, maybe I come out and see you." Marie-José, perhaps because of a lull in the conversation, has decided to buy the bread; I'm not opposed to it, but I think we can do without the tomato.

*   *   *

I know well the feeling of just wanting to move on, partly under the pretense of making good time to our next destination, partly because there is no strong reason to stay.

If we stayed, we might find all kinds of other ways to see the Torres Strait islands; Leroy might eventually "come out to see us," and who knows what interesting ideas he might have about life; but the urge to move on triumphs.

Having easily negotiated a few more channels between the islands, only Booby Island lies ahead, distinctly in our path. It is really only one large rock—the vertical column on top of it, a lighthouse, makes it more conspicuous. Having still not developed a desire to be near rocks I intend to leave Booby Island well to port on our way into the Arafura Sea.

I'm a little surprised that our fishing line is taut. I'm a little disappointed that we have a shark on the line. Perhaps it is because of the high prices on Thursday Island, and the idea of making up for it by getting a meal for free that I'm considering whether we should eat the shark; it might be all right. It is small and pink ... "Oh, I'm in no mood, I'll let him go." I am a bit troubled to see that its jaw is wrecked and it might not survive.

Lowering the anchor near the edge of the coral reef that reaches out from the west side of the rock contradicts my earlier plan, but with the wind having completely disappeared, it seems a comfortable way to await its return.

A small boat, a dinghy with two occupants, is steering deliberately towards our anchorage, distracting me from attending to the anchor. An invitation to come ashore for a cold beer on such a hot, windless day prompts a swift answer, "We'd love to." The two lighthouse keepers are our hosts, and before we go ashore they want to show us Post Office Cave, Australia's first post office. It was in this cave, in a big iron trunk, that, in the days of the tall ships, there used to be a mail exchange—the very stuff that my romantic youthful dreams were built on.

We have looked at lighthouses from many perspectives: we have had to make room for them in our emotions, often welcomed their lights to guide us, dreaded their proximity when their rays screamed out "Danger." With the keeper of Booby Island light showing us about the tower, I'm face to face with one of these lights that so mysteriously and dutifully blink from their lonely spot; actually it is a piece of cleverly constructed machinery.

* * *

The air is stirring—it is nearly midnight. I'm waiting for the drugged feeling of waking up to pass. There is a favourable south-east wind in the making. "Marie-José, we're going to up anchor!"

Booby Island light flashes brightly astern as I watch the water gurgling under our transom. A fine steady breeze is sending us on our way as smoothly as one can dare to hope.

Gratitude for the continued calm conditions that allows us to sleep, eat, and gaze around at will, within the confines of our small boat, seems to have taken the fight out of me. It will be another three days to Darwin, seven or eight in all from Booby Island at the present rate of smooth sailing.

We are sailing over the top of Australia, a whole continent. What are distances? They are relative to our physical and mental capacities. Our boat is slow, which is why a hundred miles has my respect; and since our minds are also slow we never really arrive at a final conclusion—or maybe there are no final conclusions to be made and our minds are doing just fine. Maybe that's why I'm not all that concerned here in the quiet Arafura Sea, during these days so fine that one could believe that they will never change; where I make an official comment in the logbook on how easy it is to fix our position by the stars, moon or sun.

I am careful not to spook the two birds that have settled themselves on our taffrail for the night. They are silhouetted against the night sky. If they want the rest, I'm not the one to deny it to them. I'm doing the habitual 360 degrees to check for shipping ... no shipping—my eyes inevitably focus again on the birds, and I sense their eyes are on me too. These two dark shapes are actually living things—in fact they can spread wings and soar—they represent the mystery of life.

I look up at the sky—the glitter makes my heart leap; I know the lights that don't twinkle are planets ... the sails are setting fine, they need no adjusting. I crawl back into my bunk a little melancholy, because I just don't know.

CHAPTER NINETEEN

With the Whole Indian Ocean to Cross ...

*I*n Darwin the tidal waters rise and fall by as much as twenty feet, and so even though we find ourselves ready for the Indian Ocean crossing, we must wait the turn of the tides. Our stopover seemed so unusually purposeful. We needed to give the ship new bottom paint, secure some charts, fuel and provisions; we sold some of my scrimshaw work, installed a little VHF radio, and felt the need to renew several acquaintances. It all took eleven days.

The tide has begun to turn, it is time to weigh anchor. We wave to Laurel and James on board their yacht *Laurel-James* and shift our gaze to buoys and landmarks that will guide us safely offshore.

*   *   *

The day is closing and we have not gone far. It is my turn to keep the schooner heading into a feeble head wind. Oh, no! I made an accidental tack. We have already noticed an onshore current. I won't lose time; I'll use the engine to bring the bow of the ship back. Oh, no! Now I have fouled the propeller with the trailing rope.

One thing that always surprises me again and again in the tropics is the water temperature. I expect to be shivering and I discover that I'm not cold at all.

The sun has set, which makes for a dim light, and I'm hanging on to the rudder of a heaving ship with one hand and to a long sharp knife with the other. The propeller has wrapped the rope around itself, the shaft and the stern tube. Should I try and save as much of the rope as possible? A splice in a rope can be as strong as the rope itself. I have made a half-dozen or more cuts; the knife is beginning to dull.

It is so much darker now. My mind has drifted into the shark department. Time is impossible to measure. The fact that the rope has not fallen away with all those cuts, creates a new phenomenon.

It is a fifty-foot rope knitted into a complex pattern around the sterngear. It does not unclinch.

I'm contemplating abandoning the scene to return to it tomorrow with daylight. What is wise? Should I not take advantage of the calm? My cuts are too frantic; I must be more precise—there, that was a good one; and that one did something ... Ah ... exhaustion, in the light of success, is dispelled by relief.

*   *   *

Our spirits were high when we set out on the Indian Ocean crossing. It was good to have wind and to be moving, especially since we were a bit late in the season. Now that the wind is disappearing, leaving us wallowing in the Timor Sea, we are reluctant to let our spirits fall.

One, or even two, days of calm is not the end of the world, it's part of this world; it's part of trying to sail around the planet. Even three days of calm should not make one negative.

There is no need to draw a line, but six days of calm ... eight days of calm ... ten days of calm ... are they also not enough to be taken negatively.

The windless days go by. We are thinking about our water supply and foodstuff: we are consuming water and food that is to last us for over 4,000 miles, yet we have not made a dent into this vast distance. We have stopped reading books, although their contents interested us until now; they cannot substitute for the pleasure of making fair progress along our course.

Marie-José keeps excellent meals coming out of the galley; but they would be more enjoyable if we were sailing along.

I'm sitting down below for hours on end, drawing little pictures of sailing ships on cards—I make their sails billow out, I make them heel gracefully; I listen for wind—I think I just heard a different sound from the sails ... Marie-José is on deck. She would tell me right away if there was wind. I think I'll sell these cards for a few dollars a piece...

...We are away from society with all its trivial problems. We are on the ocean which is wide, and we have an unrestricted view of the skies. But the ocean has become familiar, a little like a backyard—it is not alien anymore and I have caught myself thinking about trivial things, like selling little cards for a few dollars. Perhaps anything is trivial if it is not related to the large canvas, the universe, whose boundaries are unknown to us.

138

* * *

I'm taking it calmly this windless morning—the port kerosene lantern is not in its box; it could not have been secured properly; in that case I won't have to blow it out. Here is the consolation, a bit of wind from the north-east. It has disappeared; but perhaps it was the forerunner of the real wind. These small puffs have uncanny power to instill hope in us.

Wind we don't have, but time we do and for the first time I take time to teach Marie-José celestial navigation. It adds special flavour to the strangely happy atmosphere on board to have Marie-José's calculated position make one more cross and circle near the others. We celebrate with some wine; surely, wind will have to come sooner or later.

* * *

The sea is glossy again today. Huge turtles go about their business. These sea snakes, let me guess, how long would they be ... eight feet and as thick as a man's arm? There are several; it seems they are travelling in groups. All the snakes we have seen so far were striped, but this one isn't. I wonder why. Why have we never seen such snakes anywhere before? I know the answer: when we have wind, we see the sails billowing out, we see the wave tops and we see ourselves arriving at a new place. When there is no wind we gaze endlessly into the calm water, maybe to detect some ripples, maybe just to gaze, and we see snakes.

There you have it! We live in a world of generalization. If there is wind, there are no snakes, if you see snakes there is no wind, and it's not a question of whether we wanted one or the other. I'm happy about not having wind, now that I'm convinced that we wouldn't have seen the the great snakes had we had it.

* * *

I want to see if the three little fish are still by our rudder—they are awfully faithful to us. The water is transparent, but it turns deep blue at a point way down. A small shark cruises in the depths—slowly, in circles and figures-of-eight; then it rises to the surface. This much bigger shark, with spots all over it, is certainly not of the same family. It keeps in our ... no, we don't have a wake.

I am acutely aware of this very faint breeze, but there are no wavelets or even ripples on the water.

There are dark clouds, all kinds of clouds, even clouds that are supposed to indicate wind, but no wind. I know about the dark clouds that bring no wind—and I know about the snakes ... and I know now that it is entirely possible for us to be here forever! Everything is in motion: the snakes, the turtles, the sharks, the clouds—everything except *Sea Helen*. We just sit, as if we are superfluous, as if we have not been counted in. To restore some feeling of motion we have agreed to use the engine for a few hours each day.

*   *   *

Today, a very black bird circles us several times.

Today, a school of blue-back tunas ripple the water, to port, now to starboard.

Today, a large bird with an oversized painted bill make several attempts to land on our boomrest: it makes very low approaches and lifts itself just a short distance before its target, only to fall just a bit short—its huge bill and neck hang over the plank while the feet try frantically to get hold. It has to let go ... and into the water it goes. Finally, it has made it—I'm glad. Neither God nor evolution has provided it with the right kind of feet or the sense of balance needed for the occupation of our boomrest, and we see another big splash.

Marie-José, with a great burst of inspiration, states that this should be regarded as a holiday! And so it should be, except for one nagging thought: the season of tropical cyclones is approaching! At this point I would rather have wind and be moving along, even if it means being a little seasick.

I'm back to drawing more little ships on cards, to sell, or just to send to people we know, or just to draw them; but damn it, we want some wind! A glass of water mixed with a little white wine is truly a refreshing drink.

*   *   *

Something in the air spells "trade winds." There are ripples and wavelets on the water, our sails have quietened, now that they are filled with air. Water is gurgling along *Sea Helen's* sides; we are leaving a wake.

It is October 4. I calculate what I need to know for a journey towards the western horizon: How many miles have we gone so far? How many more have we got to go? How much food and water have we left? Already, I'm looking upon the past twenty days as just a passing moment in our lives.

140

Our daily progress hovers at ninety miles—I'm anxious to plot it on the chart. We are not as thirsty anymore. We have observed that there are no sudden squalls during the nights and simultaneously, Marie-José and I have the daring thought to keep up the big genoa.

Our daily runs have increased to 100 miles in twenty-four hours—twice we have reached the 120-mile mark.

The wind is coming from astern—what more could a sailor wish for? We could wish for a wind coming over the quarter. The sails are winged out and we hand steer, and I break my head over how I can possibly make the boat steer herself without sacrificing speed. My bum is truly and entirely sore from sitting in the cockpit. A small car tire provides some relief in that area, but my eyes, my arms, my everything—.

It's funny, there was a way all along: a rope from the genoa to the wheel—a rubber strop on the opposite side to counter the pull—find the perfect balance—it's working! What a relief! We are free to read and sleep and stretch and eat with two hands. Time does not seem to exist when one sleeps, but it is pitiless to the one with a sore bum, a stiff neck and weary eyes.

CHAPTER TWENTY

Chances Are a Million to One

I mumble something and sink into the cockpit to let calmness come over me.

"It could be worse!" Marie-José is saying. Whether she said it conversationally or intentionally is hard to tell.

"Yes, we could be dead now," I answer.

It is like cancer or some other dreadful thing: it happens to others, not us ... somebody else is a candidate for it, "but not me." But it happened to us.

That night, when it came time to take my watch, 0100 hours, I put on my safety harness and a light top over my T-shirt. Although the wind seemed light and the skies were fairly clear, I placed my foul weather gear within easy reach, just in case. I sat in the cockpit gazing about, mulling over a thought or an idea and even trying out a song, "Sailor stop your wondering ..." to see if, as a sailor, I still liked it. After a while I sought out the vacant bunk for a cat-nap. Marie-José was in her bunk. Usually a change in the wave pattern, the sound of the wind, a sail flapping or any other unrhythmic sound or in fact total stillness, will bring me on deck before I start to dream.

At around 0330 hours I was in my bunk, cat-napping in full dress and safety harness. A pilot light glowed faintly inside the cabin; above decks I had seen our running lights shine brightly when I checked a few minutes earlier. *Sea Helen* was winged out, running beautifully almost dead before the wind.

The sound of grating or scratching registered in my brain. If I had not considered a backwinded mainsail, held by its preventer, potentially dangerous and damaging, I might have stayed in my bunk for a few more moments to figure out the source of the sound before looking for it. Groggily I climbed the companionway ladder.

The mainsail was fine. There was a train—no, we were on a train and the wall of a tunnel was racing past us. No, we were on our boat! Our main boom, seventeen-and-a-half feet long and winged out to starboard, was scraping itself along a wall.

A ship! We are being run down by a ship!

"Ship!" I cried out, with sadness, for our lives were just coming to an end.

"Marie-José!"

"Yes," she replied softly.

"There's a ship," I said with a mouth too dry. "There is a ship," I started again.

"We've been hit by a ship, a big ship!" I yelled over what seemed the roar of the racing wall. The gravity of the situation was sinking into me.

I was so preoccupied with the grotesqueness of the scene that I forgot to tell Marie-José what I meant to tell her—to put on her life jacket. I was forcing the wheel to port in a vain hope of edging *Sea Helen* away from her formidable opponent. But nothing changed. Smooth and grey the wall remained. I made feeble attempts to see how high it was, but I couldn't see its upper limits.

We seemed to be suspended in space and time, Marie-José halfway out of the companionway and I, a twisted figure at the wheel, like a clay figurine dropped to the ground without first being fired. Our gazes were fixed on the wall, as if held by a strong current.

Strangely, I was aware and alert as I waited for our yacht to be torn apart, for this great force to finally lay hands on her and make her somersault—the masts would obviously topple. I believe I was in a state of shock, devoid of fear or pain, thinking only in monosyllables: ship, boat, life jackets, Marie-José's life, damage, disaster ...

Was I thinking straight? I did not order Marie-José into her life jacket as I intended to do when I first realized that this was a collision. Or had I realized that the worst was over and I should concentrate instead on minimizing the damage to our boat?

My state was transformed when I saw stars where the wall had been, and the unsettling scraping sound had stopped. No final assault had come from the stern of the ship, which was now an array of lights moving away from us.

I mumble something and sink into the cockpit to let the calmness engulf me. Marie-José is right, it could be worse, we could quite easily be dead now, in Davy Jones' locker, as the saying goes. "No, we could be fighting for our lives. We could be struggling in the water, badly hurt!" Marie-José is replying impatiently.

Nodding eagerly, I try to show her I realize in such a terrifying situation there are many gruesome possibilities.

For a few more moments I look toward the large ship, which nonchalantly continues on her way. We, too, are moving, sailing in fact, on a reciprocal course. I want to know what damage we have sustained, if we are sinking! I want to call the freighter and ask them to stand by; I want to stop our foremast from swaying and take down the genoa. All of this needs simultaneous attention. Oddly, at the same time, I have a strong urge to go to sleep; perhaps to be able to wake up and find it was only a dream.

I make my way forward, bending gingerly over the rails, and steal a look at our topsides. My God, is it possible that we only brushed together? Our topsides are still in one piece. The high toerail is pushed far inboard and the rubrail, a half pipe welded at the sheer, is squashed. I'm now less interested in sleep and more in confirming that the damage is minimal. I have an idea, I will turn on the masthead light—it does not come on. Is it a coincidence that the bulb has burned out; am I cynical enough to think it has nothing to do with the freighter.

The VHF! I must try and call her. "This is sailing vessel, sailing vessel, sailing vessel—calling ship, sailing vessel calling ship! Over."— No reply—"This is sailing vessel calling ship, ship come in please we have had a collision! Over." There is no crackle through the set. I direct the beam of the flashlight to where I mounted the VHF antenna, at the masthead together with the tri-colour light—the stainless steel rod shows up, bent sharply to port.

We are on our own. I'm making my way forward to tighten up on the slack stays to stop the masts from whiplashing. The bowsprit grabs my attention. It is bent up. Already the electric flashlight is weakening, but I can see the bowsprit's underside, the gaping wound, the cracks; it is like a splintered bone. Now I notice the slack forestay.

We are running before the wind, so it is actually safer to hold onto our canvas—to keep the sails up—thus not allowing the boat's motion to become uncontrolled. I will, however, take down the genoa to avoid pressure on the bowsprit which, after all, seems to want to hang on.

A great desire for sleep has returned, but obediently I crawl into the engine compartment and extract a board from it. I splint and bandage the bowsprit in very much the same fashion I was shown to splint a broken bone. This will have to do for the remainder of the night.

Marie-José has volunteered to take the watch and so I lay on my back in the bunk. I'm unable to sleep but grateful for the rest. One thought has escaped neither Marie-José nor me: if ever a three-hour watch—which in mid-ocean we keep purely to avoid being run down by big ships—is disposable then surely it is this one, since the odds of colliding twice within a few hours must be long. Still, Marie-José is keeping a watch, if only to steady our nerves.

The odds against winning a million on a lottery ticket are staggering, not unlike the chances that two ships arrive at a point on the ocean at the very same time—to collide without having had a prearranged rendezvous.

We have now sailed our little ship for quite some distance. A number of times we have come close to ships at sea, or they to us, and in several situations I was so nervous I trembled when the seeming danger had past.

Nobody can say whether close calls are accidents averted, or whether a crisis never existed. A close call is a lottery ticket with five of the six winning numbers. This time we drew all six. Are we winners? If so then our prize must be to live to tell about it.

It is true, we cross the oceans on small modern yachts, carrying our secret fears with us. Front and center is the fear of being run down by one of the many freighters, tankers or super container ships some of which reach speeds of up to thirty knots. Storms and reef-strewn waters need only be feared when they are at hand, and one normally knows when. The chances of a collision with another ship, however, are perhaps greater in a storm when the visibility is poorer and one is inclined to seek shelter below.

In Fiji, when we were anchored in the quiet lagoon, I had pricked up my ears as a yachtsman told of his collision with a large ship. It sounded awful; but somehow I was strangely relieved. It occurred to me that if the chances of being run down are so slim, a million to one

145

as some people claim, and I personally know someone who has already been run down, my chances of being run down must now be even smaller.

Light has crept into the sky. The sun is breaking on a new day, and it is exactly that—a new day. Our ordeal last night was not a dream, I know quite well—but it is also not happening now. It has all the qualities of another bit of history.

I'm no more agitated now then a boy who gets up with the sunrise to start a camping trip. I look along the decks, and cabin top, finding the brown specks all over them quite peculiar. If these flakes were white, I would possibly think that it snowed during the night which in itself would be mind-boggling in a tropical latitude. This big brown flake does not melt in my palm. They are rust scales, thicker than the plates of our own steel hull.

I see now that not only are the starboard rubrail and toerail bent and squashed, but the deck is buckled.

With the fear of seeing more than I'm prepared for, I take my first look at the bowsprit in daylight. It has survived this long and so I have reason to believe that it will support my weight—I venture out on it.

My curiosity is satisfied: the tip of the bowsprit is squashed and paint and muck is stuck on it. It was virtually a head-on collision. The foremast is strangely twisted and the radar reflector atop it is broken. Our new tri-colour light atop the mainmast is gone.

Marie-José is pointing to a ship, a large ship on the horizon. The VHF is useless without the antenna, but ... "This is sailing vessel *Sea Helen* calling ship, sailing vessel calling ship."

"Thease is sheap ..."

Oh gee! the radio that I thought dead coming alive has startled me; a voice has spoken to me over our broken radio; our radio is in fact not broken but working. "This is sailing vessel *Sea Helen*. We have suffered a collision during the night. Over."

"Paerdon?"

"We have had an accident with another ship!"

"Paerdon?"

Well, it's no use; he would probably understand "Mayday," but we are not sinking so it's not a Mayday.

"Thank you for the radio check. This is sailing vessel. Out."

"Paerdon?"

Our radio is operational! It means that the ship we collided with had no-one on watch, or no radio watch, or worst of all, that she avoided taking responsibility. Perhaps the officer on watch spoke no English and refused to respond.

We continue to ponder this as our boat sails on westwards. We still have more than 2,300 miles to travel. The bowsprit has not broken all the way through—a layer of unbroken fibres remains. The bobstay is hanging slack, despite the fact that the bowsprit is bent up; the chain stretched by two links. I must shorten the chain before tightening up on the turnbuckle. The starboard whiskerstay was also stretched, though by only about half that of the bobstay.

The few pieces of spare wood we have on board will become a makeshift splint. I place the various pieces over and under the damaged bowsprit and attempt to parcel the whole lot with three-eights-inch rope. In order to get the benefit of a tight, continuous winding, I dare not cut the ropes too short. So I find myself struggling with an unwieldy coil, passing it under and over and under while trying to keep the tension. "Ah, shit, damn it!" The coil has slipped out of my hand and forty-odd feet of rope is now trailing astern, my arms are falling off any moment, as well, and the flanges of the bow roller, that have always been sharper than they should have been, are digging into my pelvis. But I must try again, with more coordination and calmness. Inner calm, yes, I'm on the right track— how good it is to catch oneself in a bad state and be able to change it. I consider it a blessing that our situation is not worse than it is, and the ocean could be a lot wilder.

I have lost track of time. All stays and lifelines are readjusted, and the genoa rehoisted, but it is four and a half hours later.

I'm content to just sit in the cockpit. The cosmetic damage to our little ship doesn't bother me. The bowsprit will have to be replaced and our cruising funds will feel the strain; but, really, it's worth a smile when considering what other prizes a ticket with the six winning numbers could have delivered.

"Do you think it's going to last?" Marie-Jose has already asked me several times. Am I too arrogant, or ignorant, to answer, "I think it will," with a little smile. We have 2,300 miles to go.

CHAPTER TWENTY-ONE

The Island of Rodrigues

*I*t has becomes part of the daily routine to clear the decks of flying fish. This morning I count more than twenty. I'm seriously wondering about the possibility of being hit in the eye by a flying fish—one has sailed past my face—one has crash-landed on the mainsail. The noise they make struggling on our steel decks is enough to pull us from our sleep, and we feel obliged to get up and help them back into the water. A fishy smell inside our cabin can only mean one has come through the hatch.

It has been a month since we left Darwin—we are craving for the taste of something fresh, like fresh meat, vegetables and fruit. We have not caught a fish in all this time, and even our tins are getting few. My eyes are on a flying fish that is much bigger than the usual sardine-sized ones. With five other larger ones, fish cakes are on the menu today. Marie-José has discovered that there are just enough ingredients for date squares. "Hmm! Fish cakes coming up, date squares to follow, we have good wind—the world looks mighty fine."

Just enough ingredients for date squares means we have used the last of the dates; we have used the last of a lot of foods!

"We can only have meat dishes every two or three days now," Marie-José looks at me unblinking.

"But we had lots ..."

"Yes, but you haven't been sick—you've been eating a lot more."

It is true. When I was sick, rationing was not a problem. Now that I feel good enough to enjoy the meals—"Wow, I never thought that we'd have to ration the food." Well, I'm not the least bit unhappy about that, now that I grasp the significance. I know that on a cruising boat there are usually all kinds of foods that we wouldn't ordinarily use, but that could be used. There are herbs and spices, coffee and tea.

One meatless dish that appears rather frequently is rice with a few dried peas or beans and soy sauce—I love soy sauce. "We have lots of rice and soy sauce?"

"Hmm, enough for two or three more meals."

Marie-José is becoming extremely inventive in the galley. It is a challenge every day to create a recipe rather than follow one. She meets the challenge head on and I anxiously await the results; I'm hungry—but I'm also curious.

I have always maintained that we should eat our favourite foods first, then, if we run low and are really hungry, the unfavoured foods will taste good too. Besides if any food spoils because we kept it too long, it'll be the one we didn't like. It is quite amazing how some of the foods that we never cared for taste so good. There are some, however—particularly a certain dried meat substitute—that tastes as bad in lean times as in times of plenty. This papier-maché excuse for meat will never again find its way on board this ship.

* * *

October is the official start of the cyclone season, but in November the season is definitely here, according to the pilot charts for the Indian Ocean. It is November 1. Cirrus clouds have appeared, as have altostratus and altocumulus clouds, the surest signs of an approaching storm. I try to recollect other factors that can indicate an approach. Is there a long swell or an increase in the wind? Is the wind backing or veering? What is the barometer needle doing?

I'm happily confused. I have anticipated the worst a sailor might have to face on this earth, but the wind has all but died. The sails flop. There is obviously no cyclone. The weather is frustrating, but we are still moving westwards and should not be too far from the island of Rodrigues. Originally we intended to pass it by because of the advancing cyclone season, but we are now eager to make it because of the advancing empty spaces in our food lockers, and the bowsprit; besides, we've been a long time at sea.

* * *

"I'll do all the laundry—you'll have to get rid of that T-shirt."

"I hope they have lots of vegetables."

"I'm not going to cook in port—just eat raw vegetables."

"Hope they haven't some kind of a holiday."

It's our fifty-third day at sea. The silhouette of Rodrigues is just a shade different from the clouds and we know now that we won't make it before nightfall. The winds are light and the skies promise to clear. Unfortunately there will be no moon; however, there are leading lights for the principal bay in the north.

It is after midnight. The leading lights are coming into line; but the wind, probably deflected by the land, has swung to the south; we are faced with a hard beat. Even with the engine contributing its power, we are making more leeway than headway. I try to determine from the chart how much we can open the leading lights and still be safe. The chart shows an area of raised ground and submerged rocks in the middle of the otherwise deep and large bay. It would be easy to move into the bay if only the conditions were not so difficult, if the wind suddenly died and the swells stopped throwing our bow off?

"Does the engine sound all right?" Marie-José wants to know. I'm suddenly aware of the way the engine is sputtering. It is overheating and we have no choice but to tack and head out again. It's preposterous that after spending fifty-three days at sea, we despair at spending a few more hours tacking back and forth until morning to enter the anchorage. Was there no island, we would have no choice but to keep sailing. Was the bay less generous than it appears I would not attempt an entry. But here is an island and a large bay with leading lights!

Let's try it again. Nine fathoms! It means that we have entered the bay, even if it is still rough; in a few seconds we'll have a rain squall upon us. I have the small anchor ready but I want to tie on a buoy to float the rope in case it goes slack on the coral bottom. The squall is here; our immediate concern is leeway and drift, which we can no longer determine for we can no longer see the leading lights. "Should we anchor here?" I ask Marie-José.

The anchor takes a long time to find its way to the bottom; the wind is taking us down faster than I can pay out the 300 feet of chain and rope, and I get the whole lot tangled up. The sounding I get now is a disappointing fifteen fathoms. It is most likely west of the nine-fathom patch. We are holding! A little apprehensive and a little glad, wet and tired, we roll to sleep.

*   *   *

Marie-José's persistent urging wakes me: "Klaus, it's light out. We should move in before the wind gets stronger." She is right, it is time to head for real shelter.

150

My head is pounding, straining against waking up after three hours of sleep. I struggle on the pitching foredeck. The little engine, screaming away, can barely move the boat against wind and swell; I'm astonished that we have anchored here! The anchor seems to be fouled in the coral. I'm not ready to cut the line—I justify my reluctance by convincing myself that we are not in any immediate danger. It's only my headache and this awful pitching that makes me think of such a thing.

I'm straining my back taking up every inch of slack. My back is sore, but here are the fruits of my labour: the anchor has broken out. The flukes of the anchor are broken and bent out of shape; I put it down to good fortune and things I cannot change.

With all sails drawing and the propeller turning, we are back on a hard beat. Progress is slow, but so far the range marks are staying in line, and besides, we now can see the edges of the reefs.

There is a boat coming in from the west—it is making beautiful progress. Look at that! It was only a small speck a short while ago and now it is almost upon us. Her crew are making signs—they are going in and want us to follow on a course that ignores the lead beacons. This new course is off the wind and the going is better; but we are nearing the edges of the reefs much more quickly—we are anxiously looking for new signs from our "pilot."

The fishermen, which we now see they are, raise their arms up and down several times, a signal to drop our sails. A line is passed and we are under tow, heading up a channel through the reef that leads to the town and harbour, protected from all but a cyclone.

That was nice, getting the tow, otherwise we would still be out there, instead of in here where the water is quiet and where fresh food and fruit and maybe a shower and a bottle of wine are within reach. "You go here!" An outstretched arm from the fishing vessel points to the spot on the dock where a crowd has gathered. We have arrived on a local public holiday.

The immigration officer, Ahkee, is putting the finishing touches to his paper work: "Now you would like to borrow some money, today is a holiday." He said it all in one breath. Withdrawing his hand from his trouser pocket, he holds up several bills. "Is this enough?— I can get you more."

We have no idea how much one can buy with the money he offers—our hesitation in accepting it is simply the time required to

151

marvel at this heaven-sent gesture.

Ahkee is personally taking us through the town of Mathurin, showing us what to get where. We open a "spirit account," not to waste precious cash; the bottle of wine is secured, our spirits are high. A greengrocer has our order for three dozen eggs. In a restaurant we breakfast on lettuce and eggs that have the yellowest yokes we have ever seen.

There are many names to remember—Ahkee, Pa Paul, Andrey, Assam, Massiff ... People come to the boat to talk—they do not ask for anything and they are not pushy; a leisurely conversation is all they ask, except for Assam who, with great sensitivity asked if we would like to trade sea shells with him.

In a few years Pa Paul will be old enough to be called an old man. Were I still a youth I would be sympathetic to his advanced age. Now I accept it as natural. Pa Paul has always worked around ships and is about to retire. He has a passion for ships that, I think, exceeds my own.

Pa Paul works in mysterious ways; he brings dreams to life. For example, we find a beautiful bunch of bananas on our decks. And then comes water. On a small island water must be conserved; here on Rodrigues, it is only turned on at certain times, and the nearest tap is far away from the wharf. I had hinted to Pa Paul about this problem a few days ago; today we find a hose leading to our boat. The mangoes left on our deck are so ripe and large—a pleasure to the eyes.

One does not leave a fish lying around in the tropics. Pa Paul is on the wharf holding up a fish, which he calls "Capitaine." I declined his first offer for fear of taking advantage of his passion for ships and their crew (I have observed how quickly the fishermen sell their catch to a waiting crowd), but we now accept the "Capitaine" for fear of hurting his feelings. He stands tapping the fish, reassuring us that it has a fine flesh.

Ahkee comes around. Pa Paul, he says, would like to come on board, but not by himself. Ahkee will accompany him for a little party in the evening. When I did not have a ship of my own, I would gladly have crawled into the cabin of any ship, to feel and smell, to touch and to dream. I have forgotten that there are people who would want to cramp into a tiny cabin—except now I am reminded by Pa Paul's delicate request, or was it Ahkee's own idea? Either way it suits us fine. We know we can buy a little wine where we have our spirit account.

As it turns out, there is one other yacht that is late in the season, a very unusual one that carries blue sails. I assumed this was the latest in sails, but I was proven wrong. The yacht docks behind us. Her name is *Chinook*. Her sailors are Gordon and Sylvia whom I admire for making sails out of common tarpaulin.

A party with live music is seldom disagreeable—a little wine, or even a shot of whisky with friends ... Pa Paul and Ahkee came armed with bottles, as if to prove that they did not come to drink on our accounts. "He would like to invite all of you for dinner at his house tomorrow," Ahkee is saying, relaying Pa Paul's wish.

* * *

Sure, we have each brought a little present, but we are all speechless at our reception in Pa Paul's house. I have always felt that the people who brave the world's oceans, and not just those sitting on thrones, should be treated like royalty. Pa Paul seems to see things like this, too. The dining-room table is large enough to accommodate not only us, but also his family members of several generations, down to pretty young girls whom he directs to serve the food. Pa Paul is serving the more important dishes himself. This is French dining at its best, and we are the diners!

Andrey, the fisherman who gave us the tow, and who received a pound of New Caledonia coffee in return (one thing we did not run out of), is here to fulfill his promise to take us for "a strong one." He is every bit as enthusiastic about it as Johnny Moa was about his kava house in Tonga. We follow him through field and town and back alleys. The strong one stands before us in the guise of an innocent-looking bottle of clear cane spirit.

Marie-José and I have got to do some serious shopping for supplies. It is not a simple matter of choosing but of finding out what is available and distinguishing the cheap from the unusually expensive.

I have never been interested in collecting antiques, but I like places that take me back in time. We find ourselves in a musty old store which recalls a picture in a story book, from the worn wooden floors to the smooth wooden counter, and an adequate number of prim men attending the business. We choose our goods from bins and sacks on the floor; a few have to come from behind the counter. The prices are added up on brown paper, and I am wondering how we will get this load to our boat? The solution lies within the time warp: the store has a sturdy wooden cart and a boy to push it to the wharf. The rice has bugs in it, one can see that right away, but what's to be done? They are only bugs.

It would be easier to hand my money for five gallons of diesel fuel to a retail outlet sales clerk than to bear this kindly face telling me in French and broken English that five gallons is too little to charge for—Pa Paul's fondness for boats knows no bounds.

At the market, a young boy selling vegetables is already living in the future and does not hesitate in raising the price of his cabbage, seeing that I am going to buy it.

Rodrigues conforms with my image of how islands should be. An island should be small enough to warrant being called an "island"— one has to be able to sense island life. It should be self-sufficient. It does not need most modern gadgets, but it must have plenty of life-sustaining fruit. Things will not change much from year to year, for there is little room for expansion. A coral reef is a definite asset. It should have a harbour for ships, and the people should appreciate them as their link to the rest of the world. To have pretty women is not a must but makes common sense. A hostile young boy who sells his cabbage for high prices to a stranger can be tolerated, for he too will grow old. And finally, it is a true island when it gives me the impression of being surrounded by the vast ocean, the way the earth itself is an island in the vast spaces of the universe.

We would stay for a while, did the seasons not bid us move on.

CHAPTER TWENTY-TWO

... *And on to Africa*

Our new bowsprit is protruding as proudly as its predecessor. The exotic timber was not available in the proper thickness but it looks very capable just the same. The cosmetic work can easily wait until we haul out for bottom painting.

Assam's expression is hard to read as we greet him with, "Hello, we are leaving today!" It's an awkward situation; we arrive as he is leaving. No, that isn't it. He is concerned about an approaching cyclone! He offers to drive us in his brother's car to the meteorological station.

The cyclone "Adelaide" is to the east and moving our way but is still far off. A request for further information from a larger weather station on the island of Mauritius suggests that if we can maintain four to five knots we should reach Reunion Island before it catches up. This scientific information and helpful advice are tempered with, "But the decision is all yours," and a weak smile.

This tropical storm, being weak and far to the east, is not an immediate threat, but it verifies that we are now sailing in the cyclone season.

Our original plan of motoring through the narrow channel in the morning, when the winds are often light, is useless. It is now midday and the winds are up. The channel twists straight into the wind. We need another tow. We have already been told that the pilot boat that normally provides tows for yachts with no engines, or engines too small, is under repair—there is one boat available, a huge tug that ordinarily assists larger ships. Ahkee has a word with her crew who are warming up the engines for one reason or another.

When we are through the channel, the tug casts off our line and we are on our own in an ocean that is somewhat rougher than we remember it on the day of our arrival. But we do not have to beat against the wind; we can sail away on a beam reach.

During the past few weeks we have been indifferent towards the sea with her swells and whitecaps, but we are fully aware of her again. I, for one, wish that the swell wasn't as big. I attribute the gusty winds to the island's mountains; now the glare of the sun prevents me from finding the range marks again.

The sails are not yet set, but I must leave Marie-José struggling with the wheel to stand on the cabin top—I think I saw discoloured water ahead over our starboard bow. This could be the "middle ground" with shallows and rocks! "Fall off, fall off!" How did we get that close? Here they are, right here, and us nearly on top of them! A flat rock face is looking straight up at me. It is like being eye to eye with danger.

Knowing now exactly where we are, we can sail out of the bay with the wind over our quarter. With a stiff following breeze, we set a westerly course for Reunion.

* * *

After three days we see the lights of Reunion Island. It is strange that in the daylight we cannot see the 10,000-foot high mountain. But now, a hunk of land separates itself from the mist and the highest peak is piercing the clouds. We make for the harbour, Port de Galets.

The port captain looks very official in his all-white uniform with stripes. He gives us a berth and a form to fill in. The police and health inspector are close behind, anxious to have their forms filled in, according to regulation.

Chinook, too, has arrived. She is directed to tie alongside us.

The island keeps its mountains veiled in clouds; only on rare occasions is their beauty exposed. Captain Michael of a large fishing vessel hails us to ask if we will be busy half an hour from now. He will not say anything further until he hears our answer, whereupon he is pleased that his free time coincides with our's. The afternoon with him and his beautiful Creole wife in a cozy restaurant for a dinner of cous-cous, and later at their home tasting exquisite cane spirit liqueur is so pleasant that I am glad I hadn't answered, "We have some repairs to make and then some shopping to do?"

Captain Michael is concerned about us sailing to Africa in the cyclone season and asks us to consider staying over until the period when tropical storms are born is past. But Reunion is an expensive place to live and now that we have duly worried about the cyclones, we will make a dash for the South African coast.

Chinook is going to leave at the same time and together we obtain clearance and visit the weather station for last minute weather details. The helpful meteorologist knows of a new tropical depression which, he says, should not affect us—apart from that the weather is close to ideal. However, there is a strong local wind which makes us reluctant to slip our mooring lines lest we are unable to cope in the confined harbour. We prefer to wait till evening when the wind, created by the sun, goes down with the sun.

The wind has indeed gone down. *Chinook* and *Sea Helen* are rolling with limp sails in the dark a few miles offshore.

Sleepily I crawl into the cockpit; I was right, we have a breeze. I hoist the main and free the sheets—gradually the ship's head is responding to the rudder; we are sailing.

*   *   *

There is a song in my head I have known since childhood: it tells of a ship that is becalmed near Madagascar—the sailors begin to die for want of water and the ship is finally swept onto a reef. It is ten days since we left Reunion Island and, rather than being becalmed, we are rounding Madagascar under a breeze so strong we dare not present to it our full sail area.

We are leaving the region most frequented by cyclones and so we are less apprehensive. The wind, however, has become a mixed bag. It builds up to where we have to reef, then drops and changes direction, leaving the sea agitated. Early morning is always a good excuse for sliding back the hatch to see how things are developing ... a wave—I didn't hear the usual breaking or gurgling sound—has climbed up the side of the hull to deposit itself squarely on top of my head—plonk, splash. I'm soaked—I have the urge to protest.

Often when we chance to look out like this we see a ship somewhere closer than the odds should allow. It's a blue sail—it's *Chinook!* They are coming closer; but so is a squall. It is so strange to be looking from our little vessel at Gordon and Sylvia on their little vessel with the elements all around. And we must each look to our own to prepare for what has all the signs of an approaching gale.

The weather carries on. We are beating and pounding and falling into troughs between waves, getting a headache from it. Now the wind has gone again. "About 320 miles from Durban," I announce to Marie-José, who is always eager to hear of our progress. The cyclones are no longer our worry; it's the coastal current that could sweep us past Durban harbour.

*   *   *

"The fish have arrived!" Marie-José puts a lure over the side and all the dorados come to investigate, but not to strike. I'm going to see if I can repeat my trick with the gaff.... It doesn't work; they stay just out of reach. I give up. But here is something peculiar: the fish are gathering behind the submerged gaff hook in a perfect V-formation. I take the gaff from the water, they scatter. I pull the gaff through the water again—they make another V-formation. Why that perfect V-formation? Yet they keep just far enough away so that I can't reach them. They will repeat it for as long as I want to go on. Perhaps they have no choice. It has been observed that grains of sand on a metal sheet will arrange themselves into geometric patterns when exposed to sound frequencies, vibrations. Are these fish responding to frequencies from the gaff, like grains of sand? There is no other species of fish with so many surprises.

I often rationalize that if I'm willing to buy fish from a fisherman to eat, then I should have no qualms about catching them myself. I take the lure from Marie-José and throw it out far then pull it in fast in an effort to trick them. Several fish dart towards it, but none take it. I change the lure to an orange one, a brown one ... they have already figured out my game. How about a white one? I throw it out far—there! one fish goes for it—a tug—a solid strain on the line!

These fish both amaze and puzzle me. I have my catch alongside—the others make the water boil around it; are they feeling sorry for their brother? Are they trying to help, or do they think the commotion means food, and react to a basic instinct?

*   *   *

I have long suspected that the world is defined only by how we look at it, and how we see it is probably a result of how we are made. Someone might be contented to sit in the cockpit of a boat for ten hours, enjoying his immediate surroundings; not me, I never last that long. The world is both beautiful and harsh; it is striking and shocking. It is cruel and gentle, it is everything. When we sleep, where is the world? It is lost to us.

I'm awake, the world is back. But I have no idea how long our ship has been heading the wrong way; I have no idea when the wind changed direction. It is not fun to take a large headsail down when one is not quite awake, but I have the urge to do it this minute. In fact, one should not rush into it, but must wait until one is completely awake. Besides, I must put my foot down! Who—except for some yachting people and that's their opinion—ever said that it's fun to change sails? We have probably been going the wrong way for hours so a few more minutes shouldn't make a world of difference. After all, I might have woken up later—then it would have been a few more minutes anyway.

We have agreed not to shock one another out of a sleep. I try to speak calmly:

"Marie-José ... Marie-José."

"What?"

"There is no rush, but we'll have to take the genoa down."

I now notice that the weather is a bit on the unfriendly side. In fact the ocean is beginning to look ugly.

I'm always astonished at how differently the world looks when we are beating instead or running. Now that we are beating into this mess of a confused sea, we are frequently being boarded by water. I heard a plink on the deck and a plonk on the cabin roof—it's a bolt and a wooden block that have fallen from the gaff of the foresail. That settles it! I was undecided as to whether I should take the foresail down or not, now I know it must come down.

I don't know how to describe it, I just know how it feels, when it blows all night and everything spills in the galley. Everything is wet and cheerless. There are salt crystals sprinkled on the mast and layers of salt on the decks, since the water runs off but the salt doesn't.

I feel that the boat will ride easier if I hoist the foresail—the minor repair has been completed—to a new wind from the west. Marie-José's opinion differs.

"We should leave the fore down," she insists. "This wind is going to last for days!"

"You don't know that at all. You said yesterday that the north wind would last for three days and it's already finished today!" I credit the nasty ocean with this heated exchange of views in the cockpit. Crash—splash! Solid water from the top of a wave is in my face;

Marie-José got it on her back. I feel—and I think Marie-José does too—that, at least symbolically, I have lost the argument. For once we are able to laugh about it.

Wow, how we can look differently at the world! I didn't know a few years ago that I could laugh about a wave boarding my boat. I always felt it such an intrusion; well, it still is; it's the wave in the face I'm laughing about, not the wave on the boat. I must keep things in perspective. It is the extraordinary circumstances that make us laugh, not the ordinary ones.

* * *

Marie-José seldom misses her breakfast, not the coffee anyhow—I don't know what she was thinking when she put her cup on the table … that we are in some kind of restaurant. She didn't watch her coffee for a moment and it's all over her. The T-shirt helped protect her skin from being burned; I recall the effort it took to brew this cup of coffee.

The wind is now coming from the south. Too bad, I counted on a north wind and kept north. But it is of good strength and we are able to hold our westerly course.

I knew that we were nearing land but I was not prepared for so many lights so suddenly. There is even a flashing light. Unfortunately our charts do not show such a light; this light may be new, our charts are not. Morning twilight is at hand: I have the hardest time bringing the stars to the horizon—Sirius is the only one I can manage; now the sky is too light. The position line Sirius gives is sufficient; it's Richards Bay, seventy miles north of Durban!

The South African officials are pleasant, but the entry procedures are lengthy and complex. The novelty of being treated like a commercial ship wore off long ago, in Australia.

Christmas, the time that was so meaningful as a child, is only days away. We will not rush to Durban but will spend it at Richards Bay.

The wind now blows almost exclusively from either south-west or north-east. A nor'easter has deposited us at Durban but already it has turned 180 degrees, as if making a return trip.

Durban reserves an international jetty in the heart of the city for yachts that arrive from elsewhere. The local population is well aware of that fact and make time to view the congregation of peculiar craft preparing for the haul around Africa's southernmost point. The well established Point Yacht Club is next to the jetty, and, as good things always come in pairs, we are allowed to use its facilities free of charge, for one month.

As a starting point for rounding the Cape of Good Hope—the thought of which leaves one tingling with excitement and tinged with uneasiness—Durban is, in one word, convenient. It is a big city that has almost anything. Things cost money but there is a chart agency that gives away cancelled charts.

To prepare for this upcoming voyage is to calm down and anticipate what lies ahead. I have begun to view the barometer with new eyes—never before have I seen its needle move around and back in regular leaps. After a lull, the wind always starts again from the south-west. It stays there for several days and then slowly backs to the south. The barometer that has been rising, begins to fall as the wind swings round to the north-east. After several days, one can expect a return to the south-west.

The idea is to start heading out with a dying sou'wester and make the most of the following nor'easter.

* * *

We are ready to go, the weather is fine; it is Friday the thirteenth. We are not superstitious, not really, but we are not going to leave; it just so happens that there are some unpleasant rain squalls. We'll leave after midnight, that's what we'll do.

Sea Helen is bucking a heavy swell in the narrow channel leading from the harbour basin as the first grey of morning replaces the night. Ahead of us lie the most feared waters on the South African coast, a stretch some 250 miles from Durban to East London, known as "The Wild Coast." South-westerly gales opposing the strong Agulhas Current are said to create sixty-foot waves. In Durban, the port liaison officer showed me a photograph of a large ship that had a chunk of its bow ripped off by such a wave. The north-east wind is already up; we are running before it with a reef in the main.

Night is upon us—we carry on under jib and foresail. Dawn has broken—my pulse quickens ... the inevitable sou'wester, first light, now fresh! Nothing shields me from thinking about sixty-foot waves. Yes, the inevitable sou'wester! "We must get out of the Agulhas Current!"

Two hours have passed, and so have my fears. The south-west wind is dying already! A fluky wind remains. What to make of this? With the rudder amidships, the mainsail and the jib sheeted in for comfort, we simply drift, stern first, with the Agulhas Current, a river in the ocean, towards East London.

The morning is cool and misty. Noon is clear and still—we sit, like ducks, outside East London.

At the dirty, noisy berth allotted to us in East London (no offense to the friendly people), we take another deep breath—the sou'wester is dying, the barometer is falling; we are setting off for the Cape.

Port Elizabeth would be a possible shelter from a south-west gale. Feeling that we may regret not putting in and waiting for the weather pattern to start anew, we leave its blinking light behind.

The day is clear—we are close to Cape Saint Francis. We leave it behind, too. It would also be a possible anchorage and shelter in the event of a south-west gale.

Fog! With our ears pricked for thumping engines or breaking waves, we drift in thick fog. There is news on the radio that two ships have collided near Cape Saint Francis.

It's the third morning in the fog—I think I hear noises, like the distant rumbling of a train ... It's the land, it's mountains resonating! With the aid of the sound, I can see faint contours through the shroud of fog. We seem to be inside a huge bay, Plettenburg Bay. We lower the anchor to the sea floor behind Seal Cape.

The night was roly; morning makes us think, "If there is going to be a breeze, it'll be perfect!" There was a little wind, but now it is dying; thoughts of entering Knysna, eighteen miles further along are born. Knysna is reputed to be the most beautiful place along the South African coast, but the entrance to it is forbidden in all but the finest of weather.

Spectacular and narrow and guarded by towering cliffs on either side, the entrance to Knysna provides the situation for which such words as nervous, apprehensive, alarm, and anxiety were invented. We enter by keeping beacons in line, which takes us close to the rocks and over the outer and inner bars into a lagoon that says: "Well, here you are. Welcome!" Having left the transits, we are no longer able to see the open sea. It is as if the gate has been shut.

We watch emus stalk the drying sandbanks—we take a motorized dinghy up the river. The two days we planned to stay have turned into two weeks.

One waits nervously, one hopes ... I'm speaking for myself. For several days we have waited for the right conditions near the narrow pass in order to exit into the open sea. We don't have much engine power and must negotiate the pass with a chance of making it. The tide is starting to come in, but a light wind is blowing towards the sea; no south-westerly is forecast ... should we go? We should go!

Two hours have gone by since we left the spectacular entrance to Knysna triumphantly behind; the radio announces a south-west gale. It blows at once. I am not surprised; I wonder what good planning, waiting, hoping and being nervous does?

It blew for just one day. Now there is little wind on our way to Cape Agulhas, the southernmost point of the African continent. There is just enough wind to keep our sails filled as we round the Cape and we watch a small boat coming up behind us. "Do they really just want to give us a fish?" One of four crew is holding up a fish. They want us to pass a bucket—for an instant we almost collide. We repeat the manoeuvre to get the bucket back. The bucket has five fish in it. Their outboard motor rattles as they disappear, amidst the long swells.

The wind sends us along at a good clip tonight, and the light on the Cape of Good Hope winks in the early dawn. We take a more northerly course for the last thirty miles to Cape Town and Table Bay.

Only moments ago I considered hoisting the genoa to harness more of the feeble wind, but now I'm reefing the main because of too much wind. Hot and cold air are streaming off the mountains. Still before nightfall we enter a port that is unmistakably Table Bay Harbour, backdropped by the fully exposed Table Mountain.

CHAPTER TWENTY-THREE

St. Helena Island

*I*t's amazing how time slips by; and it's equally amazing how one's outlook and evaluation about a place can change over time. It's July 19 and we arrived at St. Helena Island on April 30, more than eleven weeks ago. Originally we allowed a generous two weeks for our stay.

Why are we staying so long? Is it because of the character and charm of little Jamestown, or the serenity and morality of its people? It couldn't be the sinfully expensive beer, nor the anchorage which, mind you, is not half bad, considering that it is the open water of James Bay.

We have begun to take for granted the barren cliffs flanking the bay. The same is true of the wreck protruding above the water only a few hundred feet from our mooring.

Circumnavigating the globe from east to west, it was clear that we could visit St. Helena, although we didn't know anything about the island, apart from what Harry Pidgeon wrote when he visited here in his yawl over fifty years ago. I made a mental note to ask some St. Helenians if they still remember Harry Pidgeon. The fact that the island had been visited by hundreds of old-time sailing ships made it more fascinating to me.

After twenty days of uncomfortable but fast sailing from Cape-town, we expected to raise St. Helena's grim cliffs. Heavy banks of clouds concealed the land for a long time, but when they were off guard for a moment, we caught our first glimpse of this isolated, majestic island in the Atlantic Ocean. Rain squalls frequently obscured our view of gorges and valleys, the flanks of which rise over 2,000 feet. Finally, our little engine inched us into the lee of the land where all sorts of small craft and brightly painted buildings came into focus.

In the fading light we moved into the anchorage and we were

lucky, as we often are, to have a boatman help us. "Over yonder," he pointed and before darkness fell we were snug between two forty-five-gallon-drum moorings.

The most prominent feature of the waterfront is the seawall which defines the head of the bay. On the east side, where all commercial cargo is handled, there are steps for landing and the wall runs alongside the sheer cliffs. The same cliffs form the back wall of the narrow storage sheds which presented themselves so colourfully when we arrived. From the water's edge of James Bay, Jamestown extends for over a mile inland and upland in a narrow valley.

We took an instant liking to the town, with its medieval architecture and its friendly people. Invariably, when a local inhabitant lays eyes on a visitor, he greets him or her with at least a hello. We quickly pick up the habit.

Jamestown boasts a staircase—Jacob's Ladder—consisting of 699 concrete steps, reaching from the valley floor to a height of 602 feet, the top of Ladder Hill. The view is magnificent, and well deserved after reaching the top with sea-weakened legs.

In another direction is the Briars, where Napoleon lived in exile until his permanent residence in Longwood was ready. To get there, one takes Napoleon Street, which after a short distance becomes a steep and narrow mountain road laboriously wrenched from the rock. The scene changes suddenly; one ascends the stony, sterile side of the mountain to reach its lush and fertile face. Astonished, we turn and look back to absorb this contrast.

The island is almost entirely mountains and valleys, with no level ground, so if one leaves Jamestown, one must go up, one way or another. One afternoon we were offered a sightseeing drive. We again climbed a narrow road to one of the high points on the island and then headed into the country. At first there were only cactuses in profusion, but again there was that sudden transition to lush greenery. We stopped at Plantation House, the governor's residence and also the home of Jonathan, a huge tortoise said to be over 250 years old and a one-time pet of Napoleon.

St. Helena was at one time renowned for its flax industry which now no longer exists. Nevertheless, flax, the plant that yielded the fibres, grows densely alongside the roads and elsewhere in the country.

I can only marvel at the variety of scenery within this forty-seven square miles of island. Presently, we are overlooking the Gates of Chaos, an area where bare mountains display dabs, dashes and streaks of every imaginable colour and among it all, two huge basalt columns, named Lot and Lot's wife.

There is no shortage of postcard scenes, and we can easily see how place names like God's Box of Water Colours or Artist's Palette were chosen. Green Hill, Blue Hill, Silver Hill, Deep Valley and Dreaming Valley are natural choices. Most scenes are set against an expanse of blue, one constant feature of this comparatively small island.

We notice one huge tree—a Norfolk Island pine. In the days of the big sailing ships it would have been planted to provide a new spar. Our host and guide is showing us ferns and cabbage trees indigenous to St.Helena. Marie-José cries out in joy when we encounter a donkey. The few still on the island, not used as beasts of burden are as motor transport has taken over. We point out to each other Diana's Peak, the highest peak on the island at 2,704 feet, situated on the rim of a great crater whose southern part has disappeared into the sea. We also point to a prominent rock, called the Barn. With a heart-shaped waterfall and High Knoll fortress in view, we descend into Jamestown, on a road so narrow that cars cannot pass each other.

Many scenes on St. Helena can be viewed through one of the numerous gunports. Ruins of gun emplacements and general fortifications are all around the island, but especially in James Bay and other stretches on the leeward side.

St. Helena is said to have been unknown until Portuguese navigator Juan De Castella discovered it on his way back from India in 1502. The island is now British. After the departure of the Dutch, who also had a hand in it for a while, the British established a garrison in 1658, using the island for replenishing and refitting their ships.

Captain Cook paid his visit in 1775 and Bligh was here in 1792, while Charles Darwin is said to have arrived in the Beagle in 1836. To commemorate the visit of Joshua Slocum, the first solo circumnavigator of the planet, in 1898, a plaque has been placed in the park. But the trump name is Napoleon! The island was his place of exile from 1815 until he died in 1821. Many people associate St. Helena with only this one fact.

Before Napoleon, this volcanic outcrop had housed slaves and, later, Boer War prisoners (1899-1921). At one time labour was

166

imported and some Europeans made this island their home. Now there are about 5,000 inhabitants, called Saints.

As we walk about the town and waterfront now, many Saints comment, "You have been here a long time!" And it's true, we have already stayed longer than the average visitor. Now and again a new yacht rolls into the bay; the figure stands at around eighty for this year so far. Saints say that yachts are coming in greater numbers each year.

I look across to *Jonathan,* a yacht from Gabon, and see Serge walking along the deck with his cooking alarm clock around his neck, resembling a bar of shower soap; he has invited us for dinner. Because Serge understands only a little English, but wants a guided tour of Napoleon's house, in the absence of the French consul, Marie-José will translate. The house is in Longwood, about five miles inland and while we are prepared to walk or hitchhike, Serge insists on taking a taxi.

Maybe there is nothing wrong with having one rate for the locals and another for visitors, but it does not sit well with me; maybe I don't consider myself a tourist, as the locals do, but a traveller. One cab driver finally offers a middle rate, apologizing that the high rates for tourists are regulation; he could get into trouble if anyone found out that he was not charging the full tourist rate.

Napoleon's stay on the island is well documented. The house contains many of his personal articles—the musty smell of history pervades it.

* * *

We have known Jake, senior attendant of the swimming pool, since the day we arrived. An invitation to his house deepens our friendship. He has no transportation of his own, so he hired a cab, at the local rate, to take us up to his lofty dwelling in Deadwood, where his wife and daughters prepared a typical St. Helenian Sunday feast, fit for a king. From Jake's place one can see halfway around the island. We watched a yacht approach from the south, disappearing behind the island's eastern point, and then reappear to the north. Jake offered to get another cab to take us back to Jamestown but we drew the line and started walking the nine kilometers to James Bay.

The evening air is exhilarating as we walk along the mountainsides, among bushes and flowers. Below the peaks, nature is unrestrained— the earth is still and scented.

We have made friends on the waterfront with Terry, an oldtimer on the island. "Yes, I remember Captain Pidgeon well—he used to show slides," Terry answers to my question. I am bursting with delight. Terry also knows of Gerbault, another single-hander of Pidgeon's time. Marie-José, however, is disappointed: she found out that there is no longer a lace school on the island. She had set out from Capetown with visions of enrolling in classes to learn the very delicate lace work for which St. Helena is well known. Pidgeon speaks of the lace school in his book. A copy of the book has gone to Terry with the inscription: "To Terry, who remembers Harry." I don't know who got the bigger thrill, me giving the book, or Terry getting it. In any case, Terry bought us a drink.

These days St. Helena is visited by very few commercial ships and liners. Modern ships, except for the ones our size, no longer consider it an oasis. As there is no airport, the only link with Capetown and Europe is the island's own ship, the R.M.S. *St. Helena*. When she is in, sooner or later just about every Saint will take a trip to the waterfront. At such a time, Jake and I are sitting on top of the wall outside the main gate watching traffic go past. Most people greet us or wave, and we wave and greet them. Being there matters more than the conversation:

"She is anchored a long ways out today ... Hello!"

"Hello!"

"Carrying a lot of passengers this time ..."

"Hello"

"Hi there! How long ... Hiii!—is she going to be in for?" I'm astonished at how many people I've come to know, and the number of faces I recognize.

We often coax Jake out to the yacht for coffee. Like most Saints, he has never been aboard a yacht before. I try my best to get some of the island beauties aboard and I am moderately successful.

At other times, when the boat is rolling, we scramble ashore for some peace and quiet. When it's still we watch extraordinary sunsets, or gaze into the horizon. Now and again a turtle will appear.

On occasion, we have been pulled out of our slumber by the thrashing of a flying-fish on our deck. Over the lapping of waves against the hull we hear the breathing of porpoises—they had obviously given chase. We encounter flying-fish in all oceans, but the first one we saw here was a surprising twenty inches in length. These large fish, in their flurry to escape a predator, will quite often land on top of the seawall, only to be picked up by a lucky Saint.

Equally surprising is the fact that local fisherman quite happily catch the conger and moray eel, even though there is good offshore fishing. Boats often return with formidable catches of tuna, bonita and barracuda. During the high season the island even exports some of these.

An invitation by a couple of fisherman for a diving and fishing expedition comes unexpectedly. The seven crew members of the yacht *Bella Del Mare,* all keen divers, also receive the invitation. Our destination is an off-lying rock, a few miles down the coast, called Egg Island.

There is always jubilation when sailors encounter their best friends, the dolphins. Every time they leap there is a happy communal cry from our open boat. One of the yachties promptly lowers himself over the side and tries to swim along with them. Egg Island looms ahead and the boat is manoeuvred in behind it. There is a noticeable surge, and I'm fascinated by the skill of these fishermen with their craft. With a faint splash, a little grapnel finds its way to the bottom and we are anchored just where I was sure we weren't going to anchor. I was going to mention the extremely short scope we were using but I remembered that local fishermen know the waters.

Stuart, skipper of *Bella Del Mare,* wastes no time in diving, equipped with his spear gun. He must have met a fish on the way up, while he was on his way down, for I'm still considering the risks of anchoring where we are, when a fairly large fish (supper for at least five) wiggles above the gunwale on the end of a stainless steel shaft. A second one follows soon after. Our hosts are skillful with the hook and land a variety of species.

I had told Stuart about the moray eel, and he must have remembered, for with the next dive this is what he dumps in on us. There it is—in all its ugliness, or, in all its glory. We all back away a little, and the fishermen, who like to catch them, look alarmed! Wordlessly, they club the eel all along its back bone. It seems strange for professional fishermen to hit a fish like that, when one blow should have killed it. However, a moray is difficult to kill outright and they know that it might stand up on its tail and spring at them, like a snake. The idea is to weaken them first, starting with their backbones. After all

169

the excitement I also dive to view the underwater world, including gigantic squarish boulders and a large cave.

In high spirits, for which a nip of brandy is partly responsible, we take the spray in our faces on our windward return trip to James Bay. Supper is heaps of fried fish. The meat of the moray is pure white and good tasting, but soft. "Has to be deep fried," is one comment. I take bigger helpings of the firmer meat, like cavally and grouper.

*   *   *

Throughout our stay the swells in the bay are seldom unpleasant and we can always land our dinghy. Only once, when I rowed Jake back ashore, was the landing awash and a small group of people there to watch the spectacle. Jake, fully dressed, had no intention of getting wet and with his experienced eye and my practiced oarsmanship, we effected a smooth landing, depriving young Saints of some free fun. I smiled as I pulled hard to get clear of the concrete: one slender girl had turned around and moved her posterior conspicuously. Everybody in the group either grinned or giggled.

Although the sea in James Bay is usually calm, there is such a thing as Roller Time. Around February, rollers created by storms far out at sea reach the bay and play havoc. Waves have been known to climb over the seawall and smash into the warehouses. However, if yachts and small craft anchor further out, in about one hundred feet of water, they can ride it out safely. I shuddered when I read that, in 1846, thirteen slave ships were lost in the bay during Roller Time. However, hurricanes are unknown and when there was a short thunderstorm one day, it was the first many of the residents had ever experienced.

The climate of this island, lying in the tropics at sixteen degrees south, is always temperate, and would please almost anyone. It suits a vegetation so varied that the English oaks can be found growing alongside bamboo and banana plants.

Setting a departure date has pinpointed our next destination. It is to be the island of Ascension, 700 miles north-west of St. Helena. At St. Helena one can get some practical information about Ascension. Many Saints have lived and worked there and are able and willing to provide a first-hand account.

Ascension is blessed with an airfield, due to the American satellite-tracking installations and its level ground. It can send and receive mail at short intervals.

With my departure date firm, I go to the post office and offer to take the mail to Ascension. There isn't another ship expected to go that way for several weeks and my offer is welcomed. That evening, a news item on the radio startles me: "Captain Klaus Gehrig, of the yacht *Sea Helen,* who intends to sail from St. Helena Saturday morning, has kindly offered to take letter mail to Ascension Island..."

Saturday morning has come. I watch as a bag of Royal Mail is sealed and I sign the delivery bill. I am ushered into the office of the postmaster, who expresses his genuine gratitude.

I am aware that on at least two occasions when yachts carried mail for Ascension, it was never delivered. One batch ended up in Brazil, while the other was never heard of again. But the Saints are undaunted, and one would be hard pressed to find another place in the world where small ships' captains are held in such high esteem.

Numerous good-byes have been said to numerous people, everything is aboard, including fruit and vegetables and even several presents. The only thing left to do is slip our mooring lines.

The wind is light—it will take a long time for us to dip over the horizon—but a small group of people, including our friend Jake, remain clustered at the seawall for as long as we can see them.

As the land behind us disappears it occurs to me that one day, when someone mentions the name St. Helena, we will say, "Yes! I remember it well—grim cliffs and green country, Jamestown, friendly people—met a fellow there who remembered Harry Pidgeon."

CHAPTER TWENTY-FOUR

A Landscape a Bit Lunar

*I*t is not hurricane weather, the trades are steady—not a worry in the world. This whole sail has been a classic: the canvas spread generously to the wind, the boat steady under our feet and the heavenly bodies visible for navigation.

Through the binoculars, I can see features of Ascension Island: one large peak in the centre, a low one on the right and a small one on the left. Now, half an hour later, it is no longer visible; it was only a moment of clarity in the setting sun. Night has fallen; shore lights are flickering.

Having risen from the ocean a lot later than St. Helena, Ascension presents a landscape of barren hills, and mountains of different shades; I consider it "a bit lunar." The only green is on Green Mountain. Umbrella antennas and other paraphernalia for space craft tracking stations on its shores, make me blink.

The boat landing makes me think of St. Helena, where it was only half as rough. I wonder how waterproof the mail sack is; I think of what I'll do if we don't make it, if Marie-José loses her step … We have made it! We are safely ashore.

The black fish make a stop at Ascension Island worthwhile. This fish, about the size of a man's hand, will eat almost anything biodegradable and so does a fair job of cleaning a ship's bottom. Empty a bag of garbage into the water, and within minutes only a few synthetic items will be left. Banana peels are their favourite.

The trades blow freely over the island and after three days, the maximum time allowed, we sail on, at a good clip over the shallows patched with coral, into the deep sea.

* * *

Our feet on the ground, we find ourselves on a dusty uphill road. Lest we end up wandering aimlessly in this heat, I ask the first person we

172

meet where the police station is. We have arrived at Fernando de Noronha, an island off the coast of Brazil.

This angular youth did not expect to be addressed by strangers. He is reluctant to break his stride and indifferent to our very first effort to speak Portuguese. Still, he retraces his steps, turns and motions for us to follow. He leads us off the dusty road along a shady trail—an enchanting short cut. Finally, we emerge by a big old church close by a stately building, the Palace. Inside the Palace I sit at a huge table, like a conference table, but with only one chair. Marie-José stands beside me while, with a flourish, I fill in one simple form. These are entry procedures in their purest form. The young officer—he has a friendly smile—indicates that he will keep our passports. "Finito!" he is saying.

We are back on the dusty road. Where it begins to descend steeply, a Jeep stops to offer us a lift. Our hair streaming behind us, I inhale the tropical air, watching the dust clouds, as the car skids and sways. I try to see how much further it is to the bottom. I'm sure that the driver has done this many times before, but I hope that he is not trying to show off because of us.

We are anchored in St. Antonio Bay, but there is a small bay further along that has a swimming beach and lush green plants lining its shores; it has a little creek where we can do the laundry. A young boy appears and speaks, first in Portuguese, then in sign language. We understand fairly quickly. "No washing hair in creek," he is saying, "Bugs!"

We have been told of a small farm in the south of the island where we may buy fruit and vegetables. After sauntering for miles, we have found a cultivated patch among the wild growth, complete with a small shack. The farmer, sitting in a chair, answers that he has a little. First he gives us a drink of cool water from his refrigerator. He makes us sit down while he readies himself, changing his shoes and finding a knife and a tin container.

His vegetables are scarce, but when searching through his plants the first green tomatoes and beans sound like tiny gongs when they meet the bottom of the tin container. Parsley, green onions and green peppers crown a little heap that exceeds our expectations. Papayas are the only fruit—the farmer is apologetic. Everything is carefully weighed—he motions for us to pay attention to the needle

173

on the scale—the price for all of it falls short of what we judge hard-to-come-by vegetables are worth.

Business done, the gardener again turns host and offers us coffee. It's not good to drink it without sugar, he indicates. I think he is right; it's strong Brazilian coffee. Would we like a small meal, a soup? Ah ... we are not sure. It's very good, our host insists. It's from the cow. "Yes, cow, muh." We understand. "No, not cow, stomach from cow." Yes stomach, intestines, that's what we thought. It really does taste good—a lot better than "stomach" sounds.

Happy with our day's achievement, we begin the long trek back to St. Antonio Bay. Despite the size of the island, we lose our way and end up cutting across the airfield, stumbling upon a small group of dwellings, passing a few long-eared goats. From the shade of some bushes we re-enter intense sunlight. A voice hollers after us. There is a crowd gathered; the one who called is mimicking somebody driving; he points to a small bus parked under a tree.

The bus serenely makes it way along with a load of people. It stops indiscriminately to pick up anybody walking along the road, and nobody pays a fare. (The island is controlled by the military.) I stop being nervous about not having paid a fare.

* * *

We have chosen an unfavourable time to sail for the mainland of Brazil. Natal, south-west of Fernando de Noronha, and still sixty miles distant after one and a half days of sailing, no longer seems worth the struggle against the coastal current, an unseasonable south-south-east wind and rain squalls. I repeat to myself the unsavoury-sounding name of Fortaleza, a large port in the north, and find that it starts to sound a lot better. Sharp gusts of wind spank us as we turn tail on Natal and follow a new course to Fortaleza.

We are coming into a bay cluttered with fishing and sailing craft and our steering cable has either broken or slipped. Under full sail and without a rudder, we are barely in control. How close are we to the shore? We must not let the sails gybe; but how can we stop them? Oh, watch out!—we gybed! We have ropes leading from a lug on the rudder to our stern; we should have thought of that first! The main must come down so we can manipulate the rudder by pulling the ropes. This would not do for a fancy manoeuvre but it will get us in behind the breakwater.

174

We did well, all considered, I'm pleased. A small harbour boat has spotted us and is giving us directions. The skipper gesticulates that he wants to tow us. We pass a rope. Good lord, he is towing too fast; heavens, he is putting us in an impossible place to anchor; shit, he's got us tangled up with another yacht! Now I have even less control than before. We are scraping all along our side; he's bumped the bowsprit! That's it. "Stop pushing, we can't go there, there is not enough room! We will anchor at the end of the line, over there, over there!" I'm yelling in English. (My Portuguese is limited to "Good day" and "How are you.") The skipper is eager to comply. It's hardly believable that the harbour authority has no experience with boats or the anchoring requirements. I tell Marie-José not to worry about the scraped paint and worry about it myself for a while.

*   *   *

Fortaleza is windy all the time. This wind is the life-giving force for hundreds of local fishing craft that put to sea under sail every morning to return gracefully before sunset with their prizes of blue-water fish.

A young Brazilian has appeared alongside with a dinghy. "I'm here because your boat looks a lot like mine," he tells us in good English, pointing out a converted fishing boat. It is not a schooner, but the hull shape, yes, if one takes a broad view ... "My name is Carlo," he reveals.

"My name is Klaus."

This makes him grin broadly. "It is a lot like my name." I look again at Carlo's boat to see if the hull is remotely like ours.

At the Fortaleza Yacht Club, the waiter carrying a tray full of drinks stops midway to the tables to smile at us as if he knows us, and is glad to see we have finally arrived. I have never seen him before. How could he possibly know us? Are we celebrities or a novelty? I'm blond and rather good looking. The waiter's eyes are shining—it is nice to see somebody so happy ... he repeats the same words. It sounds like "dalla-dalla," but I'm sorry we don't speak ... he shows us money; he is willing to pay 110 Cruzeros—I got it! "Dollars." He wants to buy dollars. "No, no dollars for sale right now." He is perplexed; the smile fades from his face, his eyes lose their shine—now he definitely doesn't know us.

A word of caution from a person who speaks English and is a

director of the club (a luxurious club) darkens the bright tropical day. "Bring your dinghy on board at night, take laundry in at night— move the boat in closer, leave somebody on board at all times!" The director also wants to buy dollars.

"Take your laundry in at night?"—I don't know if I should be alarmed or surprised that someone might want to steal a bleached pair of shorts or a well-worn T-shirt.

One skipper has shot at thieves who fled with his radio when they boarded his boat while he was asleep. Another skipper tells us that his yacht has been broken into five times in two years, once while he had a guard on board—the guard wanted more money if he had to stay awake.

I know Fortaleza isn't paradise, but this is one hell of a worry to live with. Our green decks will soon need repainting anyhow, so I bring out the yellow paint ... I paint: "Honni soit qui mal y pense," just a little curse. It's nicely visible; I feel better, now that our boat is protected.

This writing on the deck is like the writing on the wall: it has a startling effect even on invited guests. They never fail to tip-toe around it.

I just remembered I left a towel in the shower room—I must get it and at the same time I'll buy some groceries. It's always colourful on the streets. What's that? A tiny bluish coffin filled with flowers, and a baby, whose head is lolling from side to side; the four girls carrying it are yapping incessantly. Groceries in hand, I'm curious about this bizarre sight, or is it bizarre because I haven't seen it before.

There is no towel in the shower! I didn't write "Honni soit qui mal y pense" on it.

*   *   *

If it was more important to me, I would speak up and say that two Brazilians are rowing away in *Le Petit Prince*'s inflatable dinghy. Maybe they are guests of the owner? They smile and wave at me rowing our leaky old tub; they are outgoing, smiling people with heavy gold chains around their necks.

I'm having a pleasant conversation with a lady on another yacht, but Marie-José motions for me to come quickly: "That is *Le Petit Prince*'s dinghy, they are taking it away!"

176

"You know, I thought that! Where are they now?"

"They have gone that way, they are way over there!"

"Keep them in view with the binoculars." I wish I could be sure that they are stealing the dinghy; actually, I *am* sure! I need an outboard motor to chase them; our dinghy rows so poorly that I'll never catch up! I noticed a yacht with a dinghy sporting an outboard motor. A pretty young girl responds to my knock on the hull; Daddy is not on board. They are getting away! Well, it's not my dinghy; no one else seems concerned. There's Daniel coming back from the dock in his sailing dinghy. I row to his yacht to tell his wife in English who translates quickly into his native tongue.

"Should I come with you?"

"No, it will be too heavy."

Although the dinghy's owners and Daniel are present, the thieves, after a humiliating return to the club jetty, glower at me ... they know who did the damage, the one they smiled at so amicably. A young Colombian who can speak French and Portuguese reluctantly becomes involved as translator. The two thieves have gone from being defensive to being aggressive.

I sense an unspoken warning: that if you get involved there might be an accident, and we wouldn't care if you found out that it wasn't an accident. That's it, isn't it? We are in their land and they have friends; we only know a few yachties who, with reason, prefer to have the thieves glowering at me than at them.

I instruct the owner of the dinghy who speaks French and English, to ask the Colombian to ask the thieves why they took the dinghy.

The Colombian is flabbergasted at their reply. "They were looking for *Minstrel*" (a yacht that was reported dismasted 300 miles northwest several days ago), the Colombian explains.

I know that not all Brazilians are like them; they are members of an élite scum whose only abilities are to hate and covet.

I won't sleep easy from now on. It is quite possible that they will seek revenge. Revenge for what I didn't let them do. Yeah, that's the way they will look at it. The word soon spreads that one of them is the son of a yacht club director.

* * *

A walk on the beach is a walk through colours. Fishing craft, *Jangatas*, pull up on the sand leaving their sails up to indicate that they have returned with a catch. Now and again we pass a small kitchen made up of stray stones and a plank. Outside a small craft shop, a saleswoman keeps talking to me, although I make it clear that I don't understand a word ... she laughs. She shakes hands with Marie-José in a masculine sort of way before we hurry away.

In the city of Fortaleza, high-rise buildings mingle with back-alley kitchens. Modern buses and modern cars weave around donkey-carts. Sometimes a cart is pulled by a human, sometimes a human rides a donkey. Among all of this, a young Brazilian tells us that his American name is Franklin.

He comes to visit us on the boat and gets seasick, but continues talking in English, French, and German, the three languages he is endeavouring to learn, all at once. He is sixteen and can make himself understood in all three. His wants to teach us Portuguese. Thanks to Franklin I can now go into a store and produce this special sound that somebody suggested I could achieve by pinching my nostrils and saying "pang," meaning bread.

On a crowded bus I sit rubbing shoulders and thighs with a girl carrying an English textbook. She is happy that I have asked her if she is studying English; in turn, she makes sure that we make our way forward in the bus in time to get off at the right stop. She takes me through the city and gives me her phone number—"If you like to see me again—to speak English."

I think of Marie-José, who braves the seas with me, and the young girl who has intrigued me for the past half-hour, and I'm torn, looking at the decorative writing on the small scrap of paper.

Devil's Island

*D*evil's Island has been on our minds a lot lately: is there something devilish about this island? Will the currents in its vicinity be vicious; does the ocean bottom drop away around it so that one cannot anchor? Will a ship going near it come to grief?

It is the same Devil's Island on which Papillon and Dreyfus were imprisoned. Papillon became famous when he wrote an awe-inspiring account of his years in the French prisons in Guyana, his attempted escapes and his final successful one from Devil's Island. Long before Papillon's time, Dreyfus earned a place in history books by being wrongly accused of a political crime and was forced to spend four years and three months on Devil's Island.

The island is one of three close-knit islands lying about ten miles off the coast of French Guyana. So it's not just one fearful island, it's a group of three, and while each has its own name, together they are called Iles du Salut.

In Fortaleza, we made a sketch from someone else's sketch, and so we have some information about the position of the islands relative to each other and where to approach them. Happily it also indicates a lighthouse.

The easiest thing for us would be to plot a straight course from Fortaleza to any one of the islands in the Caribbean. However, curiosity about these small specks of land gets the better of us, so we plot a course that will take us near them and if the weather is fine when we get within reach, we will call there. Besides, it isn't going to be much out of our way.

We weigh anchor at Fortaleza on October 18 and clear the harbour limits as early as 0830, local time. Frantic cheers from a cluster of people aboard another yacht, returning from an all-night beach party, send us on our way.

The South Equatorial Current runs in a north-westerly direction, about 80 to 100 miles from the shore, just the way we are going, so why not get in it and ride along?

The schooner doesn't seem to want to steer herself—I can't leave the wheel until she does; in any case, we have to dodge some of these things that make me nervous and that are not marked on our chart—oil rigs.

There is really no way to tell that one is crossing the equator, except by some spherical calculations. We are three days out of Fortaleza and now, after four years in the Southern Hemisphere, we have subtly crossed over to the Northern Hemisphere again.

Light winds have reduced our speed to about two knots. That should amount to forty-eight miles in twenty-four hours; the rest of the 110 miles we are actually making must be credited to the current. Marie-José emphasizes her comment on how quietly we are sailing by baking a pie.

October 25 is a day of heavy clouds and finally, rain. Rain is welcome for it cleans our decks and rigging, which acquired an unwelcome coat of dust in Fortaleza. The wind has veered and although light, now blows stubbornly against us.

It is October 28. We have not had a commanding breeze for several days and we find ourselves much further north than we hoped. A drastic course change is necessary if we are going to make these islands before the currents sweep us completely past. Fortunately, the prevailing north-east wind has returned just in time.

A noon-sight shows us to be forty miles due east of the Iles du Salut, in a good position from which to approach. The weather promises to be fine; however, with only light winds and another forty miles to go, we should put off making a landfall until daylight returns. But since one island, Royal Island, has a lighthouse on it and the general direction of our approach is clear of danger, we will keep the boat on course and perhaps feel our way into the anchorage.

A moonless night is a dark one; I wonder if I have made a wise decision. I re-evaluate our position, studying the simple pencil sketch intensely. The sketch seems somehow a little too simple at the moment—but that is all there is—apparently there are no dangers so long as we don't run into the nearest island, St. Joseph. In any case, the islands are shown close together, less than a mile from each other.

180

My heart pounds, I have seen the flash of the light. "So there are the islands, out there in the ocean—in the dark!" Our speed isn't great but I no longer have to stand up to see the flashes. Steadily we creep closer. For once I am glad of our slow speed, for it gives me plenty of time to let things fall into place.

Through the binoculars I can see the top of the island synchronized with the rotating beam. My heart is racing again: I have picked out the dark land mass—somehow a different shade from that of the sky and the ocean. I make another slight course change to port; under no circumstances do I want to end up on the wrong side of the islands, or in between them—they have to be left well and clear to starboard.

I can tell by the brilliance of the flashing light that we are getting close. But I can still only pick out details with the binoculars. So far only two of the islands are accounted for—Royal Island, with the light, and St. Joseph, in front of us. I'm looking for Devil's Island with a sense of urgency … where is it? Was it named after the devil because it plays tricks on sailors? … I see it! And now I can make out the channel between it and Royal Island. The isle of the devil is the lowest of the three; I guess it was there all along.

St. Joseph is looming just ahead to starboard—I'm relieved, I can distinctly see the water's edge around its shores. Oh my god! What is that? Are those breaking waves? Are we going to run aground? I'm sure I'm right with my course! Standing on the cabin top I try frantically to squeeze a clearer vision out of the binoculars.

"Oooh, dolphins!"

"What, what?" I yell back to Marie-José who is at the wheel steering a strict compass course; she is only a shadow, it is so dark. And why is there so much wind all of a sudden, I ask of no one in particular, thinking that the wind will make it hard to manoeuvre if we get into trouble.

"Dolphins!" Marie-José cries again.

"Oh, only dolphins," I mean, how great, dolphins, a sailor's best friend. How good of them to welcome us in the middle of the night—and chase away the butterflies in the stomach. Surely, they wouldn't swim in less than four-and-a-half feet of water, or near some nasty rocks lurking just below the surface?

We know that we have moved into the lee of the land because of

181

a lower swell—it has lessened our apprehension. Down come the sails and on goes the engine.

Our inclination is to us head for the more prominent anchorage at Royal Island where the lighthouse will help determine our position relative to the land. It is a disappointment to realize that with the wind as it is, a little in the south, this anchorage would be choppy so we are compelled to favour the lee of St. Joseph.

"Hey, I can see some masts in there! Ah well, these boats will be anchored in about the right place." I let the anchor rattle down a depth of twenty feet then pay out another eighty feet of chain and rope.

Ah, what a beautiful dark night! All the stars are out; it wouldn't hurt to have a little less swell.

*   *   *

It is so difficult to judge distances at night. We have stepped up on deck in brilliant sunlight to find ourselves anchored ridiculously far from the other boats and from the island. The first task, then, is to anchor closer to the shore—but it still feels great to be here. The islands are all lit up and look like little jewels, so green and gay and lush. Over there is Devil's Island, the low one. It looks like it is completely covered with grass; they are actually coconut palms thickly grouped together.

Half a dozen yachts are anchored in the lee of this small island called St. Joseph, two of whom we have already seen on the Brazilian coast. So this is it, Iles du Salut and Devil's Island, a mystical place on our globe, and every Tom, Dick and Harry finds his way here.

St. Joseph is wonderful! It is a miniature jungle, but without any of the parasites or hazards. There are coconuts, everywhere! The palms are extremely close together, and new shoots compete with each other. A huge mango tree claims a large piece of ground by the boat landing. The fruit it yields though is of a small variety and mostly still too green to eat. Further along, past some of the ruins of brick buildings, is a similar tree with even smaller fruit, but they are bright orange and pleasant to eat. I derive great pleasure from sucking on tangy pulp while facing the sea breeze—its warmth caresses my face and neck.

The ruins of old buildings are proof that the island was once inhabited, as we know, by prisoners and their guards. This doesn't take away from the tranquility of the scene—in fact, it adds its own quiet philosophy. Nature is reclaiming the ground the buildings stand on. Plants grow inside them almost as well as they do outside them. Doorways are barred by trees and accented by flowers. A graveyard set back from a rough beach on the windward side exudes peace. A low stone fence surrounds the modest gravestones, most of which are still standing.

A brisk walk along a broad trail, bordered in places by walls, takes one around the island in twenty minutes. Every day I spend some time on St. Joseph with my hatchet (I prefer it to a machete), husking coconuts. With this many nuts all around, we don't have to hold back, and, among other uses, we make fresh cream for coffee every day.

One of the yachties has speared a fish big enough to feed fifteen people and has invited us to join in a feast. The fish is called "merou."

"This type of fish is very lazy," the hunter comments, "even after you spear them, they don't react, they just carry on as if nothing has happened."

These are unusual islands that house fish in their waters that don't react when speared! The white flakey meat feels good between the teeth, and in the stomach, while stories are being told. A good helping of cheap Brazilian cane spirit, mixed with lime and sugar, complements the fish.

There are doctors and scholars among us and if some of us went sailing to escape or to get away, then it must have been to return to a primitive life. Nobody can escape his human nature.

*   *   *

We would have visited Royal Island eventually, but word has reached us that the island has many mango trees with ripened fruit, so we feel that now is the time. If Royal Island and St. Joseph were any further apart, I would decide against a row, but as the distance is just within my limits, the two of us set out this Sunday morning in our eight-foot dinghy. I keep close watch for a current in mid-channel.

Royal Island is civilized compared to St. Joseph. It boasts more buildings, some of which have been cleaned up, but all of them date back to the time when the French government operated a prison here, including the one that has been made into a small hotel.

Prisoners are said to have been free to walk about and many of

183

them spent their time planting flowers which grow profusely all over the island. Even now we can see evidence of former cultivation.

We don't know who planted the mango trees bearing magnificent fruit. While some are clustered together at the center of the island, others are found at various locations and in different varieties. Nothing is privately owned, so it is not an offense to harvest some of the fruit. One jolly Frenchman, a fireman from Kourou who spends most of his holidays on these islands, assures us that no one will hold it against us if we take some fruit. He takes us to a papaya tree lest we should miss it. The lemon tree, he explains, is no longer here.

There is not much drinking water to be had. If it has rained, there might be some in a corrugated iron tank beside the building near the little dock. One must snatch a few gallons quickly before a thoughtless tourist spoils the tank by washing his picnic knife and fork, and for good measure his feet. The hotel draws non-potable water from a pond. We are surprised to find a crocodile in the pond. In fact, now that we recognize one, it looks like there are two—there are five in all. Actually they are caymans, we are informed. But the pond is walled in and there is little chance of them getting out.

With the mangoes falling off the trees in greater numbers every day, it is time to start making jam. To do this we have anchored our schooner, now a temporary jam factory, at the Royal Island anchorage.

Another familiar yacht rides to her anchor not far from us, as I step on deck to greet another brilliant day. Splash! Splash! A couple of bottles complete their arc in my direction. "Hey, Klaus!"

"Yeah?"

"Come over for a beer."

Oh boy! Who can blame someone for having a cool beer on a hot tropical morning. In any case, from Royal Island one can have a commanding view of Devil's Island. The channel separating them is actually quite narrow and on both shores are remnants of a cable-car link.

Our opportunity to visit Devil's Island is here in the form of a newly-arrived cruising couple who like our company and want us to join them for the trip. They are going to take their twenty-nine-foot yacht *Don José*. I point out to the skipper that nobody has taken any sort of deep-draft vessel through the channels in all the time we have been here ... and point out the alarming words, "No passage," on my pencil sketch.

"Hah! we came through the channel when we arrived. My echo sounder registered plenty of water!" I have often observed both channels at low tide and have never detected signs of an obstruction, and so I will not press the point.

The channel between Royal Island and St. Joseph negotiated, we are drawing level with the northern extremity of Devil's Island. Rounding it, the echo sounder shows a bit less water, but every brown patch I suspect is a sandbank remains brown water. We lower the anchor in the lee of the island.

Now that we have dragged our little rubber dinghies up over some boulders, one of us voices what we are all thinking: "Gee, we anchored far off—we could have come in a lot closer!"

Fortunately, the island is so small that we couldn't get lost, even if we tried, but it is wild for all its size. Whatever trails there were have been almost completely erased. Coconuts that have fallen off the trees over the years are so thick that only small areas are free of them. The dry and rotting ones disintegrate under our feet. We select those in their prime to take back to *Don José*.

Were there clear trails, it would have been easy to reach the famous single dwellings, but the terrain is such that we have arrived in the spirit of explorers. I try to imagine how the prisoners felt in these surroundings. I have the same thought as we sit on the Dreyfus Bench, a group of neatly arranged rocks at the north end of the island, which faces France, Dreyfus' homeland.

As far as Papillon goes, it is obvious the movie makers took considerable artistic license. To make his escape on a sack of coconuts, Papillon made a spectacular dive off a formidable cliff. Here, at Devil's Island, the highest place to dive off is a boulder and even that wouldn't be necessary as one can reach the water's edge from almost any point on the island.

Near the Dreyfus Bench I fetch us some drinking nuts off a palm with a classic curve in its trunk. With our cargo of selected nuts, we make our way back to the dinghies.

"Devil's Island," I repeat, nose to nose with a fat spider sitting in a web strung across the best path through the jungle.

Arbitrarily I assumed the island was uninhabited.... Then what the

185

devil is this a pair of eyes looking at me? Thinking quickly, in true sailor's fashion, I conclude that they belong to a goat; I have to take my own word for it, since the rest of the animal remains hidden.

We again emerge into the bright sunlight by the boulder-strewn shore—the red-hulled *Don José* is a bright splash of colour.

It feels ominous and dramatic to see shark fins in the murky waters between the shore and the sloop. In his book, Papillon describes how dead prisoners were rowed out to sea and fed to the sharks which were already waiting, apparently having had advance notice of a body by the ringing of the bell.

* * *

Don José has long gone, but we have stayed on. Some days we are alone here, then more yachts find their way in. On weekends one can count on small motor boats arriving from Kourou or Cayenne. The French police and customs boats have also paid a visit. We were concerned about visiting the islands without first checking in at Cayenne, but, the French are, as usual, lenient and simply jot down some information about us and our boat.

A philosopher has arrived on his Tahiti ketch. He offers us a small history book on French Guyana and the Iles du Salut. One chapter explains how Devil's Island came to be included under the general name of Iles du Salut: it was decided to establish a colony at Kourou. A few hundred immigrants were expected, but 1,400 arrived, including ladies with long crinoline dresses, carrying ice skates in their baggage—into the swamps of the tropical equatorial zone. Prostitutes and adventurers arrived as well. During the 1763 rain season, there were epidemics of dysentery, syphilis, mash and yellow fever. About 1,000 people died. Most of the others left the swamps and found refuge, of all places, on the "islands of the devil." When health was restored, the appropriate name of Iles du Salut, "Islands of Safety" was given to the group.

* * *

The winds are right; we still have a long way to sail in this season. So, well stocked with coconuts, mangoes and mango jam, we regretfully bid the islands farewell.

Although we have made no special friends, I feel a lump in my throat. Have I begun to appreciate the little places on our globe— tiny patches with a bit of paradise—tiny patches that challenge us to know ourselves in a world which, now that we have almost sailed around it, has become smaller? Yet, with the next storm, it will be so mighty.

We have made our way around Royal Island, heading for a stretch of brown water. A boat, a ship, is in pursuit! It is coming so fast that I can identify it as a French naval vessel. I find myself looking through my binoculars at someone looking at me through his binoculars.

I regret having been so hasty in lowering the French courtesy flag. My mind is alternately concerned with the navy ship behind, and the brown water ahead. They wouldn't want to warn us of some danger we are standing into? It won't take much longer to find out, for the vessel is almost upon us. The ship slows ... the faces of several bare-breasted men break into smiles and in time with their waving arms, the powerful engines roar again—the ship rapidly increases her distance from us and changes direction at high speed in the heaving ocean.

My worries about the patch of brown water are over—for the navy ship has gone straight through it.

CHAPTER TWENTY-SIX

Barracudas, Rum Punch and Other Flavours

Barbados, shaped like a pear, stands noticeably alone and furthest to the east of all the Caribbean islands. It is a clean sail towards it. I don't even make entries into the logbook, they would always be the same; I keep track of our position by making little circles on the chart, giving them a date. The wind is mostly constant—a few extra clouds now and again pull across the sky, but I'm not concerned. I catch myself spinning thoughts about the globe we have more or less sailed around, the places we have seen; some names seem more important than others ...

The chances of arriving at a place during daylight hours should be fifty-fifty, but it seems to me that we arrive more often during the dark. We are approaching the bottom of the pear and it is nearly midnight. The lights from an airport on this part of the island are a source of orientation.

There is no need to be tense when approaching a bay as straight-forward as Carlisle Bay. Marie-José steers on with the propeller turning, while I slacken the halyards and begin to stow the sails. The labouring sounds of the slowing engine reach my ears together with Marie-Jose's voice, "Something's wrong with the engine!"

"Something's caught in the propeller! Take it out of gear!" My swift movements in rehoisting the sails are not from fear, but because I don't want to drift away from the anchorage and lose ground that would have to be regained with a series of tacks.

We sail in as far as we dare in the darkness and drop the anchor. We are not as far inside the bay as we would be if the engine had not quit, but we are reasonably content, with glasses of Brazilian cane spirit in our hands and the thoughts of our cozy bunks in our heads. It is almost 0300 hours. A little boat moves past and a voice calls out.

"What did he say? Was this meant for us?"

"I don't know what he was saying."

* * *

The next morning burns brightly with the suggestion of a hot day. We are being hailed by a voice ... he is warning us? "I am warning you. You go in there!" It's a little harbour boat; it's the voice from last night! He means for us to go into shore to clear with Customs; but why warn us? I wonder if his grey uniform and his official cap have gone to his head?

"I got the propeller fouled!" He doesn't understand, so I point down to the rudder and shout it again; but I refrain from jumping up and down on the deck. A crew sets to work with a boathook and soon pulls a huge piece of plastic away from the propeller. The plastic is, naturally, thrown back into the water while the harbour authority still fumes.

This is not Polynesia, because a Polynesian would be smiling instead of frowning. I'm pulling up the anchor, and he is angrily waiting, but I am getting angry too. I will not break my back, even if it is your bloody island, your anthill, we have come to! He is not waiting for me to break my back; he's steaming off.

At every place we notice one thing in particular; here, it's three. Besides the impatient harbour patrol, we take note of the large population on such a small piece of land, the high prices in the stores, and the large number of yachts.

Carlisle Bay is a generous indentation that can accommodate many ships, and there are many. They all roll forever and ever, because such a large open bay can not keep out all of the ocean swell, not even on the best of days. Nevertheless, it is here that a person beautifully accompanies, on his flute, my singing and guitar-playing. The swell is less than usual tonight, and the party boat is larger than average, so we roll in moderation.

And it is here in Carlisle Bay that I can say, "Hurrah! Marie-José can swim!" Sure, I had a little to do with it, but under my supervision she has never been able to do more than a few strokes before her feet desperately sought bottom. By chance, a lady on a neighbouring yacht, who used to be a swimming instructor, applied her skills to Marie-José, while people on the beach wondered what the commotion was all about (there was a lot of shouting involved in the teaching). There was Marie-José doing the breast-stroke in deep water, and then back into the shallows—I saw it with my own eyes.

* * *

189

Entry procedures are more relaxed on the island of Martinique. It makes for a more open, freer world. One can buy a cheap bottle of French wine, contemplate how long one should study a topless beauty on the beach, or admire a nude body traversing the ocean on a windsurfer.

I'm not laughing at the story that everyone hears when he visits St. Pierre, a little way up the coast from Fort-de-France; I find it ironical. Once, during a volcanic eruption, St. Pierre was obliterated. There were no survivors, except one, a prisoner in the local jail.

It's another Christmas! Daniel, the fellow who retrieved the dinghy in Fortaleza, and his wife Betty are here. Daniel plays the trumpet. "It's not a trumpet," he reminds me again, "It's a cornet!" I blare out the lyrics to a familiar tune, and Daniel follows with a jazz version on his trumpet—cornet.

*   *   *

The channels in between the string of islands are rougher than a tropical day in their lee would suggest. With wet decks we move in behind Guadeloupe. Having been warned about violent gusts of wind that spill off the mountainous island of Dominica, we keep a close watch as we sail its length to a generous anchorage at its northern end during the dark hours.

The wind is blowing lightly from the west for the third day now; it is unseasonable and makes a reputably good anchorage into a poor one.

Christian is pulling hard on the oars of the heavy wooden boat that he is rowing towards us—the unusual flag he is flying off his stern carries the French colours; Dominica, formally British, is independent. The wooden boat has bumped alongside, and we quickly climb down into it from our boat, eager to push off to cut down on the number of bumps.

Christian's muscular body is again straining at the oars as he heads the boat for the mouth of the Indian River—the bow of the boat is uncomfortably low for he is forced to use the forward rowing position, not having replaced a broken thole pin for the aft rowing position. "Why are you flying the French flag?" Marie-José asks him.

"Because it was given to me," he finally stammers. So simple, who would have thought.

Christian got our business because he excelled in good manners.

190

Several other boats were alongside, each of them bumping us more often then was necessary. Some of their offers were offensive: "You can change your mind and go with us; he (Christian) won't make any trouble," one said. And when we refused, "You can do what you want, it's your boat!" accompanied by a dirty look.

Christian is successfully avoiding fallen trees, roots and rocks, as well as the steel from a collapsed bridge, presumably because of his vast experience with the Indian River. But back in the ocean he cannot avoid the angry rivals we didn't engage for the trip. They are executing a tight circle around us in a boat with a smoking outboard motor.

Innocent us, protesting against a tow we thought they might be offering when the bandits had no such intentions. With a dangerous manoeuvre—I'm surprised we are not swamped—they have ripped off Christian's flag. The pirates always seem to have the faster vessel. Christian's words of protest are drowned out by the noisy engine.

Christian, aside from being fairly shrewd, is also naïve. He' off to see the police who, I'm convinced, will do nothing.

Few islands in the Caribbean are as lush as Dominica. There is no shortage of water, nor of fruit and vegetables. In the many little stores in Prince Rupert Bay (the only decent anchorage), one can find almost any common item at moderate prices. But in this generous bay with a lush shoreline backdropped by splendid mountains, yachts drop anchor, and then never lower their Q flags, and their crews never go ashore. They have been discouraged by the pushy and ill-tempered people who escorted them to the anchor spot.

Yachties that steer a course for Dominica have either not let stories of theft and dead bodies cloud their sense of adventure, or they didn't hear the stories. Unfortunately the first people they meet are not reassuring—they are pressured to take an escorted trip up the river—something they might gladly do themselves—and encouraged to pay in U.S. dollars. (We claim we took the trip of our own 'free' will.)

Some boats in the bay seem to have settled in. They have black people aboard who run the errands; it is as if they have bought insurance against being pestered. In our case, the word seems to have gotten out that we did the Indian River trip; and we do have a stalk of bananas dangling from our main boom, and no, we don't have cold beer, or warm beer or old T-shirts.

If one does make it ashore, there is a striking, and worrisome absence of yacht tenders. Within moments a self-confident youth offers to watch the dinghy, for a fee. But I spy a one-eyed old man mending nets by his patchwork shack ... couldn't we leave our fragile dinghy on his beach front and lean the oars against his shack? "Bring it closer. They will steal them!" His voice is squeaky, but his toothless mouth screws up into a smile.

In this little town, half the people have good-natured faces—they greet you with a friendly smile, while the other half looks through you, stares or glares at you and even mouth a short word which you don't understand, but which sounds terrible.

The old man's face contorts into a smile. The smiling old man is the first person who has made us feel welcome here. "Do you like cookies?" I ask him. We make him a present of the bag of cookies, to his delight.

While Dominicans desperately look for ways to earn tourist dollars, dim-witted racketeers intimidate yachties from stretching their legs ashore, where they might just spend some money. The cruising yacht beside us, with several passengers aboard, will simultaneously lower her Q flag and clear the bay early tomorrow morning.

There may be a dozen yachts in Prince Rupert Bay at one time, but none of them flies the Dominican flag from the spreaders, as they don't consider this a serious stop. Compared with the congregation of yachts in some of the other islands, the number of yachts that come here is small indeed. Dominica is perhaps the most shunned island in the Caribbean.

Any deep or prolonged relaxation is out of the question while anchored in Prince Rupert Bay. These people, I believe, really do think that their badgering is what we come for. They never consider that for some of us sailors, the yacht is our floating home. The same boats keep coming back over and over, as if they need us for air, or to see if we have, in the last fifteen minutes or so, had a change of heart and need them to do something for us after all.

We are being offered a young boy, a child. "He is strong," we are told—the boy stands up in the boat to show us how strong he is; I feel that I'm being invited to look into his mouth to check his teeth—"He can work like a man and scrub your decks and sleep on the decks." I have seen the boy on an earlier occasion, when he was smoking like a man.

"Hello hello!" voices call from a deplorable pink dinghy. The dinghy has pulled up alongside a white sloop that arrived earlier in the day. No answer means that the boat is empty and can be pilfered. Someone uses the stanchions to pull himself up the hull; a hand grabs a diving fin from the cockpit. Now, someone has actually climbed aboard the yacht and items are being rapidly transferred. I'm blowing the horn hard … it has absolutely no effect; items are still flying into the pink dinghy. I blow again … the thieves glance over to me, but only briefly—they want to get on with the job. They have apparently finished and retreat to the beach. I'm holding the mike of the VHF, calling Portsmouth police, the harbour master, Customs. "This is yacht. Calling any authority on the island of Dominica …" There is not so much as a crackle from the receiver.

*　*　*

In St. Barthelemy we can buy overproof rum in bulk cheaper than stove alcohol. The man takes it out of a barrel on the floor of his not-so-well-stocked store. We use it to preheat our kerosene burners—it spreads a peculiar aroma through the boat—and we mix it into some fruit juices to hand to visitors with the invitation to "have some rum punch."

Although the day is fine and there are no worries, another sailing ship has put me on the alert. Her skipper anchored close in front of us, then got into a large inflatable and roared off towards shore—we are left fending off his boat, which seems inclined to settle itself where we already are. The skipper is quite apologetic, and promises to re-anchor.

The next morning the skipper, Mark, roars towards us. Would we like to go diving with him and his mother—the pleasant mature lady with him is his mother—by an underwater mountain? The decision is easy: I would go diving any day with someone that doesn't take offense when told he has anchored too close. Off we go, toward a little dark cone with seawater foaming around it: it's the underwater mountain. Mark has been here before and knows just where to throw the anchor. The outboard has coughed for the last time and now one can hear the ocean lapping against the mountain's peak. Viewed above water it is seen as an obstacle to sailors, but down here it is studded with corals and plants, enhanced by exotic colours.

I feel like a menacing street gang has sneaked up on me while I was studying the architecture. I'm looking straight into the eyes of two dozen barracudas. Some of them advance effortlessly a short distance, the rest follow, but then they back away once more. Their mouths are the meanest part, with three needle-like teeth sitting in their jaws. I don't know what good Mark's speargun will do. It's got only one arrow. I prefer to concentrate on my behaviour and on theirs. I have no doubt that these barracudas are not fully grown; I was right, they are only medium-sized ones, for now two much larger ones have appeared—they are not as curious.

Back in the big rubber dinghy, we see that the pieces of fan coral we brought up look sadly out of place. They have changed colour and are no longer swaying.

Mark's mother's bum is surprisingly firm and round! I cannot help noticing it. My face came close to it as I grabbed her legs to stop her from sliding out of the rubber dinghy. She is trying to see the barracudas with only her head in the water. She hasn't seen them yet, so she keeps looking. Marie-José and I hold her by the legs until she has seen them, or given up. She doesn't give up easily, and so her bum remains elevated for some time. Marie-José and I exchange smiles.

*   *   *

The island of St. Martin is easily seen from St. Barthelemy. A few hours of classic sailing from one windward island to another and we are in Great Bay.

Sometimes we almost miss opportunities because we are put off by something superficial: in St.Martin there is a slum on the way to town which we choose to ignore; in town we got a good deal on two hefty bricks of cheese which become the jewels of our ship's stores.

The course to the Virgin Islands is 291 degrees, distance, 105 miles. We cannot make it during daylight hours alone, so we leave St. Martin in the afternoon.

I had no expectation of how the Virgin Islands should look, but now I see them, they are not the way I would have pictured them. They are not untouched, there is no veil to lift and no extraordinary lushness. The name, Virgin Islands, is stripped of it's power to evoke mystery.

Certainly, in St. Thomas harbour, with rush-hour traffic on the

194

water, the name Virgin Islands is inappropriate. I flag down a small motor boat to ask directions to the Customs office. They don't have the time to give a traveller some brief information. Wow!

But Jack and Jean Slasor who live aboard their yacht have time to offer us, and other salty sailors, a freshwater shower at their house in the hills.

* * *

We are about to set sail for Puerto Rico in company with Peter and Liz's sloop *Usikusiku,* and I think back to Capetown. This prominent place will probably be remembered for one reason: we chanced to tie up alongside *Usikusiku* there. When I first saw a man in a wheelchair, I didn't think much of it. When I saw a lady sitting in a wheelchair, smiling, I assumed she was resting in her husband's vacated chair. When I realized they both had wheelchairs I was momentarily stunned.

The boat seemed to be undergoing a refit and I expected that at any moment one of them would get up and walk across the deck but neither one of them ever did. I had the impression that I was the only one seeing the wheelchairs. They didn't seem to be aware of them.

The fact is they were two paraplegics who had already sailed around the Cape of Good Hope, by themselves, and were about to set sail for Brazil and the Caribbean.

Here in the Virgin Islands, we set our sails together for the Island of Puerto Rico. I do not envy them, but I marvel at their will.

CHAPTER TWENTY-SEVEN

Sailing the Shallow Sea

*F*or some reason we have no great desire to visit the island group known as the Bahamas. The charts show such a myriad of shallows and other hazards that we are torn between fascination and dread. Talk of piracy doesn't do anything for our enthusiasm. Still, we have to come to a decision, for from San Juan, Puerto Rico, we are planning our voyage to Nova Scotia.

Although we never seek out difficult or dangerous places, when some islands almost lie in our way we often consider making a landfall.

I have noticed that if we study an area long enough, things fall more into perspective and we develop a strategy. Still I always hope that for a first landfall at a new island group there will be an outlying island like a beacon. The charts promise San Salvador, an island in the eastern chain of the Bahamas, to be such a one.

There is a special note in brackets under the name San Salvador that gives this island a special significance. It reads "Landfall of Columbus 1492." The prospect of contemplating man's quests and discoveries where this early navigator first set foot on the New World is appealing. San Salvador also has the advantage that, should we not want to visit more of the Bahamas, we will be in a good position to go around them. We become more and more interested. We remind ourselves that a boat with a draught of six feet or less can enter most anchorages, and negotiate practically any shoals. "Hell, we only draw four and a half feet!" It could even be interesting to cruise vast expanses of such shallow ocean.

The formidable Fort San Juan, guarding the harbour, is to starboard this mid-afternoon, May 22, as we head for the open sea— the schooner is already following her compass course. Why does the radio keeps saying south-east winds when we obviously have northeasterlies? They are less favourable, but still on the beam so we don't complain.

* * *

For eight days, shipboard life takes its course. Today, May 30, according to our reckoning, I know that we should be coming within sight of San Salvador, the island we have chosen for our landfall.

As evening approaches, I look more frequently but the elation we always experience when first seeing land after a long passage eludes us. We lose confidence about our position and shorten sail, accepting the uncertainty of the night ahead.

It is now after midnight. Repeatedly scanning the horizon with binoculars from the cabin top, I am determined to see land. These islands are low, I know, but we should be very near them. My growing disappointment and concern, is balanced by Marie-José's relaxed state. She can see no reason why a person shouldn't snatch a good sleep when it's offered by a quiet ocean. I lightly adjust the rudder to steer the boat in a direction my reckoning tells me will clear the island.

The morning grey is turning a lighter hue—I'm scanning the space ahead to either side, and even behind us. I can't believe it, the island just isn't here! I know it isn't the clearest day but still, I should have seen something long ago. Maybe I steered away from it? I regret the perhaps irrational course correction I made during the night, and I analyze once again my plotting and reckoning.

I'm confounded; I think I'll slip below and console myself with a peaceful breakfast. If the island isn't there now, we won't run into it for a while. There is a whole day ahead of us to take new sights and plot a new course; but the fact that the island isn't here, when it should be, is consuming me.

Marie-José, having finished her breakfast before me, routinely sticks her head through the hatch, making the cabin dimmer. Her voice is casual: "There's the island."

I'm tempted to jump up and yell "WHAT!" before storming up the companionway, but I'm not going to do that. I turn my head slowly, looking at Marie-José's legs on the companionway ladder. She isn't using binoculars, they are in their case by the ladder.

"San Salvador?" I ask with a mouth full of breakfast.

I hear the inevitable, "What else?"

197

The island isn't "just there," it is really very near, and the larger part is clear while its low point is just emerging from behind the haze. After having made so many landfalls around the globe, I wonder why I still can't recognize atmospheric conditions; but I keep outwardly calm.

* * *

We anchor off Cockburn Town. It is surprising to see only one other yacht in the bay. I would have thought that so prominent an island, Columbus' landfall, would be heavily visited. This island isn't favoured by the yachting fraternity because it doesn't offer much beyond more than its name and a half-comfortable anchorage. The two wharfs, or what's left of them, look forbidding because they are in bad repair and are surrounded by a heavy surge.

We know from experience, it can take a few minutes, the better part of a day, or even more than a day, for a customs official to arrive. The morning has slipped away and we are still waiting.

Anchoring necessitates a careful evaluation of the circumstances. If the water is dark and murky, I set the hook as well as I know how; but when the water is translucent, even inviting, I set the hook and then check it by diving down.

The anchor is well dug in. There is no hurry so I leisurely propel myself back to the boat. My eyes fall on the one derelict wharf with a figure in some sort of uniform standing on it. Yes, he is waving his arms angrily … I can see now, it is the customs officer.

Despite the fact that I left the boat to ensure its safety, I also feel that I'm caught with my pants down. I summon my strength to pull myself back on board quickly and hurry to put on my light cotton shirt and pants … but the figure keeps beckoning me ashore … "Good grief! Doesn't he see that I'm getting ready? Does he want me to come with my pants down?"

I'm in our dinghy feeling resentment towards this guy and grumbling under my beard. I'm barely hearing Marie-José saying, "Take it easy … be calm," as I am also preoccupied with landing the dinghy in the present sea conditions.

I have shipped some water, but I avoided some nasty steel protrusions and made it onto the ramp adjacent to the wharf. There is no longer anyone on the wharf, but there is a car with a uniformed fellow behind the wheel. I walk up to the car.

He says ... nothing. "Are you the customs officer?" I try to sound enthusiastic, but it comes out sulkily.

Silence.

A drab, shrubby, swampy little island, two broken wharfs, and this cigar-chewing authority. His eyes are fixed on the windshield and mine are on the cigar. He speaks:

"What were you doing out there?"

Looks like we have plenty of time. "What do you mean?" I ask, thoughtfully.

"What were you doing out there, in the water?"

"You mean when I was diving?—I had a look at my anchor to see if it was set." I don't detect an understanding nod, let alone any praise for my cautious anchoring tactics. Maybe he doesn't even know this to be common practice. "It's common practice."

Again, silence.

"OK... get in the car. We go across the street to fill out the forms."

When I think of all the nice places we have been to, where we never were asked to pay a penny in entry fees ... where the officials smiled and offered useful information ... On top of this less than friendly welcome, this authority would now like twelve dollars.

As we walk the roads and beaches of this very low island, we find little produce. In spite of all this we sense a special flavour to this sun-drenched spot in the ocean. Having come in contact with more of the inhabitants, we are now convinced that Bahamians are friendly people.

Deliberately we walk to the spot, indicated by a cross, where Columbus is believed to have made his landing, and discover an extra beautiful stretch of beach. (There is another monument smack on the other side of the island, the windward side, where some other authority claims Columbus waded ashore.)

We have now spent four days here and are ready and willing to leave San Salvador again. A new yacht, *Garnesh*, is in the bay, and her crew has invited us for coffee. We exchange plans, ours to visit the Exuma Cays, theirs to go to Conception Island. We decide we will sail together to Cat Island about forty-three miles away. It is a beautifully easy sail, at night, so that landfall can be made in daylight. With the wind coming over the quarter, there is little worry about leeway.

Two hours before sunrise, we are extremely satisfied with the way

199

the little ship has held her course, and yet we feel compelled to have life easier still, so we curl up in our bunks, not, however, before I have another good look around with the binoculars.

*   *   *

The motions of the ship and the sounds of the ocean are the same. I am still drowsy with sleep and I'm undecided whether to close my eyes again, or go up on deck and look around. There is more light in the sky now ...

I am stunned to see the island abeam. We seem to be moving very swiftly. It is unforgivable to have allowed an island to sneak up on us a second time; but I'm thrilled with how well the little ship has steered herself along. We are sailing parallel to the land, at a safe distance.

We can clearly see the change in colour from deep to shallow water in the sunlight—another anxious moment ... now we are over those shelves that we have pored over on the charts! We have reached the south-west point of Cat Island and must sail north-east to where the island's inverted L-shape forms a prominent bight. We will drop anchor there.

The ambience reminds me of San Salvador: a few buildings, some roads and scattered palms and vegetation. We are walking along the road hoping to buy some local produce. A car has pulled up beside us. Pineapples are available further inland, and we can ride there with them. I try to size up the three men in the car, without making it obvious. Both happily and reluctantly we accept.

We share the back seat with one of two other passengers who is nursing a bottle, "Because it is a holiday today." The driver asks the unruly passenger to settle down and the ride becomes more enjoyable.

We can now see fields of pineapples. To buy some we must go on to the farmer's houses. Several attempts to buy "pines" here bear no fruit. If we would like to order them, they will bring them in from the fields "tomorrow." But we are pleased that the people make attempts to be friendly. One unattractive lady shakes our hands and tells us her name several times, which wins my approval. "No, no pines," I notice she says between gurgles.

The driver of the car meanwhile is involved in heated negotiations over a goat. "No goat," he is told. Surprisingly happy and light-headed, but without pines, we climb back into the car.

No stone is left unturned, that is, no little house is ignored in the search for pines. Our driver, Raymond, who kept assuring us that pines can readily be bought, is obviously pleased that one lady has "only four in the house right now—they are fifty cents a piece." A deal is immediately struck. She takes our two-dollar bill and holds it contentedly; we inhale the pineapple scent.

"Do you like watermelon?" the question interrupts my thoughts as I relax in the back seat of the car, heading back towards the beach.

Watermelons? One minute we are wondering whether we can find any produce, and the next minute its a matter of choosing what we like.

"Yes, we like watermelon," Marie-José and I agree. We are really still infatuated with the magnificent pineapples in our possession.

We walk along a footpath through the thicket and find goats and watermelons, all in one place—Raymond's own little patch on the earth. The melons are ripe to the bursting—some are rotting for want of harvesting. Raymond hands me one in its prime; one can tell it is sound by snapping the fingernail against it.

I feel obliged to invite Raymond, and his companions, on board for coffee. He is grateful for the invitation and lifts another melon from the ground for us. But fair is fair, and I insist that we take one as a gift and pay for the other.

"One dollar," spoken reluctantly, makes us wonder where we are—even the two dollars I hold out to him will barely pay for the gasoline he used driving us to the pineapples.

Coffee is being served aboard our little schooner, anchored close to the beach in the big bight. One of Raymond's companions, the one that is celebrating, has got stuck repeating compass courses in points. Bent over the compass, as if hoarding a treasure, he rattles off numbers and from time to time adds "Right!" looking intently from the compass to us. Apparently he used to steer these courses in the rum-running days, and they have been engraved on his brain. Settled down once more, he mentions something I simply can't make out, but the key word sounds like "cheese." I look at Raymond, who explains, slightly embarrassed, that his friend has asked for cheese. Everyone, except the ex-rum-runner, smiles.

We all recognize when a general code of conduct has been thrown to the wind. Marie-José slices the cheese with a grin; she has never been in the situation of offering somebody a cup of coffee and having

201

them say, "Have you got a piece of cheese?" Everyone loves the cheese and everyone, especially the ex-rum-runner, praises the coffee.

Raymond announces that he has to leave and his two companions instantly jump to their feet. I have already noticed the ex-rum-runner's agility in the dinghy and on board, and as drunk as he is, he boards the dinghy with quick and practised movements. I decline his offer to row, and he casts a critical eye around the tiny dinghy, displeased about the amount of water the little vessel is taking in.

"This is only an old dinghy we picked up after we lost our other one. We will get a better one when we can," I explain.

"Then why don't you give this one to me?" he asks. So it wasn't his safety he was concerned with; he doesn't think the dinghy is suitable for us, and sized it up to see if it's good enough for him. "Because then I have no dinghy to get out to my boat with—and I need it for that until I get another one."

He agrees wholeheartedly, nodding his head, and they all cheerfully step out into knee-deep water.

*   *   *

We are sailing north and we find our friends from San Salvador anchored off another beach. Together we head for Fernando Bay because the charts promise it to be a snug anchorage.

We are actually beginning to enjoy the Bahamas. This tiny little bay offers coconut palms in profusion, which gives the place an atmosphere of lushness and plenty. There is cool juice from the green nut, meat from the brown nut, and cream from the meat for coffee and cooking.

I think the owner of a tiny store is an appropriate person to ask about coconuts. The shopkeeper is surprised at my questions. "Take as many as you want—nobody uses them around here," he exclaims. Someone in the store mentions that "some are being used," and for this receives an angry look. Happily we lay in a supply large enough to last us our entire stay in the Bahamas.

In company with our friends on their sloop *Garnesh*, we move on to the next little bay with the not very exotic name of Smith Bay. Here we drop anchor and raft together, with our sterns dead over an underwater wreck. We have heard, but now we see first hand, that underwater wrecks provide a breeding ground and refuge for a variety of fish. They defend their fortress against intruders, like us, by darting back and forth nervously.

It is mutually agreed that, G*arnesh* and *Sea Helen,* will continue to cruise in company and so together we pour over charts and discuss the advantages, disadvantages, and hazards about any suggested route. I always favour skipping a few places in order to have plenty of time to spare at the anchorages. We are all in favour of a leisurely cruise, and so a small, privately owned island named Little San Salvador becomes our chosen destination.

Our course includes getting off the shelves and back on again, which is exhilarating in itself. I never cease to watch the ocean surface, partly from habit, partly fascination, but mostly to reassure myself that there are no lurking hazards; I see a silvery fish swim the length of our hull from bow to stern—now he is fighting to free himself from the hook at the end of our braided fishing line. Supper this evening is going to be barracuda.

*   *   *

It is said that in the Bahamas a visitor finds his pleasure not on land but on or in the water. This is very true at Little San Salvador. There are no coconut trees near our powder-white beach, but one's gaze is held by an extraordinary combination of brilliant shades and tints of turquoise and emerald—mauve—blue … all melting together.

*   *   *

We like to supplement the ship's stores with food gathered enroute, on an island or in the sea. Here is our chance to look for the conchs that I have heard make very good eating. I voice the opinion to the crew of *Garnesh* that we might have to go around the point, and a bit further out. They confide that they have a small outboard motor, stored below decks.

We didn't expect to see the conches right away of course, but we did expect to start harvesting them within a reasonable amount of time, say a half hour from when we started diving. With the novelty of looking at the coral gardens and contours of the ocean bottom wearing thin, suspicion grows that maybe there aren't any conches. Not wanting to accept that the world is devoid of conches, I become more determined and look a little harder: in deeper water. I see a little trail in the sand. "Look for their trail and follow it," I was advised.

The trail terminates in a mound, or is this a conch? Yes it is, it must be!

A war cry is a strange phenomenon; it provides courage and extra strength and helps concentrate attention. My war cry is silent because, after all, I'm underwater but it is there, within me. I have underestimated the depth, my war cry has made me over-confident. I struggle for the last few inches. I spread my fingers to grab the shell, but there are still inches to go. My fingers are on the object but I cannot lift it off the sand, it is unexpectedly heavy. I'm starved for air. I grab the shell more firmly. The ocean surface seems near, but still up and up I go—my companions smiles are blurred. It is apparent that the conches live in depths deeper than we can comfortably penetrate.

Marie-José, who has stayed behind, is surprised as she is used to me coming back from diving trips empty-handed; four big conches is adequate reward for having kept faith. G*arnesh* has a meat grinder aboard—we can't believe all the things they carry with them; it is just what is needed to prepare this tough white meat. The edible parts of the conches, ground up and mixed with an egg, herbs and one potato, make just the right number of fritters for four adults and one child. The meal is a huge success.

*   *   *

Eleuthera Island is a long and skinny strip of land. We have begun to traverse the banks contained by its shape—an inverted "C." The wind, however, is dying; the afternoon is gone and we are only halfway across the shelves to the island's shores. It is an easy decision to drop anchor just where we are—the weather promises to remain fine, and we all are anticipating a refreshing swim and an early supper.

This shoal-water cruising consistently provides swimming, diving and beachcombing like we have never known before. Miles from shore, the tiny temporary community formed by our floating homes is a new experience for us.

With fair winds and no swell, not even a chop, we enjoy some of our cleanest sailing in the lee of this narrow strip of low land. The dark and light patches, appearing and disappearing under the keel, hold our interest for the duration of any sail. We can't help evaluating every patch of a different shade. Sailing over the murky depths back home, one mostly observes the surface of the water, oblivious to hazards that here, in the transparent sea, lie exposed to one's view. It can unnerve the most stout-hearted sailor. After awhile, the eye becomes trained to pick out coral heads at a distance; but whether or not there is enough water over them always remains to be seen.

In Governor Harbour a familiar sloop, *Nordly's*, rides at anchor—we met her in Puerto Rico. Now the three yachts sail together the comfortable distance to Hatched Bay.

Because of the uniformity that a stretch of low-lying land appears to have, many of the entrances to the various bays are difficult to pick out. The entrance to Hatched Bay is unusual by contrast. By Bahamian standards, with land no higher than 204 feet, it is impressive to enter a harbour between steep rock walls. Something else about this bay is unusual: seaweed, reaching up from the ocean floor like tall grass, strokes our keel.

We have chosen Royal Island as a last stop in the Bahamas. The route to it includes negotiating the Current Cut, a narrow pass at the north end of Eleuthera Island. We tried to time it to go through with the last of the ebb, but we have not yet realized how swiftly we sail under these good conditions, for we have arrived early. *Garnesh*, ahead of us, is preparing to negotiate the cut by lowering her jib and starting the engine. She is making her turn around the reefs and outlying rocks; her speed has increased—she has vanished from our view, like a gliding swan. Now it is our turn. It is like a river—the shores keep changing very quickly. Another five miles of shoal ground have to be crossed to reach the harbour of Royal Island.

We have shared few anchorages in the Bahamas with other yachts, but at Royal Island it is actually crowded. The crew of *Nordly's*, that has sailed in our wake, is curious about what we were doing before the cut. They could not figure out our zigzag course. The answer is that we had a three-and-a-half-foot dorado on the line and were trying to land it; the fish is large enough to provide supper for us all.

In the past few weeks we have hardly given a thought to the smugglers and pirates that are said to infest these waters, but what *Nordly's* crew is telling us changes that: "You see that big dinghy that came in—the fellow wanted to know if we have seen a big motor cruiser—said he was waiting for a big shipment ..."

I am amazed that anyone would want to broadcast that he is

waiting for a shipment of drugs rather than content himself with a simple inquiry about a certain craft.

Four of the yachts in the bay, including *Nordly*'s, weigh anchor with the morning sunlight, leaving *Garnesh*, us and a 32-foot sloop, at the anchorage. The skipper of the sloop sounds strange to our sensitive ears, as he inquires if we have a fitting for the fuel line on his engine. His friend loaned him the 32-foot sloop which he has sailed alone from Florida. No, the huge dinghy with the powerful outboard (a Boston Whaler) is not a problem to pull behind—he doesn't even notice it's there. (Where the huge dinghy is stowed when the sloop is at sea has been occupying my mind.) He is going to run over to Spanish Wells, a distance of about six miles, to find the part for the fuel line. It is already late in the afternoon and I can't help wondering why he doesn't get away until dusk.

I am inwardly fuming: why would anyone want to drag a huge dinghy like that behind a sailing boat and run with it from island to island in the dark? And where's he going to get the part at night anyway?

To minimize our worst fears, we are rafting *Garnesh* and *Sea Helen* together and devising a defense plan in case we should be boarded at night. We will signal each other by means of a string stretched from porthole to porthole. *Garnesh*'s crew doesn't have a firearm and agrees, to avoid confusion, not to come on deck under any circumstances. I would shoot an intruder if I thought it necessary.

It is 2200 hours and the Boston Whaler hasn't returned. Our conversation has grown quiet for we are all sleepy and anticipate an early rise. We seek out our bunks.

I am surprised to see the Boston Whaler made fast to the sloop again this morning. We each report a fitful sleep.

Breakfast was pleasant, our engines are noisy, the anchor chains rattle in the morning stillness—we move past the sloop with the big Boston Whaler, which we regard with suspicion, astern; her skipper does not show himself on deck or in the hatchway.

The wind, blowing straight into the tiny harbour mouth is cause for alarm. *Garnesh*, with more power and a sleek hull-shape, is making slow but steady progress through the pass, but with one extra large swell we are hobby-horsing. We breathe easier now that we are far enough out to fall off the wind.

The two yachts, *Garnesh* and *Sea Helen,* are to part company a few miles further on. *Garnesh* has planned to stop at the Great Bahama Island before going on to Florida, while we do not intend to stop again and have plotted a course to take us past the Great Abaco group and on to Nova Scotia.

We are about to make the transition from the shallows into deeper water and I feel a surge of dread sailing close by a large freighter; it is stranded. For a long while it looked like it was moving, for it stands absolutely upright, submerged to the waterline. But it has been thus for many years, judging by the degree of deterioration.

We change course to starboard. Garnesh is just ahead of us, the ghostly ship is just behind; *Garnesh's* crew waves, we wave—it is our farewell. It is a special moment for us; sharing these past few weeks with them in these islands was a special moment in our lives.

Clouds are rolling in and the winds are up and gusting. Although the islands still protect us, the seas are heaping up and lunging at us. It is strange to see the sun-filled islands, where we live so leisurely, display their other face just as we are leaving.

After weeks of quiet cruising, with nothing more than wavelets to lap against *Sea Helen,* I am irritated at the turbulence of the sea. I feel a trace of motion sickness, and I begin to organize things for comfort in this new situation; I'm satisfied that we are clear of danger and I'm grateful that the wind is over the quarter.

Garnesh, we can see, is heading into the worst of it. A blinding rain squall obliterates them from view.

CHAPTER TWENTY-EIGHT

Crystals of Salt Sprinkled on the Ship of Dreams

*I*t is definitely a brighter day this morning. While I'm savouring this fact, Marie-José is pointing out a huge tanker to port—it's rather close; I wonder how close they come when the night is black as coal, it's raining and we are down below.

* * *

I'm reading a book in the cockpit. Again I have arrived at the bottom of a page realizing that I have not absorbed what I have read.

Our sails are winged out. The rope leading from the genoa sheet moves the wheel as if an invisible helmsman keeps the boat on course, relative to the wind that is coming dead from behind.

We have talked a great deal about Nova Scotia, the east coast of Canada, not the west coast where we started out with our little sailing ship. Several times we have been surprised at the progress our sun sights showed, despite poor sailing conditions; we are not that concerned when progress is slow. I'm reading a book in the cockpit—rather I'm holding it in my hand, which is resting in my lap.

This time I hear it distinctly! I believe that I heard it long before, that thump thump! "There is a freighter coming straight for us!" I say it out loud in astonishment, my head inside the companionway and my hand fumbling for the metal cone. "Where's the foghorn?" I have the wish to disguise the urgency in my voice. Hell, what's this about being calm and collected when we are about to be run down by a big steel hulk. The horn is pressed into my hand; Marie-José has responded to my confused request. Maybe it is the way I'm blowing it—the foghorn sounds so feeble, so weak.

"I should have fired the rifle!" I say, shaken by the vividness of the freighter's bow bearing down on us. The officer of the watch must have decided to take a look at his surroundings for the ship has suddenly veered off to starboard; maybe he had only just returned to the bridge ... "I should have fired the rifle!" It would have made so much more noise.

* * *

I'm always a bit surprised that a single piece of refuse, such as a foam coffee cup or a floating tin can, can capture my attention on a vast sea. But since these throw-away items are becoming common here, I no longer turn the binoculars their way, considering them the unfortunate results of over-packaging.

The water is becoming an inky green, like that of a river. Are we in the Gulf Stream that sweeps from south of Nova Scotia to Europe?

The almost-full moon is haloed and high clouds gather. The genoa is no longer spread to a fair wind but a jittering jib confirms a storm is gathering quickly; we are sailing towards Nova Scotia.

The wind is very light—there is a lot of seaweed floating about; it has turned cold all at once, even though it is summer. We scramble for warm clothes that I realize we have not needed for several years.

The fog is thick, we have not escaped it. Hopes I had that the fog would not come, at least not until we are safely in port, are dashed. We hear the drone of an engine—I blow the horn—again and again ... Finally, there are two separate blasts in return; I take it that the crew of the other ship knows we exist.

This fog is different; it is caused by the warm wind from the south—and with wind the ocean is not still; I hope it will clear soon. We are coming closer to the shores of Nova Scotia.

There lies the land. Even though I can't see the smile on my face, I know it's there—the fog has lifted. We eagerly accept our fate: we are making landfall on the most beautiful of days. I cannot help noticing the absence of coconut trees, but how pleasant Lunenburg looks. Numerous wooden wharfs stand in the foreground of a cluster of buildings in solid colours, many of them deep red. I seem to know what I feel at this moment, but to accurately describe it would take either a genius or a simple person: somehow I don't fit into either category.

* * *

A person's basic nature doesn't change—I'm still the boy I used to be, but the world is heavier on my shoulders.

Tied to an old wooden wharf after a voyage around the world makes us see ourselves as we really are, or perhaps as we should be.

Some people would feel wonderful at this moment. Personally, I feel a bit low. We reached a high somewhere among the islands in the Pacific or the Indian Ocean or the Atlantic, and now we have arrived, where, theoretically, we should feel great, but actually we don't.

I look at myself objectively. I want to go on experiencing. Given the right frame of mind, life is an extraordinary experience.

When I was a child and heard or spoke the word "adventure," a fire was kindled in me. At those times, I saw myself in a picture with a frame around it that made the adventure manageable. Now I reject the frame; adventure is only part of a larger canvas.

* * *

The summer in Lunenburg is many things. It is a time for us to reflect, and a time to meet people who take an interest in us and our little sailing ship.

We are finding our equilibrium in a world that has not changed as much as we have. We search for people who can understand what is still fresh and vivid in our minds and what might soon fade into obscurity.

The word "winter" has became lodged in our heads because our hands hurt when bailing the cold water out of the dinghy, and because I find myself rushing back down below after checking the anchor in a southerly gale sweeping the harbour. We try not to be disappointed when we are refused docking space. We know it is refused by people who are not the whole world, but we are still disappointed. We walk with arms around each other along the waterfront of the colourful town.

Dressed in the heaviest clothes we have, our noses red from the biting wind, we stand before the general manager of Lunenburg Foundry & Engineering Company. The foundry has wharfage of its own, but it's an unlikely place for a private yacht to be welcomed; we will, however, accept the worst spot on the wharf, if it is offered.

The manager points out the lack of space. I nod my head. It is this fact that made me reluctant to ask. Large amounts of vacant dock under the jurisdiction of the museum is not available to us.

"We can't leave you anchored out there," says the manager. I begin to feel warm inside my bulky clothes—perhaps it's the office heat. I start to worry that maybe I'll blush too easily at his compassion.

210

A week later the matter is settled. The Foundry's tug will be moved back and the old dragger will be moved ahead and we can go "here," where there is a ladder. The manager shows us the exact spot that is to be ours for the winter.

It is obvious that the manager wants us to have the best possible spot on the wharf. I am impressed. Had I masterminded how we would moor for the winter, I could not have done better; it is like wishful thinking materializing. Granted, it will be rough living in our little boat once it gets really cold, but we can expect to be reasonably well and alive when spring arrives.

We have tied up none too soon, it is a frosty wind in my face—the snowflakes are tiny and few, but they are here. My ears catch the wind and make me think of going below, but somehow I like the crispness of this moment; perhaps for the moment I am content, if not happy.

Out of habit I reach out to extinguish the oil lanterns when in fact an electric bulb is giving the light.

The gusts of wind make me wonder about the anchor, though we are snug against the wharf in the most protected part of the harbour.

How far away those faraway places where we have travelled already seem. Although there are lasting impressions—exhilarating and frustrating experiences, the feeling of finding ourselves in the vast ocean without food, islands where we might have stayed had I not been so restless and curious—we realize these memories will also fade. Perhaps we are crystals of salt sprinkled on the ship of dreams.

What else would we have done if we had not sailed? Would we have done something more important? Would we have discovered how the Universe began and how it will end? Would we know the meaning of life on the earth?

There were times at sea when we looked at the sky and the horizon and thought our view encompassed everything. But we were only seeing the world from the deck of a little sailing ship.

*   *   *

211

Printed in Canada